Primitivism, Radicalism,
and the Lamb's War

PRIMITIVISM, RADICALISM, AND THE LAMB'S WAR
The Baptist-Quaker Conflict in Seventeenth-Century England
T. L. Underwood

THE GOSPEL OF JOHN IN THE SIXTEENTH CENTURY
The Johannine Exegesis of Wolfgang Musculus
Craig S. Farmer

Primitivism, Radicalism, and the Lamb's War

The Baptist-Quaker Conflict in
Seventeenth-Century England

T. L. Underwood

New York   Oxford
OXFORD UNIVERSITY PRESS
1997

Oxford University Press

Oxford   New York

Athens   Auckland   Bangkok   Bogota   Bombay   Buenos Aires
Calcutta   Cape Town   Dar es Salaam   Delhi   Florence   Hong Kong
Istanbul   Karachi   Kuala Lumpur   Madras   Madrid   Melbourne
Mexico City   Nairobi   Paris   Singapore   Taipei   Tokyo   Toronto

and associated companies in
Berlin   Ibadan

Copyright © 1997 by T. L. Underwood

Published by Oxford University Press, Inc.
198 Madison Avenue, New York, New York 10016

Oxford is a registered trademark of Oxford University Press

Library of Congress Cataloging-in-Publication Data
Underwood, T. L. (Ted L.)
Primitivism, radicalism, and the Lamb's war : the Baptist-Quaker conflict in
seventeenth-century England / T. L. Underwood.
p.   cm. — (Oxford studies in historical theology)
Includes bibliographical references and index.
ISBN 0-19-510833-7 (cloth)
1. Baptists—England—History—17th century.   2. Society of Friends—England—
History—17th century.   3. Baptists—Relations—Society of Friends.   4. Society of Friends—
Relations—Baptists.   5. England—Church history—17th century.   I. Title.   II. Series.
BX6276.U53   1997
280'.042—dc20   96-5508

1 3 5 7 9 8 6 4 2
Printed in the United States of America
on acid-free paper

To
Geoffrey F. Nuttall
and
Richard L. Greaves

Preface

In 1671, a certain "R. H." described Quakers as "the *fag-end* of Reformation" (see chapter 1). If this charge of extremism is correct, as I think it is, then we must ask, How did Quakers reach such a radical position? How did so many who had once been Presbyterians, Independents, and Baptists come to differ in belief so dramatically from the members of these groups? We must also ask, What, if anything, did they continue to have in common with these religious parties? Because theologically Baptists stood between Presbyterians and Independents on the one side and Quakers on the other, one would expect Baptists and their relationship with Quakers to provide a source of answers for such questions. Unfortunately, that relationship has been largely ignored by scholars. The present study is intended to fill this void. In doing so, I will take advantage of the existence of scores of previously unused tracts and manuscripts of controversy produced by "the Lamb's War" that involved hostility and conflict between members of the two groups. Examining these and other materials, the present study will undertake to analyze that conflict, to clarify some of the beliefs of Baptists and Quakers, and to discover the role that primitivism—the emphasis on the first, earliest form of Christianity—played both in linking Quakerism with the Puritan and Nonconformist tradition, and in setting Friends apart from that tradition.

This study has been made possible in large measure by travel grants from the National Endowment for the Humanities, the McKnight Foundation University of Minnesota Arts and Humanities Endowment, and the Institute of International Studies and Programs of the University of Minnesota; and by research grants from the Graduate School Faculty Research Grant Program and the Institute of International Studies and Programs of the University of Minnesota. I am deeply grateful for such generous support.

My thanks are also extended to the Royal Historical Society and the Institute of Historical Research at London University, and to the following libraries and their librarians: the Briggs and Wilson Libraries of the University of Minnesota; the Folger Shakespeare Library, Washington, D.C.; Regent's Park College, Oxford University; the Bodleian, Oxford University; the Wren Library, Trinity College, Cambridge; and in London, the British Library, the Congregational Library, the Library of the Religious Society of Friends, and Dr. Williams's Library. I am also appreciative of the very valuable advice and assistance of Hugh Barbour, Janet Barnes, Sylvia Carlyle, Kenneth Carroll, John Creasey, Rosamund Cummings, Peter Daniels, Tabitha Driver, Linda Elias, J. Vernon Jensen, May Jesseph, Neil Keeble, Josef Keith, Barbara McGinnis, Robert Milks, Edward Milligan, Susan Mills, Michael Mullett, Peter Ohlin, Cynthia Read, David Steinmetz, Yvonne Storck, Charlotte Syverson, Malcolm J. Thomas, and B. R. White; and of the strong encouragement of Wilbert H. Ahern, Raymond Brown, Mariam Frenier, C. Ronald and Freda Goulding, Judith Greaves, David C. Johnson, James Keeley, Jooinn Lee, E. P. Y. Simpson, Eric and Eve Stevens, and Dewey Wallace. In addition, I wish to record my gratitude for the enthusiasm, gracious understanding, and steadfast support of my immediate family—Judith, Tamara, and Mark—and for the lively interest, keen intellect, and pythonesque humor of my students.

Finally, I am especially indebted to Geoffrey F. Nuttall and Richard L. Greaves, who evaluated an early version of the manuscript and whose scholarship and friendship have been an inspiration over the years.

February 1996   *T. L. U.*

Contents

Abbreviations

BBQ   William C. Braithwaite, *The Beginnings of Quakerism*, 2nd ed., rev. by Henry J. Cadbury, Cambridge: Cambridge University Press, 1955.

BDBR   Richard L. Greaves and Robert Zaller, eds., *Biographical Dictionary of British Radicals*, 3 vols., Brighton: Harvester Press, 1982–84.

BQ   *Baptist Quarterly*. London: Baptist Historical Society.

BQPE   Hugh Barbour, *The Quakers in Puritan England*, New Haven: Yale University Press, 1964; reprint, Richmond, Ind.: Friends United Press, 1985.

BSPQ   William C. Braithwaite, *The Second Period of Quakerism*, 2nd ed., rev. by Henry J. Cadbury. Cambridge: Cambridge University Press, 1961.

DNB   Leslie Stephen and Sidney Lee, eds., *The Dictionary of National Biography*, 22 vols., London: Oxford University Press, 1949–50.

FGM   George Fox, *The Great Mistery of the Great Whore Unfolded*, 1659.

FJN   George Fox, *The Journal of George Fox*, ed. John L. Nickalls, London: Religious Society of Friends, 1975.

FJP   Norman Penney, ed., *The Journal of George Fox*, 2 vols., Cambridge: Cambridge University Press, 1911.

FPT   Norman Penney, ed., *The First Publishers of Truth*, *JFHS* Supplement 1–5 (1904).

GCP   Thomas Grantham, *Christianismus Primitivus*, 1678.
HBR   Roger Hayden, ed., *The Records of a Church of Christ in Bristol, 1640–1687*, Bristol Record Society Publication 27, 1974.
HSPFE   Geoffrey F. Nuttall, *The Holy Spirit in Puritan Faith and Experience*, Oxford: Basil Blackwell, 1946; reprint, Chicago: University of Chicago Press, 1992.
JFHS   *Journal of the Friends' Historical Society*, London: Friends' Historical Society.
LF   Library of the Religious Society of Friends, Friends House, London.
MBC   William J. McGlothlin, ed., *Baptist Confessions of Faith*, Philadelphia: American Baptist Publication Society, 1911.
MW   John Bunyan, *The Miscellaneous Works of John Bunyan*, ed. Roger Sharrock, 13 vols., Oxford: Clarendon Press, 1976–94.
QH   *Quaker History*, Haverford, Penn.: Friends Historical Association.
RQER   Barry Reay, *The Quakers and the English Revolution*, New York: St. Martin's Press, 1985.
UFR   Edward Bean Underhill ed., *The Records of the Churches of Christ Gathered at Fenstanton, Warboys and Hexham, 1644–1720*, vol. 9, London: Hanserd Knollys Society, 1854.
UHB   Alfred C. Underwood, *A History of the English Baptists*, London: Kingsgate Press, 1947.
WEBSC   B. R. White, *The English Baptists of the Seventeenth Century*, London: Baptist Historical Society, 1983.
WHB   William T. Whitley, *A History of British Baptists*, 2nd ed., London: Kingsgate Press, 1932.
Wing   Donald Wing, *Short-title Catalogue of Books . . . 1641–1700*, 2nd ed., 3 vols., New York: Modern Language Association of America, 1972–88.

In addition, Savoy Declaration is used for Savoy Conference, *A Declaration of the Faith and Order Practised in the Congregational Churches in England*, 1659, and Westminster Confession is employed for Westminster Assembly, *The Confession of Faith, and the Larger and Shorter Catechisms, First Agreed Upon by the Assembly of Divines at Westminster*, 1650.

Primitivism, Radicalism, and the Lamb's War

Illustration from Benjamin Keach's *The Grand Impostor Discovered*, 1675.
By permission of the Folger Shakespeare Library.

1

In a by-path he is resolv'd to go

Introduction

[Professor]
> *A Man in Habit plain yonder I see,*
> *That's turned back, now crosses o're to me:*
> *He seems to some, blest* Canaan*-ward to look,*
> *But his way thither strangely has mistook:*
> *In a by-path he is resolv'd to go,*
> *Which former Saints did never own, nor know:*

[Quaker]
> *Friend, I would speak to thee a word or two,*
> *Which by the Spirit I am mov'd to do.*

Benjamin Keach (1640–1704), *The Grand Impostor*
Discovered, 1675

The Study

The period 1640–89 in English history was marked by turmoil and change. Civil war, the execution of a king, the establishing of a republican regime, the restoration of monarchy, plots against the government, and the Revolution of 1688 were among the political developments of the time. In the religious sphere, the ferment of ideas in the 1640s and 1650s, the abolition and restoration of episcopacy, the repression of Noncon-formists, and the 1689 Act of Toleration were significant features. The two middle decades of the century witnessed the expansion of the Baptist sect as well as the rise and expansion of Quakerism. Although at its beginning the Quaker movement attracted some Baptist converts, hostility quickly came to characterize relations between the two groups. Public disputes took place and polemical tracts were exchanged.[1] Such conflicts led John Bunyan to publish his first two works, in which he censured Edward Bur-rough as "an enemie to the Truth" and denounced the Quakers as "blind Pharisees." In reply, George Fox rebuked Bunyan as a person who "had better have been silent, then to fight against the Lord, the Lamb and his

3

Saints."[2] Yet, as this study will demonstrate, Fox, Bunyan, and others in the two groups had much in common with each other and with the broader Puritan and Nonconformist tradition as well.

Apart from two brief articles in the 1970s, the relationship between seventeenth-century Baptists and Quakers has been virtually ignored in scholarly publications.[3] The present study is intended to fill that void. The importance of doing so lies in the need to clarify early Quaker views and to explain how Friends came to differ so significantly in their beliefs from other English Protestants. Because theologically Baptists stood between Presbyterians and Independents on the one side and Quakers on the other, this examination of the Baptist-Quaker relationship, far more extensive in its analysis than previous studies, allows us to identify a primary link between the two and at the same time to explain some of their dramatic differences. Such comprehensive analysis is made possible by the use of scores of previously unemployed tracts and manuscripts produced by Baptist-Quaker disputes—materials that, in setting forth accusations, clarifications, and rebuttals, shed new light on the antagonists' perceptions and beliefs.

Further distinguishing the present study from other investigations of Baptist and Quaker religious thought is the use of a new conceptualization for the analysis of the groups' views and relationships: *primitivism*, the emphasis in faith and practice on the first, earliest form or pattern as described in the New Testament that entailed efforts to re-create or imitate such a form in the present.[4] It will be shown that their zeal for primitive Christianity provided the two groups' basic link with each other and with the Puritan and Nonconformist tradition. It was also from this zeal that the primary difference between them arose—the extent or degree to which they identified themselves with that earliest pattern. Whereas in this regard Baptists surpassed Presbyterians and Independents, Quakers eclipsed Baptists. Recognizing a significant distinction between their own time and that of the primitive church, Baptists tried to replicate the New Testament model as fully as they could. However, perhaps encouraged by the current interest in the dramatic, imaginative re-creation of biblical experiences and in millenarianism, early Friends in the height of their enthusiasm appear to have believed they *were* the New Testament church. In a phenomenon similar to what Mircea Eliade has described as "the rejection of profane time" and the "recovery of the Great Time, *illud tempus* of 'the beginnings,'" Quakers seem to have entered, in imagination and re-creation, the "Great Time" of "the beginnings" of Christianity more fully than Baptists, in order to experience the New Testament Christ as they believed the primitive church had.[5]

To experience Christ immediately as the earliest Christians had, however, required an internalization and spiritualization by Quakers of outward historical events. This in turn affected their perception of primitive Christianity—a vision that stressed immediate, inward, and spiritual qualities. Up to the point of Christ's ascension, Quakers did not deny that the events of Christ's life had occurred outwardly, although they strongly emphasized his divine nature to the neglect of his humanity and they normally spoke of his crucifixion, death, burial, and resurrection as occurring within them with the appropriate soteriological results. However, they apparently perceived Christ's ascension to have been into his saints rather than into a physical heaven as the Baptists believed. A corollary was the Quaker claim that the second advent had also occurred in the primitive time when Christ came to dwell spiritually within individual Christians. In addition, Friends believed that primitive Christians had Christ as their authority since the New Testament had not yet been written, and that these earliest Christians experienced their own spiritual resurrection and judgment, witnessed the beginning of the Lamb's War, practiced silence as well as quaking in worship, allowed the preaching of women, and advocated the disuse of outward baptism and the Lord's Supper. The Quakers' entrance into the "Great Time" of primitive Christianity and their perception of it led to a fusion of time for Friends—the past and future were experienced in the present.

Baptists, on the other hand, taking a literal approach, perceived the historical crucifixion, death, burial, and resurrection of Christ witnessed by the earliest Christians to have been outward and physical in nature, and necessary for human salvation. These same outward, physical qualities had attended Christ's ascension into heaven in the past and would also accompany the second advent, the Lamb's War, and the resurrection and judgment, all of which would occur in the future. Past, present, and future were more clearly separated by Baptists. In addition, Baptists perceived primitive Christians as respecting the authority of the Old Testament Scriptures, observing outwardly the Lord's Supper and believers' baptism, worshiping without silence and quaking like that of Friends, and honoring Paul's injunction that women keep silent in the church.

Finally, it is in its use of the *Quod primum id optimum* paradigm that the present analysis contrasts markedly with previous Quaker scholarship, including the two most recent major works on early Quakerism, highly valuable biographies of Margaret Fell and George Fox that nevertheless treat Quaker theology in the more traditional manner, stressing spiritualism and mysticism.[6] As the present study will demonstrate, it was actually the fundamental Quaker emphasis on primitivism and the experience of the "Great Time" of "the beginnings" from which flowed those theological positions that sparked so many heated controversies with Baptists and set Friends so widely apart from other Christians of their time, yet also resulted in one of the most remarkable contributions to the history of Christianity in England. An expansion on some of these themes and further background follow.

The Setting: Biblical Primitivism, Meditation and Preaching, and Millenarianism

The emphasis on primitive Christianity, the practice of re-creating biblical experiences in meditation and preaching, and a strong interest in millenar-

ianism are often considered to be among the important characteristics of
the Puritan and Nonconformist tradition. It is commonly said, for example, that Protestant reformers countered the authority of papacy, church
councils, and tradition by appealing to the authority of the Scripture. In
English Puritanism and Nonconformity there was also an ardent emphasis
on the primitive state of the church as the model for current belief and
practice. The experiences of God's people described in the Bible, after all,
were thought to be of an immediate nature, issuing directly from the divine source. The New Testament narratives were to provide the pattern for
the present. They were appealed to on a range of issues, from vestments
and polity to the eucharist. Some weight was assigned to the Old Testament and to postbiblical precedents, but the New Testament church in its
purity and simplicity, unsullied by the apostasy and human inventions of
the Roman Church in later times, was considered the primary model.

That "the Church should be modelled on that of Apostolic times" was
considered by his biographer to be the guiding principle for Thomas
Cartwright's Cambridge lectures of 1570. In the first half of the seventeenth century John Dod (d. 1645), William Ames (d. 1633), and Thomas
Shepard the Elder (d. 1649) were among those who emphasized the authority of the primitive model in the Scriptures in contrast to the human
inventions of later times. Dod warned against the "Popish religion" con-
sisting of "the precepts of men," a "meere devise of mens braine," in opposition to the divine truth in scripture. Ames, appealing to "the practise
of the Ancient Church," condemned usages "brought in, in the depraved
and darke times of the Church, . . . against the rule of Scripture, and practise of the Primitive Church." Having similarly condemned the human inventions and ecclesiastical customs of the Roman Church, Shepard declared, "It is sufficient to believe this: that what the primitive churches
exemplarily practiced, that was taught them by the apostles who planted
them, and that whatsoever the apostles preached, the Lord Christ commanded." In 1659 the Independent John Owen entitled one of his works
*Of the Divine Originall, Authority, Self-evidencing Light, and Power of the
Scriptures*, arguing that in the Bible "by the Power of the Holy Ghost," divine truth "was *brought* into the *organs* or instruments, that he was pleased
to use, for the Revelation, and declaration of it unto others." In the preface
to a 1675 work by Thomas Doolittle, who considered "Popery" to be "a
Novelty," Richard Baxter declared, "*For my part, I consent to be of the oldest and most Universal Christian Church . . . professing my self of the oldest
Religion and Church that's truly Christian.*" "*We profess to stand to the testimony of Antiquity,*" he continued, "*believing as* Tertullian, Quod primum
id optimum." In the same year Thomas Gouge encouraged people to read
in Scripture "the holy lives and actions of Gods Children, not only *as matters of History*, but *as patterns of imitation*: For, for this end are they
recorded unto us," and Thomas Goodwin later declared, "We receive like
precious Faith with all those Primitive Christians, yea, with the Apostles
themselves." With respect to postbiblical precedents, Baxter observed that

"The chief use of the Fathers is to know Historically what Doctrine was then taught," echoing William Ames's earlier argument that allowed the use of the Church Fathers only in very limited circumstances, "the Word of God, and the edification of Beleevers requiring no such thing."[7] As I will show, this emphasis on primitive Christianity in the Puritan and Nonconformist traditon was not only shared but extended and amplified by Baptists and Quakers.

To the principle of *Quod primum id optimum*, and efforts to imitate the first form of Christianity, must be added the practice of re-creating biblical experiences in meditation and preaching through the use of dramatic imagination. Such re-creation employed the human senses, albeit in a spiritual way and for a spiritual purpose. Thomas Gouge encouraged such use, instructing people to meditate on the Scripture in order to remember and understand it and, when preparing for death, "With the Eye of Faith [to] look upon Christ hanging upon the Cross, there offering up his Life as an All-Sufficient Sacrifice, and full Satisfaction to Gods Justice for thy sins, and [to] cast thyself into the Arms of Jesus Christ." Demonstrating the way in which through imaginative and sensual re-creation such meditation could approach a fusion of the present with the primitive time, Baxter urged his readers,

> Suppose thou were now beholding this City of God; and that thou hadst been companion with *John* in his Survey of its Glory; . . . But get the liveliest picture of them [the saints] in thy minde that possibly thou canst; . . . till thou canst say, Methinks I see a glimpse of the Glory! methinks I hear the shouts of joy and praise! methinks I even stand by *Abraham* and *David*, *Peter* and *Paul*, and many more of these triumphing souls! methinks I even see the Son of God appearing in the clouds, and the world standing at his bar to receive their doom; methinks I even hear him say, *Come ye blessed of my Father*![8]

Dramatic re-creation in preaching once resulted in John Rogers (d. 1630), minister at Dedham in Essex, taking hold "with both hands at one time of the supporters of the Canopy over the Pulpit, and roaring hideously, to represent the torments of the damned, [which] had an awakening force attending it." Analysis of homiletic and other materials has led Theodore Dwight Bozeman to conclude that "With few exceptions Puritan sermons . . . provide copious documentation that the Puritan primordium was a real, dramatically engaging, unquestioned world of scene, society, characters, action, and moral atmosphere" and, more broadly, that primitivism itself "was integral in manifold ways to the very meaning of the Puritan vision."[9]

Such primitivism also entailed a looking forward with New Testament Christians to the second advent and other eschatological events. Whereas early Continental and English reformers thought they were living in the last days before the overthrow of the Roman Antichrist, they generally rejected millenarianism, the belief that the true church would triumph over its enemies and reign for a thousand years with Christ on earth, as it was a potentially dangerous error. But in seventeenth-century England, Thomas

Brightman's *A Revelation of the Revelation* (1615; published in Latin in 1609) and Joseph Mede's *The Key of the Revelation* (1642; published in Latin in 1627) prompted widespread interest in the subject. Thomas Goodwin, John Owen, and Richard Baxter were among those who gave it attention. The repressive activities of the Roman Empire and the Roman Catholic Church and their subsequent destruction were thought to have been prophesied in the Book of Revelation. Gradually the beliefs and practices of the true church were being recovered so that with the coming of the millennium the pure condition of the New Testament church would be restored. Furthermore, some preachers like Owen considered such traumatic events as the execution of Charles I to be signs that the millennium was fast approaching.[10]

Baptists and Quakers: Rise and Progress, Primitivism, Radicalism and Moderation

Although there is evidence that there were Anabaptists in England during the sixteenth century, they were few in number, were often aliens, and were repressed or banished soon after their detection. Consequently, the origin of the English Baptists is usually traced to the English Baptist church established in Amsterdam in 1609 by John Smyth, a Separatist minister who had moved there from Lincolnshire in the previous year with many of his congregation. In Amsterdam, Smyth concluded from his study of the New Testament that "Infants are not to be baptized . . . Bicause ther is neyther precept nor example in the new Testament of any infants that were baptized, by John or Christs Disciples; Only they that did confess their sinnes, & confesse their Fayth were baptized."[11] Smyth's group adopted both Arminian principles and the practice of believers' baptism and were rebaptized, but when Smyth planned to merge with the Mennonites, Thomas Helwys and others broke away, objecting among other things to Anabaptist views against taking oaths and holding public office. Helwys and his followers returned to England in 1612, settling in Spitalfields, London. In *A Short Declaration of the Mistery of Iniquity* (1612), Helwys pleaded for a remarkably broad religious liberty. "Let them be heretikes, Turcks, Jewes, or what soever it aperteynes not to the earthly power to punish them in the least measure," he argued. But he also declared that Christians should not flee from persecution, "for the disciples of Christ cannot glorify God and advance his truth better, then by suffering al manner of persecution for it." Helwys was soon imprisoned in Newgate, and by 1616 he had died. His congregation continued to worship together, however, and by 1626, at least six such General (Arminian) Baptist churches existed in England.[12]

Particular (Calvinistic) Baptists developed from a series of secessions beginning in 1633 from an Independent church that had been established in London by Henry Jacob in 1616. The subject of baptism seems to have played a role in these secessions, although it is not clear until the withdrawal of 1638 that the issue was that of *believers'* baptism. Of that occasion it was reported that several persons departed, "being convinced that Baptism was not for Infants, but professed Believers." By 1644, London had at least seven Particular Baptist churches, for in that year they published a joint confession of faith. It declared the scriptural mode of baptism to be immersion, a practice that had not been introduced among Particular Baptists until 1641; it was in use among General Baptists by 1651. Although thus agreed on the nature and method of baptism, these groups remained separate. As the Baptist historian W. T. Whitley observed, "Scarcely ever did General Baptists try to enter into outward organization with Particulars; rarely indeed was there any intercourse, even unofficial."[13]

By the early 1650s, a third but comparatively small group, the Seventh Day Baptists, was in evidence. Their distinctiveness, reflected in their name, rested on the observance of Saturday as the sabbath. The Particular Baptist Thomas Tillam (fl. 1637–68) adopted this view about 1655 and ministered to a Seventh Day congregation in Colchester, Essex. He argued that the fourth commandment was not ceremonial but rather moral and perpetual, that Christ and the Apostle Paul had observed it, and that "onely the apostasizing Church of Rome . . . did communicate upon the sunday, so called." There was also among some members of this group a special interest in Hebraic tradition. In fact, an unnamed source reported to Tillam that a number of Jews regularly attended their Seventh Day Baptist meeting places in London.[14]

In the two middle decades of the seventeenth century, the number of Baptist congregations increased significantly, aided by greater religious toleration, by the practice of sending out itinerant evangelists or "messengers" to establish new churches, and by the establishment and growth of associations of congregations. Whereas in 1644 there were probably only fifty or so Baptist churches, by 1660 there may have been some three hundred congregations and perhaps as many as twenty-five thousand Baptists.[15] As a result, Baptists were "established" and yet still youthful and expansive as a movement when in the 1650s the Quakers' vigorous evangelistic efforts began.

George Fox (1624–91) secured a central place in the history of seventeenth-century Quakerism not only by his own remarkable achievements but also by the imprisonment and untimely deaths of several other Quaker leaders from the movement's earliest days.[16] Born in Leicestershire, Fox began a spiritual quest in 1643 that resembled those of others who were to become Friends. From time to time it took him on journeys into adjoining counties and even to London, where he saw that "all was dark and under the chain of darkness." His other experiences, including consultations with ministers of various persuasions, proved no more satisfying. "But as I had forsaken all the priests," he testified, "so I left the separate preachers also, and those called the most experienced people: for I saw there was none among them all that could speak to my condition." Sometime in 1647, Fox reached the climax of his religious searching and many years later recorded that "When all my hopes in them and in all men were gone, so that I had nothing outwardly to help me, nor could tell what to do, then, Oh then, I heard a voice which said, 'There is one, even Christ Jesus, that can speak to thy condition,' and when I heard it my heart did leap for joy." He continued, "So he it was that opened to me when I was shut up and had not hope nor faith. Christ it was who had enlightened me, that gave me his light to believe in, and gave me hope, which is himself, revealed himself in me, and gave me his spirit and gave me his grace, which I found sufficient in the deeps and in weakness."[17]

Thus enlightened, Fox made it his mission to "bring people off from all the world's religions, which are vain," and to "turn people to that inward light, spirit, and grace, by which all might know their salvation, and their way to God." In these efforts he and others often used the imagery of the Lamb (Christ) and his saints at war with the Beast to describe their intense prophetic encounter with the world. In the next few years such leaders as James Nayler, Richard Farnworth, William Dewsbury, Francis Howgill, Edward Burrough, and Richard Hubberthorn could be counted among Friends. The convincement of Margaret Fell, who as a widow would marry Fox in 1669, transformed Swarthmoor Hall in Lancashire into a center of Quaker life and activity. Friends enjoyed such success in the north that in 1654 they launched a major evangelistic effort in the south of England. The work of traveling evangelists—the "First Publishers of Truth," as they came to be known—was described by the Quaker historian A. Neave Brayshaw: "Speaking to large companies in crowded rooms, in barns, in the open air; conversing more closely and familiarly with single individuals or with groups, disputing with 'priests,' facing the fury of the mob, they carried out their mission as triumphant conquerors."

The "fury of the mob" was a phenomenon Quaker preachers encountered from the beginning in the north as well as in other parts of England. In 1653, for example, imprisoned in York Castle, the former Baptist Elizabeth Hooton wrote to Fox that "a great uproar" occurred as Quakers preached in the streets and that "after goeing into a friends house, ye Rude people fell upon ye house and broake open ye dore & fell violently uppon ym." Thomas Aldam wrote to Margaret Fell that in Wakefield, Yorkshire, Thomas Goodaire was beaten with a sword by an assailant who "stroke till ye sword did fly out of ye hilt." Like many others, Fox was physically threatened, attacked, and imprisoned on several occasions. Joseph Besse's *A Collection of the Sufferings of the People Called Quakers* provides moving accounts of such episodes. The Lamb's War was accompanied by casualties. In spite of such strong resistance, the mission to "turn people to that inward light, spirit, and grace" brought the number of Quakers to some thirty-five thousand by 1660.[18]

From his analysis of an abundance of Quaker records, Richard T. Vann has concluded that "Quakerism at the beginning drew adherents from all classes of society except the very highest and the very lowest." Groups most heavily represented included yeomen and husbandmen, and wholesale and retail traders. Further, among the seventy or so First Publishers of

Truth, Ernest E. Taylor counted at least thirty yeomen and husbandmen, eight artisans and shopkeepers, and four schoolmasters. Baptist records are not nearly as thorough and methodical as those of Quakers, and few date from the seventeenth century. What information we have suggests that Baptists included many small artisans and tradesmen. Of their ministers, W. T. Whitley has observed, "In the country, the typical minister was a thatcher, a farmer, a malster, a cheese-factor; in the town, the preacher had been during the week making shoes, pins, buttons, collars, hats, clothes, had been dyeing or upholstering or selling such wares."[19]

Whatever their social origins, members of both groups strongly identified with the primitive church, the Baptists more strictly than Presbyterians and Independents, and the Quakers more intensely still. Thomas Grantham, General Baptist minister in Boston, Lincolnshire, entitled his major theological work *Christianismus Primitivus* and defended the ancient Christian religion against the "Humane Innovation" and "Pretended Revelation" of postbiblical times. Elsewhere he argued that the primitive church in Jerusalem was "*the* Mother of us All" and that "all Churches, in all Ages and Nations, are indispensably bound to follow this Church, in the Observation of all things whatsoever Christ commanded them." He concluded that "The Institution of the Baptized Churches (now wrongfully called Anabaptists) *and theirs only*, is truly Apostolical."[20] William Penn encapsulated the Quaker view in the title of one of his works: *Primitive Christianity Revived, in the Faith and Practice of the People Called Quakers.* In his preface to Fox's journal, he described the postbiblical falling away, the rise of "the *False Church*," and the work of the Protestant reformers, among whom there still "was too much of humane *Invention, Tradition* and *Art* that remained . . . and of worldly *Authority*." Eventually, some Protestants went "a step farther," he explained, "and that was into the *Water.* Another *Baptism*; and hoping to find that *Presence* and *Power* of God in submitting to that *Ordinance*, which they desired and wanted." Although these Baptists "were very *Diligent, Plain* and *Serious*, strong in *Scripture*, and bold in *Profession*, bearing much *Reproach* and *Contradiction*," they also failed, for "that which others *fell by*, proved their *Hurt*. For worldly *Power* spoiled them too." It was left to the Quakers to "declare this *Primitive Message . . . That God is Light*."[21] The self-perceived identity of each group lay in the primitive church, but some of the implications of that identity had to be discovered and worked out over time. As already noted, Baptists did not begin to practice immersion until the 1640s. The Quaker peace testimony was not published until 1660, and there were also other changes among both groups, to be discussed.

Working out such implications for their own self-perceived identity was difficult enough, but coping with the outward facet of identity—the way members of both groups were viewed by others—was perhaps even more challenging, for Baptists and Quakers were considered among the religious radicals of their time.[22] In response, some members of both groups sought to correct misperceptions, to project a more moderate image, and

to distance themselves from other radicals. Baptists were seen to have separated themselves from the Protestant mainstream, discarded Christian
baptism as it had been practiced in the church for centuries, and attacked
the notion of a professional ministry. And contemporaries associated them
with the Continental Anabaptists, who were best remembered for the hor-
rendous Münster revolution of 1534. Thus, although Daniel Featley,
member of the Westminster Assembly of Divines, debated at Southwark
with *English* Baptists in 1642, his account (*The Dippers Dipt*, 1645) focused on the radical religious views of Continental Anabaptists. Samuel
Richardson protested, asking what it mattered to English Baptists if some
German Anabaptists had held extreme religious opinions and made attempts against the state, and declared, "As for our parts, we can justly
plead, *Not guilty*, and challenge all in the world to prove it against us if
they can." In addition, the titles of the 1644 Particular Baptist and 1660
General Baptist Confessions, among several other documents, referred to
their congregations as "*falsely* called Anabaptist." Nevertheless, subsequent editions of *The Dippers Dipt* (the seventh appeared in 1660) continued to concentrate on the extremism of Anabaptists.[23]

Contemporaries found even more reason to consider Quakers radical,
for they rejected the authority of Scripture, eliminated the sacraments, refused to pay tithes or to honor magistrates and social superiors in traditional ways, and sometimes went naked "as a sign" in public. Not surprisingly, in 1671 the otherwise anonymous "R. H." described the Quakers as
"the *fag-end* of Reformation." Indeed, as Baptists were maligned as Anabaptists, so Quakers were defamed as Ranters and papists. They reportedly had pantheism and sexual license in common with the former and salvation by works with the latter. For their part, Quakers condemned both
Ranters and papists, and Muggletonians and Seekers as well. Fox himself
was among those taking issue with such groups. In addition, following the
Restoration various means were taken to impose order, control potential
extravagances, and render Quakerism more respectable. The establishment
of an organization, with authority exercised by meeting clerks and "weighty
Friends," some censorship of publications by the London Second Day
Morning Meeting (even Margaret Fell encountered resistance from this
group), the expunging by Thomas Ellwood of embarrassing portions from
Fox's journals, the "loss" of Fox's "Book of Miracles," and liberties taken
with other materials, sometimes by Fox himself, all reflected this effort. Finally, as Barry Reay has pointed out, the deaths of so many of the earliest
Quaker activists left the movement "to the influences of the patrician Penn
and [Robert] Barclay."[24]

In the political sphere, Baptists and Quakers were also perceived as
radicals, for some had been active in the parliamentary army and had cam-
paigned for the overthrow of the monarchy as well as the traditional
church. Some Baptists were also Levellers or Fifth Monarchists. Thus it is
not suprising that in the politically unstable months of 1659, there was
considerable fear among some of an uprising of Baptists and Quakers and

the transformation of England into another Münster.[25] Efforts to counter charges of political extremism included those of the wealthy London merchant and Particular Baptist minister William Kiffin, who presented a petition, *The Humble Petition and Representation* of 1649, to the Speaker of the House of Commons from several London churches disavowing a tract supporting the Leveller cause and proclaiming the Baptists' desire "to live peaceably and quietly under Magistrates and with all men." *The Humble Representation and Vindication* of 1654 affirmed General Baptist loyalty to the government, and a similar affirmation was made in *A Declaration of Several Baptized Believers* in 1659. Further, in a rare act of cooperation, General and Particular Baptists issued a condemnation of Venner's Fifth Monarchist uprising of 1661.[26] In 1659 George Fox warned Friends against plotting to overturn the government, and in 1660 Margaret Fell, Fox, and others testified against "*Strife*, and *Wars*, and *Contentions*." In the following year Friends published a more complete statement of their peace testimony and their repudiation of antigovernment plots. Nevertheless, Quakers and Baptists continued to be suspected of political subversion, and as Richard Greaves has shown, after the Restoration some *did* engage in plots against the government, including the Monmouth Rebellion in 1685.[27]

Other Religious Radicals: Seekers, Ranters, and Muggletonians

Sharing the radical end of the religious spectrum with Baptists and Quakers were persons identified as Seekers, Ranters, and Muggletonians. Jerome Friedman has positioned four of these movements "in order of [their] radicalism" as follows: Seekers, Quakers, Muggletonians, and Ranters. Although such placement obviously depends on the primary criterion chosen, all stood farther than Baptists from the mainstream of English Protestantism. In this study I use the three minor "groups" for comparative purposes.[28]

The designation *groups* reflects difficulties with the historicity of Seekers and Ranters. Although it has long been accepted that early Quaker membership drew heavily from Seeker communities in northwest England, J. F. McGregor is probably correct in concluding that "there was no *sect* of Seekers in Revolutionary England." Yet some Friends remembered an earlier time when conversions had been made among Seekers, and both Thomas Edwards and Richard Baxter described and attacked Seeker beliefs, the former identifying William Erbery, William Walwyn, John Saltmarsh, and Laurence Clarkson (Claxton) as members of this supposed sect. In defending themselves, the first three described basic Seeker tenets, with many of which they were sympathetic. Clarkson admitted that he had been influenced by Erbery, had become a Seeker after leaving the Baptists, and had then moved among Seekers in London, Kent, and Hertfordshire. (Clarkson was successively a Presbyterian, Independent, Baptist, Seeker,

Ranter, and Muggletonian.) For his part, Richard Baxter identified six different types of Seekers and considered John Jackson, who explained and
defended Seeker beliefs in *A Sober Word to a Serious People* (1651), "the
most rational and modest that hath wrote for this way." Thus there are a
number of descriptions of Seeker tenets written by Seekers, sympathizers,
and detractors that can be employed in this analysis, even if Seekers should
be approached as merely "the personification of a point of religious debate," as McGregor has suggested. In brief, Seekers believed that the true
church, ministry, and worship were "lost" in the current age of apostasy,
and they were thus waiting for them to be restored by divine initiative.[29]

Ranters pose a similar historical problem, most seriously for J. C.
Davis, who has suggested that their existence may have been an invention
of seventeenth-century sectaries, Presbyterians, and Royalists. In contrast,
Jerome Friedman has confidently placed Ranters into five categories, including sexual libertines, gentlemen Ranters, and philosophical Ranters.
The term Ranter was used loosely and derogatorily to refer to a range of
persons from the morally upright minister John Pordage to Abiezer Coppe,
who declared, "I can if it be my will, kisse and hug Ladies and love my
neighbours wife as my selfe, without sin," to John Robins, who, according
to *Ranters of Both Sexes* (1651), was believed by his followers to be God
the Father of Jesus Christ who was then in his wife's womb. Ranter beliefs
usually reflected antinomianism and a mystical pantheism; included the
notion that the dispensations of the Father and Son (Old and New Testaments) were over and the Age of the Spirit was beginning; appealed to an
inward spiritual authority; and sometimes denied that the spiritual person
actually sinned in the commission of carnal acts. "And so as allowed by
God," Baxter complained, "they spake most hideous Words of Blasphemy,
and many of them committed Whoredoms commonly."[30]

Unlike Seekers and Ranters, Muggletonians do not present problems
of historicity, although it was not widely known until the 1980s that they
had a continuous existence until at least 1979. At their beginning, John
Reeve claimed that on three occasions in early 1652, he heard the voice of
God appointing him as the last divine messenger and designating Lodowick Muggleton his spokesperson. As the two witnesses of the eleventh chapter of Revelation, their doctrines, curses, and blessings were said to be the
direct will of God. They taught that God became a man (Christ) and continued as such, being between five and six feet tall and ruling in heaven
some six miles above the earth. They also believed that the human soul was
mortal and that the ministry and worship of the church for most of its history was void and thus as acceptable to God "as the cutting off of a dogs
neck." After Reeve's death in 1658 and Clarkson's subsequent unsuccessful challenge to his leadership, Muggleton was perceived by his faithful followers as God's only commissioned witness until his death in 1698.[31]

There were a few points of similarity among Seekers, Ranters, and
Quakers, as I will show, but Muggletonian and Quaker doctrines contrasted sharply, and printed exchanges were often acrimonious. Members

of each group accused the other of having Ranter connections. Both were correct. Some Quakers had been Ranters before the inner light transformed them, and Reeve and Muggleton had associated with John Robins, who they later denounced after God's commission came to them in 1652. Muggleton claimed that his and Reeve's commission "hath had great power over the Ranters and Quakers," but Fox concluded that the voice Reeve heard commissioning them "was but a whispering of Satan."[32]

Baptists and Quakers: Conversion, Conflict, and Analysis

In 1650, John Downham, rector of Allhallows the Great in Thames Street, London, claimed that Separatism led successively to Anabaptism, Seeking, Levelling, and Ranterism. Although William Kiffin and other Particular Baptists denied this, there were in fact persons like Joseph Salmon, who in recanting his Ranter views admitted "posting most furiously in a burning zeal toward an unattainable end" in his pilgrimage from Presbyterians to Independents, Baptists, and then Ranters. Laurence Clarkson's (previously noted) progression was similar. Others were also "posting up and down." Valuable insight into this phenomenon and a highly sensitive exploration of a broad spectrum of religious thought and experience were provided in 1946 by Geoffrey F. Nuttall, who both enlivened Puritan scholarship and turned upside down much of the world of Baptist and Quaker studies. In what has been called "the single most important work on English puritan divinity," Nuttall argued that a strong thread of continuity ran through conservative, moderate, and radical positions within Puritanism and Separatism, extending through the Baptists and on to Quakerism. Thus, among other things, English Baptists and even Quakers were to be viewed not, as previously, against an essentially Continental background of Anabaptism, spiritualism, and mysticism, but rather in an English setting as groups that repeated and extended the "movement toward immediacy, toward direct communion with God through His Holy Spirit" that was characteristic of English Puritanism.[33]

If not always "posting most furiously," Baptists did give evidence of an openness to the discovery of further religious truth, as reflected in the Particular Baptist statement in the second edition (1646) of their 1644 confession: "We confesse that we know but in part, and that we desire and seek to know: and if any will doe us that friendly part to show us from the word of God that we see not, we shall have cause to be thankfull to God and them." The London congregation of Thomas Lambe the soap boiler was especially known for its open and vigorous discussions on issues of faith and practice, and indeed among many such General Baptist congregations there was a lengthy dispute in the 1650s over whether the New Testament practice of the laying on of hands after baptism should be required for church membership. Some Friends considered early Baptists "tender," that is, sensitive and open to the leading of the Spirit. For example, when in the mid-1670s George Fox recounted in his journal some of the religious experiences of his youth, he remembered staying in London for a time in 1644. Noting that his Uncle Pickering was a Baptist there, he added, "They were tender then." Among the Quakers he was not alone in that judgment (as discussed more fully in chapter 8). Thus it is not surprising that when Quaker evangelists entered an area, they frequently went first to meetings of this "once tender people" to "proclaim Truth" and sometimes were attentively received. In 1654, for example, William Caton wrote from Dover that "I had as much liberty amongst the Baptists as I could desire" and that a "fire is here kindled amongst them which cannot suddenly be quenched."[34]

Our sources do not allow for quantitative analysis, but there is ample evidence of early Quaker success among the Baptists. In 1648 in Nottinghamshire, Fox himself convinced many from a community of "shattered Baptists," as he called them. In 1654, the Broadmead church in Bristol lost about one-fourth of its membership of Independents and Baptists to the Quakers. In 1655, the two elders of the Baptist church at Littleport, Cambridgeshire, and many of their congregation became Friends. In such widely separated counties as Somerset, Northumberland, and Kent, Baptists were reported to have been converted. John Beevan and Francis Howgill, who described their religious quests as "posting up and down," as well as William Ames, William Bayly, Samuel Fisher, Elizabeth Hooton, Luke Howard, and Rebecca Travers were among Baptist converts to Quakerism who made memorable contributions to the Friends.[35]

Some former Baptists, however, caused difficulties for the Quaker movement. Although Friends discontinued use of the sacraments, after becoming a Quaker Humphrey Wolrich baptized a woman with water (see chapter 5). Later he became embroiled in a controversy with the London Second Day Morning Meeting over its refusal to authorize the publication of one of his manuscripts. The former Baptist Samuel Cater was involved in James Nayler's scandalous messianic entry into Bristol in 1656 (chapters 3 and 6), but was released after interrogation by the magistrates. Solomon Eccles (chapter 6), who in London in the 1660s had several times gone naked "as a sign," denounced and prophesied the death of the Quaker schismatic John Story in 1677, but later regretted and condemned his own prophecy. Both Rice Jones and John Perrot (chapter 6) led separations from the Quaker mainstream. They "runn out," Fox said.[36]

The conversion of some Baptists to Quakerism raises the question, Did Quakers ever become Baptists? At least three cases deserve attention. Edmund Hickhorngill or Hickeringill (1631–1708) was a member of the Baptist church in Hexham, but in Scotland in 1653, he reportedly testified that he had become a Quaker. Later that year he wrote a conciliatory letter to the Hexham church declaring, "Truly how much your patience and long-suffering, after all my prodigal-like extravagances, hath wrought with me, I am not able to express," and affirming that God "hath given me a room (as I hope) in your hearts: which as I saddened too, too long, by a grievous apostasy, so now I doubt not but by an unfeigned return to rejoice you." We do not know whether reconciliation resulted, but in 1662, Hickhorngill became rector of All Saints in Colchester, Essex. Edmund Skipp, vicar of Bodenham, Herefordshire, 1647–57, may have adopted Quaker views before repudiating Friends in 1655, and eventually joining with Baptists. In 1667, an unnamed male Friend in Southwark did in fact join with Baptists and in the process abandoned his Quaker wife to marry a Baptist woman. In the ensuing dispute between the two groups a Baptist reportedly declared, "he had rather one of them should commit adultery than that hee should Marry one of our Freinds [*sic*]."[37]

Although Quaker efforts to convert Baptists enjoyed some success, when Baptists realized more clearly the nature of the Quaker message and the threat posed to their numbers, controversy rather than conversion became the usual result of their contacts. In a letter to Margaret Fell, Edward Burrough reported the great distress of London Baptists that "A thousand of us [came] out of the North to scatter their Churches." Fox reported numbers of unpleasant encounters with "jangling Baptists." On one occasion he refused to eat a meal because of the presence of an "evil eye," presumedly that of the Baptist woman who had prepared it. In Dorchester in 1655, Baptists refused Fox's request to use their meetinghouse but disputed with him at a nearby inn concerning baptism. The next day the groups broke off their contact by employing a gesture used in the primitive church. According to Fox, "The Baptists being in a rage began to shake the dust off their feet after us. 'What!' said I, '. . . we which are in the power of God shake off the dust of our feet against you.' "[38] Other confrontations and disputes between various members of the two groups are dealt with in subsequent chapters.

Such controversy between Quakers and Baptists also took the form of tract warfare. When Baptists claimed that there were none whom Quakers "have exprest more Contradiction to (in matters of Religion) then against us," Hubberthorn strongly denied it. However, an examination of Joseph Smith's *Bibliotheca Anti-Quakeriana* (1873) suggests that in the entire tract conflict carried on between Friends and the various religious elements in England, the Baptists had a sizeable share, especially considering their minority status in a population approaching five million. For example, Baptists represented about 20 percent of the writers and produced around the same percentage of the anti-Quaker works listed by Smith through 1689. These efforts were nearly evenly divided between General and Particular Baptists. It is also of interest that of the 109 sections included in Fox's polemical collection *The Great Mistery* (1659), some 19 percent were directed against Baptists. The number of tracts exchanged between members of the two groups began with seven in 1654 but almost doubled by 1656 and afterward averaged about eight per year until 1662. The Licensing Act (1662) and other measures aimed at suppressing Nonconformity meant that few publications were forthcoming from 1662 until 1672, when Charles II's Declaration of Indulgence finally provided relief. In that year twelve tracts were exchanged. The number grew to twenty-seven in

1674, the most productive year, but sharply decreased in 1675, reflecting a return to religious repression. From then until 1689, the year of the Act of Toleration, such polemical works were traded only sporadically and were few in number.[39]

The "explosion" of tracts in 1672–74 reflects several major public debates in London (see chapter 2) as well as the less restrictive circumstances for Nonconformists following the 1672 Declaration of Indulgence. Hostile Baptists "*began first with us: as soon as the King gave liberty*," Luke Howard complained in 1673. The case of Thomas Hicks, one of the most hostile of the Particular Baptists involved in the London debates, illustrates the phenomenon of tract proliferation. Hicks published in 1672 *A Dialogue Between a Christian and a Quaker* and in the following year *A Continuation of the Dialogue*, as well as in 1674 two additional tracts in response to Quaker counterattacks. A record fifteen replies were forthcoming from nine Friends, including George Whitehead, William Penn, and Isaac Penington the younger. In 1675 four of Hicks's tracts were bound together and sold under the new title *Three Dialogues Between a Christian and a Quaker*, and later Whitehead reported that one of Hicks's works was to be reprinted with a new title. Not surprisingly Fox declared that in 1673 Baptists and others in London "had given out many books against us" and that "the Lord's power came over all and all their lying, wicked, scandalous books were answered." Nor is it surprising that the London Second Day Morning Meeting, in directing Quaker publication activities, decided in December 1674 *not* to authorize the printing of an additional manuscript against the Baptists because, as the case then stood between the two groups, the committee "would not willingly have other Controversyes brought in to make more work."[40]

Printed works of controversy, of course, constituted a major medium during the Reformation. Peter Milward's bibliographic volumes on the religious controversies of the Elizabethan and Jacobean ages illustrate how extensive such controversial writing had become. From 1650 to 1689, the Baptist-Quaker conflict generated at least ninety Quaker and fifty Baptist publications. These works were often characterized by lively accusations and rebuttals, interspersed with strongly worded personal attacks and emotional appeals. The tone of these exchanges is illustrated by John Bunyan's denunciation of Edward Burrough as "a railing *Rabshaketh*" and the Quakers as "fond Hypocrites." In response, Fox condemned Bunyan's "Lies and Slanders" and, as already mentioned, concluded that Bunyan "had better have been silent, then to fight against the Lord, the Lamb and his Saints." In the 1670s, the Baptist William Russel complained that William Penn "seems to have dipt his quill in Gall and Wormwood," and Thomas Rudyard declared that had the Baptist Richard Hobbs "taken a dose of Opium, he could not have more *intoxicated* his Brains then he has by this *Occasion of Contest*." In spite of their often vituperative nature, the disputes shed much light on the convictions and perceptions of the antagonists. This extensive set of polemical materials provides the major portion of printed primary sources for this study.[41]

One must be mindful of Christopher Hill's warning against drawing lines of division between religious groups in this period more sharply than they themselves might have. And what Richard Greaves has said of the nature of Puritanism—that it is "elusive, impossible to define, label, or catalogue with crisp precision, quantitative data, or scientific accuracy"—is sometimes true of Baptist and Quaker views as well. Nevertheless, I will show that in the main, members of both groups had a strong and clear sense of their religious identity. Regrettably, in the words of Barry Reay and J. F. McGregor, Baptists have been "a group curiously neglected by historians," although a few useful, if abbreviated, studies have been undertaken. Even Geoffrey Nuttall's seminal work gave little attention to Baptists. The more plentiful examinations of early Quakerism have increasingly given up the glossing of history to project respectability and have instead recognized Friends' radicalism and the threat they were seen to pose to the established order. The few publications linking both groups and relating them to Puritanism and Nonconformity have treated such relationships only briefly, identifying the two as "left-wing" sects that had some theological similarities yet were antagonistic to each other, and observing that some Baptists became Quakers.[42] The discussion of the Scripture in chapter 2 reveals the most fundamental distinction between the two groups—the degree to which they identified themselves with the primitive church. Chapter 3 demonstrates how Friends' zeal for an immediate experience of Christ like that of the primitive Christians gave rise to those emphases that generated their strong disagreements with Baptists over a number of basic doctrines and practices. These beliefs and practices are explored in turn in subsequent chapters.

2

The sacred Scripture is our just Confines

The Scripture

[Professor]
> *But Scripture is our Rule, that sacred Word,*
> *Which first descended to us from the Lord,*
> *And was confirm'd by Miracles and Signs.*
> *The sacred Scripture is our just Confines.*

[Quaker]
> *The Scriptures are indeed a Declaration*
> *Of what Men once enjoy'd; but Inspiration*
> *Both was and is a Rule, doth never vary:*
>
> . . . .
>
> *This Inspiration is my onely guide,*
> *The Scriptures by the Spirit must be try'd.*

Benjamin Keach, *The Grand Impostor Discovered*

The Quakers Ballad: or, An Hymn of Triumph and Exhultation for their Victories, at the two late great Disputes by them held with the Baptists . . . To an excellent new Tune, called The Zealous Atheist was an anonymous broadsheet published in 1674. With humorous rhyme, it referred to portions of the most extensive public dispute between Baptists and Quakers that occurred in London in a series of four major meetings in 1672–74, drawing up to three thousand persons for sessions that, at least once, went as long as five or six hours.[1] Among those involved were William Penn, George Whitehead, Isaac Penington, George Keith, and Thomas Ellwood; and on the Baptist side, Thomas Hicks, Jeremiah Ives, Thomas Plant, William Kiffin, and Hanserd Knollys. The vigor that characterized these London debates is illustrated by the meeting held on 9 October in the Barbican when the audience often shouted and interrupted the proceedings. According to *The Quakers Ballad,*

A Rabble thrust in from each end of the Town,
And before half an agreement could be laid down
In less time than a man can a pot of Ale swallow
'twas confirm'd with a hoop, & deny'd with a hallow.

At one point people were startled by a crack that abruptly appeared in the building, forcing the speakers to abandon the pulpit for a safer location. Eventually, after it grew dark and candles had been lit, the Baptist Thomas Plant pointed out, "*The doors are broken, and several things necesssary to be repaired*" and called for an end to the meeting. Following discussion of means for arranging another debate, both sides agreed to dismiss the meeting, "it being late, and the Meeting place much Damaged."[2]

Among the points of strong contention in this extensive dispute was the nature and role of Scripture. A number of basic questions were taken up. What authority did the Bible have in faith and practice? What were the relationships between Scripture and Holy Spirit, and between Scripture and immediate inspiration or revelation? In what sense was the Bible the Word of God? Was the Scripture necessary and/or sufficient for salvation? How was it to be used and interpreted? The vigorous exchanges on these questions in person and in print in these London debates, and others to be employed in this chapter, reveal much about the fundamental element that separated the members of the two religious groups. Underlying the disagreements on these questions was the fact that Friends more closely identified themselves with primitive Christianity, seem to have entered more fully the "Great Time" of the Christian "beginnings," and thus could claim as their own the same authority that the earliest Christians had *before* the New Testament was written. Baptists, on the other hand, refused to enter the primitive time as fully as Quakers and retained a sense of "difference" between their own age and the extraordinary one of New Testament Christianity. Their authority remained the written Word, which stood between them and the primitive church.

The Authority of Scripture: Rule and Touchstone, the Spirit, Holy Men of Old, Words of Christ, Sufficiency and Necessity

Baptists' dedication to following the primitive model led to brevity and simplicity in their early confessions and to the absence of systematic discussion of the doctrine of the Scripture. However, in an attempt to display doctrinal harmony with Presbyterians and Independents, Particular Baptists published a confession in 1677 that was largely a revised version of the Westminster Confession and was thus in accord with the Savoy Declaration as well. It included nearly verbatim the chapter on the Scripture from the older confession. The General Baptist confession of 1679, also directed toward such harmony, included an article on Scripture similar to that in the Westminster Confession. However, it omitted references to the testimony to and illumination of Scripture by the Spirit and instead inserted a warning against dependence on pretended immediate inspiration and an inner light. Baptists were attempting to convince others of their moderation and their affinity with mainstream Nonconformity, and to distance themselves from religious radicalism in general and Quakerism in particular.[3] All four of these confessions reflected the belief that the direct revelation of biblical times had ceased and that now in the Holy Scripture was recorded what was necessary for salvation. Thus Scripture was the supreme authority in faith and practice, and (with the exception of the General Baptist confession of 1679) assurance of this authority, as well as the understanding of what was revealed in the Bible, was said to be provided by the inward illumination of the Holy Spirit.

When Baptists asserted that the Scripture was the authority in faith and practice, Friends strongly disagreed. The Bible, they argued, had been inspired by the Spirit, and without the Spirit people could neither believe nor understand it. Surely, therefore, the Spirit, not the Bible, ought to be the rule of Christians. William Loddington, a former Baptist from Reading, argued that he was obliged to obey nothing in the written Word "*because there Recorded*" but complied "because the Spirit of God convinceth me that it is my Duty." However, as Whitehead pointed out, "Our denying that they [the Scriptures] are the Rule of Faith is no Proof that we deny them to be any Rule at all, while in Subserviency to, and Proof of the greater." Still, Baptists who claimed the letter or written Word as their guide were believed to be guilty of serious error. Reflecting on his experience as a Baptist, William Ames confessed it had been the Devil who taught him to take the prophets' and saints' words to be his rule.[4] Quakers also objected to the Baptist claim that Scripture was the touchstone of truth. On the contrary, Friends argued, the Spirit was the touchstone and was to be used to test the Bible. Samuel Fisher alleged that Baptists were forced to admit this: "When we ask them what are ye to try the Scriptures by, whether they are of God or no? they say by the Spirit; yea, though other things may be necessary, yet the testimony of the Spirit is necessary, and only all-sufficient to this purpose."[5]

A close association between Spirit and Scripture in the minds of Baptists was evident in arguments about authority. Baptists claimed that, contrary to Quaker accusations, they did not say the written Word was to test the Spirit, but rather that the Spirit speaking in the Bible was the touchstone. Grantham explained, "When the Quakers tell us that they have the Holy Ghost, and that what they speak they speak as they are moved by the Holy Ghost, &c. Then indeed we say we are to try what they thus tell us, by what the Spirit hath said in the Scripture." Although Baptists thought of the Spirit working in and according to the Bible, they nevertheless distinguished between the two, claiming that the latter was to be the guide for the saints. According to William Burnet, God never designed the Spirit to be the rule but rather designed it to be an assistant to help people live by the rule. That Friends denied the Scripture to be such a model led Russel to speculate whether it was possible that Jesuits might encourage the introduction of Catholicism to England by promoting Quakerism. Friends were accused of popery for other reasons too, of course, and they sought to distance themselves from Catholics as well as from radical Protestants.[6]

In supporting their conflicting views, both groups appealed to primitive Christianity. Friends, more closely identifying themselves with the earliest Christians and other biblical saints, claimed repeatedly to have the same authority as "the holy men of God" did "before the Scriptures were written." According to Fox, "The holy men of God before the Scriptures was, had a rule, and a touchstone," which was the Spirit. This same Spirit led the saints to write the Bible, and therefore it was the Spirit that was the Quakers' guide as well. Of his own enlightenment Fox testified, "These things I did not see by the help of man, nor by the letter, though they are written in the letter, but I saw them in the light of the Lord Jesus Christ, and by his immediate Spirit and power, as did the holy men of God, by whom the Holy Scriptures were written." Further, the Spirit, Thomas Lawson argued, enabled New Testament Christians to know all things and to discern antichrists, deceivers, and false prophets. Surely, therefore, that which gave forth the written Word and was the rule and touchstone to holy persons before the Bible was written ought to be the authority for Christians now. This meant not that they were to live contrary to biblical precepts, but that having the Spirit as their guide, they were to live in accordance with the scriptural standards as Paul and the primitive Christians had. In fact, as Burrough pointed out to the London Baptist John Griffith, "They who witness that to bee their rule which gave forth the Scripture, walkes up in the life of the Scripture more than you all."[7]

That the Spirit had given forth the written Word Baptists agreed, but even if the Quakers had the same Spirit in the same measure as the writers of Scripture (Baptists believed they did not, of course), still the latter was to be their rule just as the written law had been the guide for "holy men" in Old Testament times. "Consider the sweet frame of that gracious soul, the Lords servant David," John Griffith wrote. "What a high estimation he set upon the Word of the Lord; saith he, O how I love thy Law! its my meditation all the day." The Scripture served the apostles and the saints of the early church in the same way, for Paul considered the Jews at Berea more noble than those at Thessalonica because they examined the written Word daily to see if the things he spoke were true, Griffith asserted.[8] Above all, Scripture was the rule of Christ, who obeyed it in the time of his temptation to overcome Satan, Burnet pointed out. In fact, Griffith argued, Christ commanded the Jews to search the written Word. In discarding this role of Scripture, Friends were abandoning the rule of the saints and even of Christ himself, an act that caused Enoch Howet to exclaim, "O subtle Devil! Will nothing serve thy turn but to disarm us and take away that weapon that Christ fought and overthrew thee with? But as he had the victorie, so must all his members in their overcoming strength obtain it, (I mean this authoritie, *It is written*.)"[9]

Members of both groups, then, believed the Bible issued from the Spirit, a fact with which Quakers supported their emphasis on the superiority of the Spirit as the rule and in which Baptists found further reason to revere scriptural authority. Another argument Baptists used to support this authority was that Scripture contained the words Christ received from the Father. These statements were not confined to the Gospels but were found in the rest of the New Testament as well, for the apostles testified of the things Christ had spoken to them. Therefore, addressing himself to all persons and rejecting Quaker claims, Griffith wrote, "If you are of God, you will hear John, Peter, Paul, and the rest that were the servants of Christ, not the fleshly conceits of these or any other men. My Sheep, saith Christ, hear my voice, and a strangers they will not hear." Persons who denied the authority of Scripture denied Christ's words and consequently denied that by which they would be judged at the last day.[10]

Friends readily admitted that Christ's statements were precious and that those who truly received Christ did not reject his words. Nevertheless, it was neither statements nor the so-called written Word that was to judge people at the last day. All judgment was given to the Son, Christ the Word, not the Bible. Surely Christ was of far more authority than the words that he spoke and were recorded in the Bible, they argued. Furthermore, as Nayler pointed out, when Christ spoke the words of God, "They did hear him carnally (as carnall men doe the letter) and could make him answer to his speech, but could not hear the words of God, as Christ plainly saith." Burrough concluded that Baptists, like the Pharisees, professed the words that Christ spoke but rejected Christ himself.[11]

Quakers used arguments similar to these of Nayler and Burrough in directly attacking the Bible's sufficiency as the rule of faith and practice. They claimed that in the past the written Word had not proved to be sufficient, for those who had it as their guide crucified Christ and judged their deed lawful and necessary. Nor did the Scripture prove to be a sufficient standard in the present, for people who used it did not necessarily act appropriately. In a 1653 manuscript, Fox accused Baptists of "turning from this light within, & obeying the command in the letter without, as the scribes & pharisies [did]." It was, in fact, no proper guide at all, for it proved to be variable when employed. Penn pointedly brought this to Hicks's attention when he wrote, "The Church unto which Tho. Hicks belongs own the Scripture to be the Rule: But suppose Tho. Hicks in some one Point believes the Scripture not to intend the same thing, the rest of the Church understand it to mean, as in [the] Case of Free-Will: I query how this Matter shall be reconciled?"[12] If, in such a case, Baptists were to admit that the Bible as the standard of faith needed the assistance of the Spirit, this would be an admission that Scripture was not a sufficient rule alone. The Spirit, on the other hand, was a sufficient guide without the Bible, but this meant neither that the truth of the written Word was destroyed nor that people were acquitted from obedience to it, for, on the contrary, the Spirit led people to the fulfilling of Scripture.[13]

Baptists acknowledged that not all people who possessed the Scripture had the authority and mind of the Holy Spirit and conceded that the Spirit was required as a guide to the Scripture. They argued that this did not weaken the position of the written Word, however, for it was the fault of individuals if they did not obey it, and although the Spirit might be the guide, the Bible was still the rule. Having admitted the need for the guidance of the Spirit, the Baptist response to the Quaker criticism of the sufficiency of the Scripture as the standard was primarily a counterattack on the sufficiency of the Spirit in this role. Grantham dramatically summarized the major thrust of the argument:

> Suppose now that a Jew, a Turk and a Quaker, should meet together, and a question arise among them about the Saviour of the World. The Quaker tells the other, That *the Eternal Spirit is the Saviour of the World, and not the visible Man exclusively considered.* The Turk saith, *It is blasphemy to say that Christ is God, or that God hath a Son: and that Christ was only a good Man and a great Prophet.* The Jew tells them, *They are both deceived, and that Christ was an Imposter or Deceiver.* And they all aver these things are evinced by the Spirit in their hearts respectively. Certainly in this difficulty, no way in an ordinary Ministery can be found to resolve the Question satisfactorily, but that which Apollos, Acts 18:28 used, who *mightily convinced the Jews, and that publickly, shewing by the Scriptures, that Jesus was Christ.*[14]

Baptists feared not only insoluble problems like this if the Spirit alone were the authority but also the wildly heretical doctrines or ideas that could be foisted on the world if the written Word were no longer the rule. People would have no security against impostors. "Then," predicted Hicks, "if George Fox do but say 'tis reveal'd to him the Earth is flat, it must be believ'd, because I have no rule wherewith to disprove his pretended Revelation." The doctrinal confusion that could result from a revocation of scriptural authority might be accompanied by moral chaos as well. Howet worried that it would bring in "a Night of Darkness, that men might take their pleasure in sin without any Light at all to shame them for it, if he [Satan] could make the Scriptures useless." The Spirit might be needed as a guide for the written Word, but the prospect of the Spirit replacing the Bible as the standard was so fraught with dangers that it was a plan of Satan himself and would, according to Howet, "shake us in our foundation, I mean the Doctrine of the Prophets and Apostles, would make the whole building of Religion and Godliness fall."[15]

Baptists thought they had good reason to be alarmed, given the beliefs and practices of others at the radical end of the religious spectrum, especially Ranters and Quakers, whom they considered much alike. According to Thomas Collier, Quaker principles were "but the principles of the old Ranters" who would have "no Scripture to be a rule." Indeed, Ranters, like Friends, appealed to a rule within and rejected an outward authority: The Ranter Jacob Bauthumley argued, "The Bible without, is but a shadow of that Bible which is within, which is the Law spiritual, the safest and only rule." It was thought that Seekers also advocated an inner spiritual authority and were skeptical of the reliability and use of the Scripture.[16] Unlike Seekers, Ranters, and Quakers, the Muggletonians appealed to an outward authority, but it was not the Scripture of the Baptists. John Reeve and Lodowick Muggletonian claimed to have been appointed by God as the two last divine witnesses (Rev. 11), the only ones who had the power to interpret the Bible and determine who was to be blessed or cursed to eternity. With Reeves's death in 1658, Muggleton declared that he alone "doth stand in God's place." William Penn denounced such assertions as "most arrogant and false." For his part, Muggleton considered Penn "an ignorant spatter-brain'd Quaker," and accused him and other Friends of taking up the doctrine if not the practice of the Ranters, and the Baptists of adhering to the dead letter of the Scripture.[17] At least with the former charge Baptists could agree.

Scripture, Inspiration, and Revelation

Although the issue of mediate and immediate inspiration was not often discussed in its own right, it was an integral part of many of the disagreements between the two groups. Quakers did not deny that God could speak to people mediately through Scripture or through other persons, but they insisted on the centrality of immediacy like that enjoyed in New Testament Christianity. As with their emphasis on the authority of the Spirit, this insistence was rooted in their own experience. Fisher testified, like numerous others, that even as a boy "before I could read the Scripture (which I could read when very young) I knew by that of God in me . . . that I should not lye." The former Baptist Francis Howgill, reflecting on his pre-Quaker years, declared that although he had been taught that it was heresy to look for the word of God to be spoken anywhere except in the letter, "Yet often I was made to doe many righteous things by the immediate power and word of God."[18]

The immediate experience of God by Quakers, like that enjoyed by New Testament Christians, placed the means of mediate inspiration, the Bible, in a secondary position. Consequently, Friends pleaded for the primacy of the authority of the Spirit above the Scripture. To rely on mediate inspiration was to depart from the experience of the biblical saints, each of whom had had immediate communication with God. In the opinion of Quakers, Baptists had fallen away not only from the practice of the saints but from their own earlier ways as well; Penn noted that immediate experiences of God "once were the great Foundation of both their Knowledge and Comfort, though now mockt at by him [Hicks] with great Derision in a Quaker." The current practice of Baptists to act "by imitation from the Letter without" was, according to Burrough, an abomination, for they followed their own wills without the moving of the Spirit and thus incurred the wrath of God.[19]

Baptists did not deny that God could speak to people immediately, but they emphasized God's mediate inspiration through the reading or preaching of the Bible. It was an emphasis rooted in experience. Referring to the Spirit's anointing, William Kaye testified, "If the Scriptures had not spoken of it, I say, that such is the sufficiencie of the Scriptures, that as Paul said of Sin, He had not known it but by the Law, so I had not known the anointing, but that the Scriptures had declared it." Grantham appealed to the personal knowledge of all "sober" Christians when he argued they would grant that the first knowledge they received of Christ as the Savior of the world came from the Spirit speaking in the Scripture or by the preaching of the gospel.[20] Such was the importance of the Bible in the experience of Baptists that they insisted on its primacy with regard to authority. Grantham noted that when people read Scripture the words had the same authority as if God spoke the same things to them immediately from heaven. However, the Baptists' emphasis on the mediate inspiration through the written Word was the result of a negative fear as well as a positive experience. There was serious danger in encouraging people to rely on immediate illumination by the Spirit, for it was far more difficult for them to distinguish their own whims from true immediate inspiration than from the mediate inspiration of the Bible. Quakers were said to fail miserably in this respect, for "They substitute in its [Scripture's] room, their own motions and impulses."[21]

A further issue was that of continuing revelation. It involved two questions. Could the Spirit reveal to people things contrary to Scripture? Could the Spirit lead persons to make additions to the Bible? With respect to the former, the Baptist emphasis on the primacy of the written Word led to the rejection of whatever contradicted it. Similarly, Burrough argued that the Spirit led according to, not contrary to, the Scripture. Penn made the position of Friends clearer when he stated, "Nor do we say that those essential Things relating to Faith and Godliness mentioned [in the Bible] are by us to be sleighted or contradicted; or that the Light and Spirit we are led by, doth or can lead to any such thing." Could the Spirit lead people to add to the written Word? To Baptists, the answer was emphatically no. Given their emphasis on the supremacy of the Spirit above the Bible, Friends might be expected to have entertained at least the theoretical possibility of such additions. However, in their disputes with Baptists they did not do so. On the contrary, in arguments concerning the person of Christ and the second advent, Quakers often accused Baptists of using unscriptural language and of asserting positions not to be found in Scripture. Furthermore, William Shewen advised that the presuming of things beyond what was written in the Bible ought to be answered with sharp reproof, and Whitehead warned that "To add or diminish be forbidden under a penalty, Rev. 22. 18, 19." Considering themselves to be the "true Church which is come out of the Apostacy, since the dayes of the Apostles, to that the Apostles was in," Friends believed like Fox that Quaker doctrine was "not a new Gospel."[22]

The Nature of Scripture: The Word of God, the Letter, and Salvation

In light of the Quaker views just discussed, it is not surprising that when Baptists referred to the Scripture as "the Word of God" or "the Word," Quakers often protested, arguing like Burrough, Nayler, and Farnworth that only Christ, not the Scripture, could properly be considered the Word of God. Fox explained: "Christs name is called the Word of God; his name is above every name, and over all things he must have the preheminence, words and names." Thus Thomas Lawson, who in 1655 debated with Matthew Caffyn at the latter's house and at the Quaker meeting in Crawley, Sussex, declared, "Thou art *Antichrist*, pulling the Crowne from off his [Christ's] head, and giving it to the Scripture."[23]

Baptists contended, however, that a collection of many words comprising discourses of the prophets, Christ, and the apostles could be called the Word of God, and that even Christ himself had used this name to refer to Scripture. True, the Bible contained some words of Satan and evil persons, but, according to Grantham, they were recorded for people's information and admonition and so were to be believed as the Word of God. To Baptists, the Word was the declaration of the divine mind and will and contained God's precepts, promises, and judgments. It also included the history of the wicked as well as the saints, and the words of both Satan and Christ. To affirm that the Word was such was not to deny that Christ was the Word as Quakers claimed, for, according to Joseph Wright, the Baptist minister at Maidstone in Kent, "Whosoever doth own the Scriptures to be the Word of God: doth not deny that Christ is the Word of God, neither can such a thing be layed to their charge, without doing great injury to them: but I say, as it is true, that Christ is the Word of God, as the Scripture saith, Revel. 19.13. So it is as true, that the Scripture is the Word of God, as Christ saith, Mark 7.13."[24]

The dichotomy of spiritual and physical, employed by Quakers in arguments over the proper understanding of the Word of God, was more sharply defined in the controversy over Scripture as "the letter," a term often used derisively by Friends. They could admit that what the Bible spoke of was spiritual, but, in the words of Fox, "The letter of Scripture (paper and inke) we cannot say it is spiritual." The Baptists' Word or Scripture "is that by which no flesh shall be justified, but is the letter that killeth, and ministration of death," Nayler maintained. Whitehead explained that Quaker references to Scripture as the letter were in the Pauline sense, that is, distinguishing between the law and the gospel, and between the letter and the Spirit. Such references to the letter were made "chiefly to those, whose Minds have been too much in the Shadows and Letter thereof, neglecting the Substance, Power & Spirit. We knowing also that in the New Covenant we must serve the Lord in the Newness of the Spirit, and not in the Oldness of the Letter."[25] To the Baptist teacher Matthew Caffyn, Thomas Lawson declared, "Thou art shut out from all the holy men of God, who were Ministers of the spirit, and not of the letter, as Paul was, 2 Cor. 3.6. but thou art a Minister of the letter, and not of the spirit."[26]

Baptists did not consider the letter itself as spiritual either. William Burnet admitted that the letter written with ink on paper was dead. However, the contents of the letter—the Word, or mind, or will of God—that "matter," as Burnet called it, "is Spiritual, and Powerfull, when carried home by the Spirit to the heart." Because of the spiritual potential of this content, Baptists objected to derisive references to the Scripture as "the letter." That Friends made such assertions led Hicks to charge that they preferred their own pamphlets above the Bible. It was reported that at the Barbican meeting of 28 August 1674,

> This was proved from the Titles they give to their own books; and the Titles they give to the Scripture, *viz. The Voice of Wisdom: Breathings of True Love: Shield of Truth: A Spiritual Glass: Light Risen Out of Darkness*. These are the Titles given to several of their books.
>
> But the Scriptures are called, *Letter; Dead Letter; Paper, Ink and Writing: Carnal Letter*, &c. 'Tis easie to judge by these Titles, to which the preference is given.[27]

Hicks made an accusation showing greater insight in his first dialogue: "It is not the paper and Ink that your spite is so much against, as the sence and meaning. 'Tis this test your souls dread." Whatever the Quaker purposes, Baptists such as the Stafford minister Henry Haggar contended that persons deriding Scripture as the Quakers did "by calling it ink and paper, and a dead letter, are false Apostles and deceitful workers . . . which the Apostle Paul, Gal. 1. 8, 9 saith, Are accursed."[28]

The Christological and pneumatological elements thus far observed in disputes over the nature of the Scripture were accompanied by a soteriological one. It involved a twofold question: Was the Scripture necessary to salvation, and was it sufficient? To Friends, it was Christ, or the spiritual Word or the Spirit, that saved people, not the written Word. It was evident, Shewen argued, that people had the true knowledge of God before the Scripture was written. But even after it was written, the Bible did not prove sufficient for the salvation of many who possessed it. Indeed, those very persons who honored the Scripture in which Moses had written of Christ did not believe it but crucified him when he came in the flesh.[29]

Not only had Scripture been demonstrated unnecessary and insufficient for salvation in the past, it was also proving to be so in the present. The Quaker William Ames confessed that as a Baptist "I was Chosen to be an *Elder*, because of my *Wisdom in the Letter*. And when I was so, there was none so forward as I to condemn Sin, and yet my self the *greatest sinner*." Shewen pointed out that people who had the Bible "may talk much of the Scriptures with their Tongues, and carry the Bible in their Pockets, and yet the Devil may rule in their Hearts." He also claimed that many of the heathen who did *not* have Scripture nevertheless lived such righteous lives that they would find it more tolerable at the Day of Judgment than many so-called Christians who *did* have it. From such observations Friends concluded that persons who believed in the soteriological necessity and sufficiency of Scripture were the Antichrist, for they were setting up another way to salvation than that of Christ.[30]

The claim that Scripture was insufficient for salvation because some who had it were not saved was to Baptists a non sequitur. They argued that if people possessed Scripture but were unsaved, it was not the fault of the Bible. At least with the Bible in their possession people were in a position to enjoy salvation, but without it where would they be? How would they know of the gospel? How would they know that Christ had been born and that he had lived and died on their behalf? Was there some other way to know these things? Quakers who thought so should demonstrate this by sharing their knowledge of divine truths *not* recorded in the Bible. Keach pointedly requested such a demonstration when he asked, "Prethee what other things were they, which Jesus did, which the Apostle says were not written?" William Russel complained that although he had asked this question many times of Quakers, they could never tell him one of them. To a similar question from Hicks, Penn replied that if God saw the need to acquaint humankind with some fact of history then God could do so. "But," he added in a later reply to Hicks, "a relation being with us, the Light of Christ doth nothing unnecessarily." Nevertheless, the former Baptist Humphrey Wolrich argued that historical facts and even the Bible itself were not necessary to salvation, for Christ was able to save in the present without the Scripture, as he was before it was written. Friends were careful to add that this was not to slight or void Scripture. Indeed, the Spirit worked not contrary to but according to the Bible, for the purpose of fulfilling it. The operation of the Spirit in this way convinced and converted, but, according to Burrough, not the Scriptures without the Spirit.[31]

Baptists did not claim that conversion or salvation came through the Scripture alone. Referring to the time when those who had the Scripture nevertheless crucified Christ, Ives affirmed that neither then nor in the present could people be saved without the Spirit. However, Baptists spoke of the Spirit working "according to" and "in" the written Word, for they stressed the close conjunction of the two, believing, as Thomas Grantham did, that the words in Scripture "as they contain the mind of God, for Men to believe and obey, are Spirit and Life; and they that reject these words, holding forth the Mind of God, do resist the Spirit, and put Eternal Life from them." Scripture "in the hand of the eternal Teacher"—the content of the letter "applied by Gods spirit to the believers heart"—made persons wise to salvation, Howet claimed. However, Burnet argued, although "God never designed that the word . . . could work true sanctity without the Spirit; neither hath he designed the Spirit to do that work alone, but by the word, John 17.17, 19."[32]

The Use and Interpretation of Scripture

If Friends, like Whitehead, believed that "the Spirit is effectual without the Scriptures, and able of it self to lead into all Truth," then what was the role of the Bible? Although denying the primacy of the written Word, Quakers often appealed to the Bible to support their views. Baptists were well aware of this. When Friends claimed that according to Scripture, Christ, not the Bible, was the Word of God, Hicks retorted, "Then it seems the Scripture is the rule of thy belief in this point. Dost thou well then in denying it to be a Rule?" On another occasion Wright lamented, "What a sad thing is it, that men should quote Scriptures, like Satan, to justifie their Doctrine of deceit, which they deliver, and yet notwithstanding esteem the Scriptures of no value?" But Quakers did *not* "esteem the Scriptures of no value." On the contrary, they thought them to contain the words of God and to be a divine declaration and a secondary guide that people were to follow. Indeed, Quakers believed their doctrines were to be found in the Bible, and therefore, according to Thomas Salthouse, the Scripture was a witness with them of what they maintained and taught. Consequently, there was nothing improper in their appealing to the written Word. To Hicks's earlier charge, Whitehead replied that although Friends denied the Scripture to be the rule, yet "We make use of them as the Spirit of God teacheth, and for the Information and Conviction of them that have a belief concerning them; for the End still that they may eye that Light and Spirit of Truth which gave them forth." To prove a point in a public dispute with John Tombes, Fox said he "desired all the people to take out their Bibles; for I would make the Scriptures bend him." And Scripture was of use not only for evangelism and debate but also for Christian living. Because the Bible was a declaration of heavenly truths, Christians were to read it, believe it, and practice its tenets. As Fox declared, "The Scriptures is for correction and doctrine, furnishing the man of God in his place." To this statement Baptists could have subscribed, for they also advocated the use of Scripture to convict people of their sins and to instruct and equip them for Christian living. However, Baptists associated the work of the Spirit more closely with the Bible and placed greater emphasis on its use in making people "wise to salvation."[33]

With respect to the interpretation of the Bible, Quakers emphasized the use of the Spirit, pointing out certain weaknesses in the method of interpreting Scripture by itself. There were, for example, numerous translations of the Bible and even multiple Greek and Hebrew versions. Penn wondered how a person could discern which was correct. Even when using the same translation, people could not agree on a common meaning. The former Baptist Samuel Fisher, learned in Greek and Hebrew, declared, "There's as many silly senses, misty meanings, and contradictory conceits in the minds of them that are Ministers of it [Scripture], almost as they are Ministers of it." By what then was the written Word to be interpreted if not by itself? Obviously, by the Spirit, as Burrough argued: "He that hath the same spirit which speaks them forth, reads them and understands them, and none else." Indeed, for those who did not rely on the Spirit to give them understanding, it was a dangerous thing even to read the Bible.[34]

Baptists did not reject the assistance of the Spirit in interpreting Scripture, but they held that the written Word was its own best interpreter. They claimed that the controversial tenets advocated by Quakers reflected serious misinterpretations of the Bible that contradicted its true meaning and proved that Friends were not really led by the Spirit. Grantham explained that Friends contradicted or wrested the Scripture and when they did so were to be rejected as vain boasters who were led by their own fancies and not by the Holy Spirit. Quakers scoffed at such charges, as when Burrough maintained, "Wee speake of nothing but what is declared of in the Scripture by the holy men of God, and neither without it, nor above it or beyond it do wee speake." Indeed, when the interpretations of the two groups conflicted, it was the Baptists who were guilty of abusing and perverting the Bible, Nayler asserted.[35]

In the great debates of 1672–74, Baptists and Quakers accused each other of being "no Christians." According to *The Quakers Ballad*,

> At first they came on like huffing Philistians,
> And needs would attempt to prove us no Christians
> When most by our wranglings, already thought much
> To believe that in truth either of us were such.

Indeed, during the last of the meetings (16 October 1674 at Wheeler Street, Spitalfields) a "neutral stranger," attempting to clarify the question in dispute, sided with the Quakers and was then suspected by Baptists of being a Roman Catholic priest. At the same time Hicks was accused of lodging himself "*safely in an Ale-House*" nearby "til his *Confederates* departing call'd him away." In the end George Whitehead concluded that he had "never met with such unfair Dealing, clamorous Work and hideous Noise in Dispute, from any People as from these Men."[36] However, beneath the acrimony of these and other disputes I have described, many differences seem to be ones of degree or emphasis.

It has been shown that with respect to the authority of the written Word, Baptists advocated the Bible as the rule and touchstone while admitting their need for the assistance of the Spirit, whereas Friends advocated the Spirit as their guide but found it necessary to appeal to Scripture. In their discussion of the nature of the Bible, Baptists closely associated Scripture and Spirit while Quakers tended to disassociate the two. Furthermore, although Baptists and Quakers emphasized mediate and immediate inspiration, respectively, they concurred that the Spirit guided people neither contrary to nor beyond the Bible. I have also observed that the two groups agreed on the general use of the Bible and on the assistance of the

Spirit in its interpretation, but disagreed about the relative importance of the two in such elucidation.

What fundamentally separated the two groups and explains these disagreements was the different extent to which they identified themselves with New Testament Christianity. As has been shown, the written Word stood between Baptists and the primitive church and thus was their authority. This was not so for Friends. Appearing to believe they *were* the New Testament church and thus experiencing the status "that the Apostles was in," they claimed that their authority was what primitive Christians had *before the New Testament was written.*[37]

To Quakers, the controversy with Baptists seemed reducible to a choice between, on the one hand, the experience with the Holy Spirit or Christ the Word as in biblical times and, on the other hand, the Scripture or written word of "paper and ink." The former was sufficient as the rule and guide to salvation. The latter was not. In a letter to Margaret Fell written from Hawkhurst, Kent, probably on 5 June 1655, Alexander Parker reported that after a meeting in Staplehurst with Fox and others, some Baptists "begun to cavill and to jangle" and "affirmed several times that ye Scriptures were the way, the only way and noe other way," but "wee affirmed Christ to bee ye way the only way."[38] To a consideration of the Quakers' "Christ . . . the only way" I now turn.

3

Christ was in them, else were they Reprobates

The Person of Christ

[Quaker]
> For Paul *to th'* Corinthes *clearly intimates*
> *Christ was in them, else were they Reprobates.*
> *And Christ in you also elsewhere he saith,*
> *From whence, 'tis plain, it was th' Apostles faith*
> *To own the Light within,*

[Professor]
> *Th' God-head consider'd distinct and apart,*
> *From his prepared body I assert,*
> *Is not the Christ, and false it must be then,*
> *To say that Light, is Christ, within all men.*

Benjamin Keach, *The Grand Impostor Discovered*

As has been shown, Quakers claimed as their own the divine authority enjoyed by the primitive Christians before the New Testament was written, and their disputes over the Scripture revealed a fundamental difference between them and Baptists—the extent to which they identified themselves with the primitive church. Friends were driven to enter the "Great Time" of the Christian "beginnings" by their zeal to experience Christ as the earliest Christians had. But this New Testament experience also produced obvious historical difficulties. Unlike the disciples, Friends had not literally heard the words of Christ or witnessed his crucifixion, burial, resurrection, or ascension, for example. However, this problem was mitigated by the Quakers' internalization and spiritualization of such outward, physical, historical events. Thus the Christ whom Baptists thought of as preaching, crucified, buried, resurrected, and ascended into heaven some sixteen hundred years before became for Quakers the Christ within them, who spoke and was crucified, buried, resurrected, and ascended—all *within*. The dichotomies present in the debates just discussed—immediate and mediate, inward and outward, and spiritual and physical—thus emerged in their disputes over the person of Christ. To have the immediate experience that the earliest Christians had, the Quakers believed, required the internalization and spiritualization they practiced. Conflict with Baptists was one result.

A number of issues were heatedly contested in the sundry exchanges between Quakers and Baptists on centuries-old questions of Christology: What was the nature of the divine indwelling? Was Christ as truly within believers as he was in heaven? What was the relationship of the human and the divine in Christ? If he were truly human, then how could he also be eternal? What was the relationship between Christ, the Father, and the Holy Spirit? However, a narrower question that perhaps raised the most trepidation among Baptists was asked in 1656 by the Baptist William Jeffery of the Quaker Thomas Lawson: "If the spirit in some man be the Christ, what hindreth him to say *hee* is Christ [?]"[1] Later that year, on 24 October, a day so rainy that they "received the rain at their necks and vented it at their hose and breeches," the Quaker James Nayler and his small party entered Bristol, he on horseback, others accompanying him on foot. The former Baptist Samuel Cater was among them. Some of the women spread garments in Nayler's path and sang "Holy, holy, holy, Hosannah." The group on this occasion reenacted an episode from the time of "the beginnings." To many the act seemed blasphemous and Nayler's subsequent indictment by Parliament and his harsh punishment fully warranted.[2] Nayler's triumphal entry provided the alarming answer to Jeffery's question. The Quaker emphasis on the Christ within was seen to lead logically to the extravagant language occasionally used by some Friends and to episodes like that at Bristol.

The Divine Indwelling: Christ Within and Without

In exploring questions so dramatically raised by the Nayler incident, it is useful to examine testimonies of former Baptists. As previously observed, their rigorous quest for a New Testament experience influenced their eventual adoption of some Quaker views.[3] A similar quest led to their Christological position; their autobiographical works often include references to their former belief in the God "in Heaven above the Skies," or in the God or the Christ "at a distance," and other phrases that express a spatial and chronological separation as well as the absence of a satisfying personal relationship. When their quest to experience primitive Christianity reached its culmination, the Christ who had been "at a distance" became the Christ whom they knew directly, as the earliest Christians had. That required that he be found *within* them. Their experiences were like that of Fox, who testified, "Christ it was who had enlightened me, that gave me his light to believe in, and gave me hope, which is himself, revealed himself in me, and gave me his spirit and gave me his grace, which I found sufficient in the deeps and in weakness."[4]

In applying their experiences to the lives of others, Quakers under-

standably associated the traditional emphasis on the transcendence and outwardness of God or Christ with the unregenerate state. Francis Howgill,
for example, testified that as a Baptist he discovered that Baptists, like others, professed that "Christ at a distance without had done all," and the former Baptist Humphrey Wolrich charged that Baptists imagined "a God
above the Clouds, and afar off, but know not the Christ who is the express
Image of the Fathers person, to reveal the Father in you."[5] Alexander
Parker observed that "the Pope and his Train, and the vilest drunkard or
wicked person that I have seen, have confest in words Christ come in the
flesh at Jerusalem, and yet are not of God." Further, Salthouse pointed out
that those who relied on an outward word, light, and Christ were in a state
of "degeneration and imperfection where they have lain covered with
gross darkness feeding themselves with the hypocrites hope and empty
shadowes."[6] Christ gave comfort, joy, and peace to persons by his revelation within them. He moved and acted and gave life to his saints from
within them. To Friends, this relationship of the indwelling Christ to his
saints was exceedingly intimate. As Fox declared, "Gods Christ is not distinct from his Saints, nor his bodies, for he is within them; nor distinct
from their spirits, for their spirits witnesse him." To some, this troubling
statement resembled the Ranter Jacob Bauthumley's opinion that God
"hath his Being no where else out of the Creatures."[7]

Baptists thought Quakers' views diminished the importance of the historical and glorified Christ and rendered Friends equal to him. Similarities
like those just noted between statements of Fox and Bauthumley led the
Baptist Thomas Collier to think that Quaker principles were simply the
ideas of the old Ranters, for both "would have no Christ but within."
Ranters did strongly emphasize the divine indwelling, and Bauthumley,
who soundly rejected the notion of Christ having a body in heaven, declared, "God is in all Creatures, Man and Beast, Fish and Fowle, and every
green thing." In linking Quakers with Ranters, Collier reminded his readers of the Nayler episode in Bristol and in doing so may have additionally
had in mind the published report that followers of the Ranter John Robins
believed he was God the Father and that his wife was about to bear their
son Jesus Christ. The views of others at this end of the religious spectrum
are of interest here. Seekers, for example, were thought to stress the divine
indwelling also. William Erbery declared that the fulness of the Godhead
was manifested in the flesh of the saints, and criticized Baptists for opposing the appearance of Christ in his people. Muggletonians, on the other
hand, believed that God had given up immortality in becoming human,
then assumed it again "in the very same flesh or person that dyed, and now
reigneth in glory in the highest Heavens." God, then, was between five and
six feet tall, and the heaven in which he ruled was some six miles above the
earth. In an autobiographical manuscript, the Muggletonian Thomas
Tompkinson described an apparently gentle dispute with Quakers in which
he argued against their notion of God as an infinite spirit. However, Muggleton and Penn exchanged more hostile words, both in person and in

print, that, as reported by the latter, led Muggleton to declare of Penn, "I care not a Fart for Him, nor his Friends."[8]

For their part, Quakers' descriptions of their experiences of the divine indwelling were not limited to the Christ within, but also included references to the Spirit of Christ, the Word, God, and the Spirit of God. Nor was the defense of their position limited to relating their own experiences, for they claimed that theirs were the same as those of the earliest Christians. Christ himself spoke of being in his disciples, and Paul had testified to Christ's presence in him, they argued. Furthermore, Paul informed the Colossians that Christ was in them, the hope of glory, and the Galatians that the Spirit of the Son was within them. In fact, as Burrough apprised Bunyan, unless people were reprobates, Christ was in them.[9]

The significance of Friends' strong emphasis on the spiritual nature of the Word and their insistence on its identification with Christ rather than the Scripture was again evident in arguments over the indwelling of Christ. In defending their doctrine of the Christ within, Quakers often appealed to the biblical experience of the Word, for in both the Old and New Testaments the Word was said to be near and even in the heart. Paul himself "directed every one to the word within in the heart," which "ingrafted word," according to Fox, "is able to save souls, and that is *within*."[10] On other occasions Friends also spoke of the divine indwelling in terms of the Spirit of God or God within. They pointed out that God had promised to dwell and to walk in his people, and that Paul had referred to God's having shined in human hearts. Terms were used interchangeably with little attempt to draw distinctions. Indeed, when Caffyn, as reported by Lawson, protested that it was not God but his Spirit that dwelt in people, Lawson charged him with imagining "God to be one where, and his Spirit, another where."[11]

In their arguments supporting the Christ within, Quakers not only appealed to the biblical experience and to their own but also displayed, on rare occasions, an explicit reliance on reason, as when they argued that the divinity of Christ and the omnipresent quality of the divine logically necessitated the presence of Christ in all. Whitehead, for example, declared that to be omnipresent God must in some sense be in all people, and further pointed out that "Some Baptists themselves have confest, that Christ in Respect to his divine Nature, is everywhere; therefore he must needs be in Man." Whatever the basis of appeal, however, the conclusion was the same: The indwelling Christ was necessary for salvation. In the words of Burrough, "Till Christ be revealed within, there is no salvation nor life partaked of." Consequently, as Farnworth asserted, "We are required to hold such accursed, as denies Christ within."[12]

Other Protestants also spoke of God's presence within, of course. The nearness of the Holy Spirit, for example, was often described by Presbyterians and Independents in terms of the divine indwelling. The Spirit of Christ operating in people's hearts enabled them to have saving faith and sanctified them, and the Holy Spirit working within these persons empowered them to do good works. Although the divine indwelling was usually ascribed to the Spirit of God or the Spirit of Christ, it was not uncommon for Christ to be said to dwell in believers.[13] Baptists also subscribed to this tenet. They too preferred to speak of the indwelling of the Holy Spirit or of the Spirit of Christ. Russel, having granted that Christ was said in the Scripture to live in his people, added, "but the Scripture saith it is by the Spirit, 1 John 4.13." This indwelling of Christ's Spirit, however, was not of the fully intimate nature advocated by Quakers, for it was not "to be understood of the Essence, but of the Gifts and Graces of the Spirit," Russel explained.

Baptists were not opposed to speaking of Christ's indwelling. As John Wigan declared, the Christian "knowes and hath a witness in himself, that Christ dwells in his heart, Eph. 3.17. and lives in him, as Paul witnessed, Ga. 2.20. *Nevertheless I live, yet not I, but Christ liveth in me.*"[14] But here again the indwelling was not identical to that claimed by Friends. Caffyn, comparing John 17:21–22 with John 15:10 observed, "Our being in the Father, and in the Son, is meant, in their love." He concluded, "Even so Christs dwelling in the Saints, is meant, his dwelling in their love, in their affections." More typical of the Baptist position was the explanation given by William Jeffery, General Baptist minister at Bradbourn in Kent, that "the Spirit of God doth dwell in the Saints, and that Christ doth dwell in their hearts by faith; but note, that faith is the substance of things hoped for, and the evidence of things not seen, Heb. 11.1. so the just live by faith, and look for the Son of God from Heaven, whom he raised from the dead."[15]

It is not surprising then that in a letter written to Margaret Fell, probably in December 1654, Howgill and Burrough complained that Baptists near Bristol "had reported all ye country over that we . . . denied Chr[ist] and ye Scriptures, and soe had incensed the country." The strong opposition of Baptists to the Quaker emphasis on the indwelling Christ resulted partly from the perceived danger of not drawing a clear distinction between Christ and his saints, and partly from their impression that Quakers were denying the existence of the Christ without. As noted, in 1656 Jeffery asked, "If the spirit in some man be the Christ, what hindreth him to say hee is Christ[?]" Later that year, replying to a charge that Fox claimed he was the way, the truth, and the life, Nayler declared, "Where Christ speaks in Male or Female, he is what he testifies himselfe to be." Still later in 1656, Nayler made his messianic entry into Bristol. Baptists' distress over this event may have been intensified by the knowledge that Samuel Cater, the former Baptist elder in Littleport, Cambridgshire, was among Nayler's party, and that once inside Bristol, the group made its way to the house partly owned by the Quaker Dennis Hollister, formerly an Independent member of the Independent-Baptist Broadmead church. In any case, the episode proved their point, Baptists thought, and nearly twenty years later Thomas Hicks reminded Quakers of this in the disputes of 1672–74.[16]

Perhaps equally dangerous in the opinion of Baptists was the Quaker disposition to diminish the importance of the Christ without. To Baptists such as Burnet, the presence of Christ in the heart of a saint did no more "unthrone" Christ or void his existence at the right hand of God in heaven "then the beams of the natural Sun shining upon the Earth, or into a House, doth unthrone, nihilate or make void its body or essence in the Firmament." In their various disputes concerning the divine indwelling, Baptists maintained a balance between the "inwardness" and "outwardness" of Christ. He was to be known both within and without, Thomas Ewins, the Baptist pastor of the Broadmead church, argued. The soteriological significance of this balance was evident in Bunyan's assertion that salvation was obtained for people by "the man Christ Jesus without" and was affirmed to them by his Spirit, which dwelled within. It was, therefore, dangerous for Friends to use the doctrine of the inner Christ "*to fight against the doctrine of Christ without, Ascended from his Disciples into heaven, by whom salvation was obtained, neither is there salvation in any other*, Act. 4:12."[17]

In the opinion of Baptists, the Quaker doctrine of the Christ within threatened the Christian belief in the historical and the glorified Christ. The Christ described by Scripture was not, as some Friends claimed, a type of what was afterward to be accomplished in people, and those Quakers who spoke of Christ's crucifixion and resurrection *within* were said by Collier to "slay the true Christ if ever any people in the world have done it." In 1668 Burnet reported a dispute in which he, Caffyn, and the Quaker William Bayly were involved.

> Matthew Caffin being in a discourse of God and Christ, Matthew said, he owned no God nor no Christ to be his Christ but that God and Christ that was in the Heavens above; at which words, William Bayley made reply, and said, *What [?] is thy God and Christ yonder above the Clouds*, pointing up to the Heavens with his finger? *Yes* said Matthew Caffin, *above the Clouds*. In contempt thereof he uttered these words, and said, *that Christ that was without was not his Christ, and that God that was without was not his God.*[18]

In reply to Fox's affirmation that Christ was not distinct from his saints, Hicks, defending the presence of Christ in heaven, inquired, "Can any man be more plain in denying the person of Christ without him?"[19]

Quakers responded to such charges by insisting that their emphasis on the divine indwelling was not a denial of the Christ without. Christ was a being distinct from the saints, and with respect to a statement by Fox like that just quoted, Penn explained, "G. F. only opposeth Christ's being at a Distance, as divided from the Saints, because they who know not Christ to be in them the Apostle terms Reprobates; and not that Christ and his Saints are in distinct Beings."[20] Penn and Burrough further asserted they did not deny the outward glorified Christ of the present ("he is ascended far above all heavens who fills all things, yea and without us too"), or the historical Christ of the past, or the Christ crucified in the flesh.[21] (However, Baptists were suspicious that there was only a spiritualized meaning in such statements.) Friends also held that Baptists wrongly supposed that Quakers' doctrine of the divine indwelling rendered them equal to Christ. In the body of Christ prepared by God, the fullness of the Godhead was made manifest, whereas Christ was known in them only in measure. Nevertheless, this inward presence was of ultimate importance for salvation. Indeed, they argued that they themselves experienced the Christ as the disciples and other Christians in the primitive time had, for the historical Christ who was crucified and risen was the same as the Christ within them. Therefore, Fox declared, echoing Paul's words, "If Christ that's crucified be not within, and Christ that's risen be not within, I say that you are all Reprobates."[22]

The Incarnate Christ: Humanity and Divinity

Quaker attempts like those just described to allay the fears of Baptists concerning the orthodoxy of their Christology were unsuccessful, for their assurances that their emphasis on the Christ within was not a denial of the Christ without, and that the two were indeed the same, served only to focus suspicion on the Quaker doctrine of the incarnation. Wright, for example, complained, "Instead of giving direction and encouragement, by their Doctrine and Example, to confess Jesus Christ come in the flesh: they do the direct contrary, neither making confession of the Person, Office, or Administrations of Christ: nor his person, nor his Divine and Human Natures, personally united, and personally distinguished from the persons of all other men."[23] Although not providing a full solution to the Christological problems, around which great controversy centered in the post–New Testament church, the Chalcedonian Creed furnished a basic statement against which orthodoxy was often measured. Presbyterians and Independents were in accord with this statement, ascribing to Christ two natures united in one person, "very God, and very Man." In their earliest confessions Baptists did not normally include such theological phrases, but chose rather to make simple affirmations using the language of the primitive church.[24] Nevertheless, that Baptists were in basic agreement with the Chalcedonian formula was evident in the controversy concerning the incarnation. Thus it seemed to Baptists that Quakers repudiated the union of the divine and the human in the incarnation and that in doing so they denied the human nature of Christ.

In accordance with their primitivism, Friends, like Baptists, were reluctant to employ terms not used in New Testament times and objected to the use of the words *person* and *human* on such grounds. However, they insisted that they did not reject the incarnation of Christ. They believed that he had been miraculously conceived in the Virgin Mary by the power of the Holy Spirit and had been born "according to the flesh." The former Baptist Humphrey Wolrich argued that Christ had taken upon him the body prepared for him in order to do the will of God. In this holy body he had preached his gospel, worked miracles, and attracted many to him. Indeed, Whitehead affirmed that "he took upon him a real Body (and not a fantastical) and that he was real Man, come of the seed of Abraham."[25] However, Friends distinguished between Christ and his body, pointing out that he existed prior to his body and that the latter, not the former, had died on the cross. Surely, therefore, Christ could not be said to consist of a personal, created, human body. Furthermore, they objected to the concept of a hypostatic union of divine and human natures as not part of the primitive church's belief. Burrough explained that the two natures "are two distinct things, that which is humane is of the earth, as the first man was . . . but that which is Divine is from above, as Christ is, who is Lord from Heaven." He went on to point out, "We never read that Humane nature is Christ, nor that the flesh and bloud is Christ by temporal generation; for to assert that is all one as to say that Christ (who is Lord from Heaven) took upon him Christ in time, (but Christ in the flesh we read of and own)." Furthermore, in the opinion of Wolrich, Baptists who insisted on the human nature of Christ did not know him any further than did the Pharisees, to whom his flesh and blood were insufficient to reveal him to be the Son of God.[26]

Baptists, of course, did not believe that Christ was merely human, but they supposed that Quakers thought he was only divine. Burnet observed, "They preach that he is come in the flesh, but not that he was flesh, or that the flesh taken in the womb of the Virgin was Christ, but that Christ was in that body." Baptists were even wary of what Friends meant when they spoke of Christ's body. Grantham told of a meeting with John Whitehead in which the latter reportedly said:

> *Well*, Thomas, *I will satisfie thee if I can, I say, Christ's Flesh was such flesh as* Thomas Grantham's *flesh, all corruption excepted*. I began to hope we might agree, but presently perceived his Cheat, and therefore told him, if he could answer me one honest Question more, I should be satisfied; which was this, Dost not thou under these words, *all Corruption excepted*, except my whole Body, and the flesh of all Men. Here he would not answer me by any means, but instead thereof, Cursed me in these words:
> *Thou whited Wall, God shall smite thee; the Plagues, and Curses, and Vengeance of God is thy portion.*[27]

Such Baptist skepticism was justified, as I will show.

For their part Baptists strongly enunciated their belief that Christ was human as well as divine. They were cognizant of the fact that Scripture sometimes spoke of the body of Jesus, but they pointed out that this did not mean the body was not part of Christ. On the contrary, Scripture gave proof that the body born of the Virgin Mary and crucified near Jerusalem was the Christ. Furthermore, to those Quakers who claimed Christ had never been seen with mortal eyes, Baptists declared that although the Godhead of Christ had never been seen, yet his manhood had been. Caffyn pointed out that those who had seen him did not have "any other

eyes, as invisible and spiritual eyes," as Friends might claim, but human
eyes. However, his human nature was evidenced not only by his body but
also by his soul and human spirit, both of which were like that of Adam before he sinned. Indeed, Christ exhibited all the properties of a human person and was, therefore, a true man.[28]

Baptists agreed with Quakers that only the bodily or human nature of
Christ, not the divine, had died, but they held to that widely accepted
principle, *communicatio idiomatum*, that the two natures being united,
the properties of one were sometimes ascribed to the other, so that although only the human nature had died, it could properly be said that
Christ had died. This was of great soteriological significance, for in the
opinion of Baptists, salvation depended on the death of Christ, and therefore, if only the divine nature in him were the Christ, then Christ had not
died and salvation had not been achieved for humankind. Howet declared
that Quakers "denie the Lord that bought them, if they denie that bodie
that was crucified for them, for he bought Lordship over all things by his
death," and Collier exclaimed, "You own no flesh but all spirit: therefore
you shut up the way to the Kingdome." Grantham asked with alarm, "And
now what is more plain, than that thou here deniest that Christ died upon
the Cross? And then if Christ died not, he was not buried, he rose not
again from the Dead; and then what is become of the Christian Faith?"[29]

In addition to their protests against the Quaker denial of Christ's
human nature on Christological and soteriological grounds, Baptists raised
objections arising from fears evoked by the Nayler episode. Did not the
Quakers believe that only the Spirit or light that was in his body was the
Christ, and that the same Spirit was in them also? Hicks asked, Why could
not Penn and Whitehead "be as truly and properly called Jesus Christ, as
well as that outward Person or bodily appearance? And why may not Divine Worship be given as well to you as to him?" Such worship had been
directed not only toward Nayler but to Fox as well, Hicks declared, for in
a letter to Fox, Josiah Coale had referred to him as "The Father of many
Nations, whose being and habitation is in the power of the highest, in
which he rules and governs in righteousness; and that his (*viz.* G. Fox's)
Kingdom is established in peace, and the increase thereof is without
end."[30] In fact, Coale sometimes did employ extravagant language, referring to Fox on one occasion as "ye beloved of my soule, whos life I always
feel present with mee, which is my stay, and strength in all my undertake-
ings."[31] Such language was in letters found on Nayler at his interrogation
in Bristol. But a letter to Nayler from Margaret Fell in which she referred
to Fox as "him to whom all nations should bow" was not among them, for
the Quaker George Bishop of Bristol opened it, saw "what that might
prove" and thus did not deliver it.[32]

The importance Baptists placed on the human nature of Christ in
these controversies seemed to Quakers to be inconsistent with Baptist belief in his divine nature. The latter was of primary significance for Quakers,
for they claimed to experience Christ immediately just as the primitive

Christians had. Christ was the Word, the eternal Spirit, who was before the world was and was one with the Father. Whitehead argued that no person could see the Father with the carnal eye, and whoever saw Christ saw the Father. Therefore, he concluded in *The Christian-Quaker*, Christ was not to be seen with the carnal eye. Indeed, he stated in another work, it was "both Unscriptural and Absurd to assert, That Jesus Christ consisteth of a Humane Body of Flesh and Bone, or is Finite," for that was inconsistent with "the Eternal Glory of the Son of God."[33]

Although Quakers denied the body of flesh to be Christ or part of Christ, they did not deny that he took upon him a real body, so that to this extent they did not deny Christ to have come in flesh, as some Baptists charged. In answering such accusations, Friends sometimes spoke of Christ's body or flesh as spiritual and as a divine indwelling in his people. Christ was said to have a spiritual body in glory and to be the spiritual Son of Man of flesh and blood of which people were to partake. Nayler described a pre-incarnate spiritual body that came down from heaven and ascended to heaven. With respect to the divine indwelling, Friends spoke of Christ's taking upon him the flesh of all his people, who were said to be members of his body, so that, in the words of Salthouse, "the Life of Christ hath been, and is made manifest in mortall flesh; and we have this treasure in earthen vessels."[34] In these ways, while accepting only the divine nature of Christ, Friends could nevertheless declare that they believed him to have come in the flesh.

Did the Quaker doctrine of the nature of Christ have the disastrous soteriological consequences anticipated by Baptists? Certainly not, Friends argued, for surely God was able to save without the assistance of human nature. The body of Christ was a coworker, but the divine power and life made it serviceable to the work of suffering. Indeed, it was not the dead body on the cross but the Spirit that was the Savior, "as it lives, quickens, gives life to the Soul &c." As Penn explained, "to believe and obey the Light of his Life, . . . is both the best way to know the Sufferings of his Body, and to receive the Benefit of them."[35]

Baptists agreed with them that Christ was the divine, eternal Son of God, but they insisted that the divine nature alone was not the Christ, the Savior of the world. In such arguments, they generally described the divine in Christ as the Spirit or Word, which was not the Christ apart from his body. Scriptural references to his birth, circumcision, baptism, and death could not be true if he were Spirit alone. Indeed, Christ had shown his disciples that they were wrong in supposing him to be a spirit and had invited them to handle him to see that he was flesh. For Friends to distinguish Christ from his body was absurd, Grantham claimed, for neither the body nor the Spirit, distinct from each other, was the Christ, but in conjunction they were one Christ. According to Wigan, it was "not the Word alone, nor the flesh alone, but the Word and flesh in union, that is called Christ, Joh. 1.41." As Burnet declared, "That Word, or Eternall Spirit, became or took flesh, and so became both the Son of God, and the Son of Man, not by confusion of substance, but by unity of Person, for the Godhead was joyned and united to the Manhood; so that either of them have their properties remaining, and yet of them both is made one Christ."[36]

In response to the Quaker emphasis on the spiritual quality of Christ's body, Baptists admitted that the Church was sometimes referred to as the body of Christ, but as Wright explained, "When it is so given it is to be taken mystically, believers being understood to be the Body of Christ and Christ to be the head of that Body: this mystical sence destroyes not the proper sence, for Christ is a distinct person from all other persons." Furthermore, with respect to Friends' references to the spirituality of Christ's flesh that was to be eaten and his blood that was to be drunk, Grantham argued that the flesh and blood were real and the same as were nailed to the cross, but that they were to be eaten and drunk in a spiritual manner. In these and similar arguments Baptists defended the existence of the divine and human natures united in the incarnate Christ, a union that was, in Russel's words, a "wonder of Men and Angels that cannot be resolved by any Man." However, that this mystery ultimately could not be resolved was no reason for Quakers to reject its truth, for, as Burnet proposed, "Would it not be sad to say Christ is not God, because he is man, and is it not as sad to say he is not Man because he is God, or to conclude that he is neither, because he is both?"[37]

The Eternal Christ: The Pre-incarnate Christ, the Trinity, and the Glorified Christ

As discussion of the Christ within raised difficulties pertaining to the incarnation, so disputes about the incarnation evoked questions concerning the eternal nature of Christ. The Baptist insistence that Christ was both human and divine led naturally to the issue of Christ's pre-incarnate state. This topic was raised on numerous occasions but perhaps never more poignantly than in the London debates of the 1670s, when Penn asked, "Was he the Christ of God before he was manifested in the Flesh?" and in the former Baptist Stephen Crisp's response to Thomas Hicks, when Hicks told him:

> That the Christ I believ'd, was no other then that person the Scriptures speak of. The Word made flesh, God manifested in the flesh, called Emanuel, God with us, not the meer Godhead of the Son, nor the meer manhood, but God and Man united in one person, that is the Christ.
>   To which Crisp, replyed, *Then I know the beginning and Date of thy Christ*.[38]

The Quakers' stress on the eternal nature of Christ was consistent with their claim to experience Christ directly as the earliest Christians had. As Friends saw the issue, if Christ were not Christ without human nature, then Christ was not eternal, for the human nature was not eternal but rather taken at a specific historical moment. Baptists experienced difficulty finding a satisfactory answer to this problem. Their responses were not un-usual in reserving the term *Christ* for the union of the human and divine natures. Russel, for example, argued that "Christ" was a name of office that could be applied only to that union of natures, and Wigan, using the same approach and referring to John 1:1–14, explained that the eternal Word was the Creator and the Word made flesh was the Christ, adding, "Till then, there was no such thing as a Christ, or a light to the Gentiles, but only in a promise."[39]

However, Baptists often referred to the pre-incarnate Son of God as the Christ. Their justification for doing so may have been the previously noted principle of *communicatio idiomatum*, or perhaps was the principle implied in Wigan's use of the term *promise* and made more explicit in state-ments by Russel and Bunyan. The former explained that "He was never called the Christ of God before, but with respect to what he was to be, when, and after he was manifested in the flesh," and Bunyan maintained that Christ could be said to have been slain or crucified before the world was created, "according to Gods purpose and conclusion, which he pur-posed in himself before the world was."[40]

Friends did not believe Christ to consist of human nature but held that the pre-incarnate and the incarnate Christ were the same. Whitehead expressed this view when he declared, "The true Christ was in being from Everlasting, and in time universally shining and manifest in some degree throughout all the Generations of the Righteous, since the World began." He had created all things, and his day had been seen by Abraham. Christ had been that spiritual rock with the Jews in the wilderness, his voice had been heard by the prophets, and his form had been seen in the furnace by Nebuchadnezzar. Christ had testified to his own eternal nature in claiming to have existed before Abraham and in praying that he might have the same glory that he had with the Father before creation, Quakers claimed.[41]

Disputes concerning the person of Christ also raised the subject of the Trinity, although only implicitly in most cases. Presbyterians and Independ-ents utilized the formula *una substantia, tres personae*, but there was an emphasis on the mystery of the doctrine and a recognition of human in-ability to express it adequately. John Owen, for example, distinguished be-tween the original revelations and the expressions of those revelations, al-though he held that to reject the latter was to deny the former also.[42]

Seeking to duplicate the primitive model, Baptists were reluctant to move beyond the language of the earliest Christians. They employed nei-ther the term *Trinity* nor the *tres personae* formula in their confessions until 1677, when they were trying to appear as mainstream Noncon-formists. Misgivings concerning the use of the formula were evident among the early Baptists, and Edward Drapes pleaded that the words might not "be imposed on any as a snare: let us more look to things than words." Similar reservations were voiced in the Restoration period. Thomas Collier did not doubt that those who used the formula did so to express the distinction in the Trinity made in the New Testament, but pro-

fessed that he tried to avoid the phrase because it was not biblical language. Grantham hoped for much the same thing, and although he
claimed to see no "inconveniency" in referring to the Father, Son, and
Holy Spirit as three persons, he admitted that he could not determine
whether it was proper to do so. In light of these opinions, it is not surprising that this topic arose less frequently in Quaker exchanges with Baptists
than with others. Nevertheless, Baptists lodged strong protests against
confusing the members of the Godhead, for it seemed to them that in the
various arguments supporting the Quaker doctrines of the indwelling
Christ and the incarnation, Friends failed to distinguish sufficiently between the Father, Son, and Holy Spirit. Caffyn, for example, objecting to
Quakers equating Christ and the Holy Spirit, pointed out that "The Eternal Spirit, which dwelt in the Man Christ, which afterwards the Apostles
received in them, is called another Comforter, and that by Christ himself,
which would not come unto the Apostles, unless he (the true Christ) went
away."[43] Collier, attacking the Friends' doctrine of the incarnation, declared that those who argued that Christ filled heaven and earth and
dwelled in the saints "do account the very person of Christ to be the infinite God; and owns no Christ of the seed of David according to the flesh."
Touching on both of these doctrines, Wright considered it vain to make no
distinction between the communion of the Holy Spirit with believers and
the union of the human and divine natures in Christ. Henry Grigg identified soteriological implications of the problem when he asserted, "Neither
the Comforter, *viz.* the Holy Spirit, nor the Deity of our Lord Jesus, distinct
from his Manhood or Humane Nature, could be the Saviour and Mediatour
which died on the Cross, or was crucified between the two Thieves."[44]

Like some Baptists, Friends objected to the *tres personae* formula.
However, they emphasized the unity of the Godhead and dismissed distinctions drawn by Baptists as foreign to the experience of the primitive
church. They referred, as did Burrough, to Christ as the comforter, for, as
Whitehead pointed out, Christ had promised that he would not leave people comfortless but would come to them, and thus was himself the comforter. When, as reported by Wolrich, Caffyn protested that there was a difference between the Christ and the comforter, Wolrich replied, "There be
diversities of administrations, yet is there but one Lord, who is the same
and changeth not," and when, in an exchange reported by Whitehead,
Grigg denied that the comforter could be the Savior, Whitehead declared
that to deny the comforter to be the Savior was also to deny Christ "in his
spiritual Appearance" to be the Savior.[45]

Quakers were also opposed to Baptist attempts to distinguish between
Christ and the Father, believing like Fox that "Christ is not distinct from
the Father, for he and the Father is one." It had been foretold in Scripture
that the Savior was to be the Prince of Peace and the everlasting Father,
and Christ himself had stated that he was one with the Father and that he
who had seen him had seen the Father. When, according to Whitehead,

Grigg attempted to explain that Jesus was truly God in substance and essence but was distinguished from the Father with respect to his personal subsistence, Whitehead called his statement "nonsensical and confusedly intermixt with those unscriptural Terms." In response to Grigg's question, whether there were three who bore record in heaven, Whitehead replied, "I say yes, and these three are one; and is not Christ (the Saviour) that Word, which is one of the three, which are but one divine Being, Thing or Substance, though revealed under several Considerations and Diversities of Manifestations, and Degrees of Discoveries?"[46]

The disputes concerning the indwelling of Christ and the incarnation also raised the topic of the Christ of glory. The Quaker emphasis on the Christ within seemed to Baptists to deny the glorified Christ without. Baptists believed, like Burnet, that the Father and the Son "hath their being in the Heavens above the Clouds," and they opposed any internalized interpretation such as that reported by Caffyn of a Friend, who, "being several times asked by mee, where that Heaven was that Christ ascended up into, and now was in, he answered, clapping his hands upon his breast, saying, WITHIN ME, WITHIN ME." The heaven into which Christ ascended was not in the disciples, because he departed *from* them, and the disciples looked up to the clouds and to the heaven without. There in the presence of the Father, Christ continued to intercede for his children, and there he remained until the time of the restitution of all things.[47]

Emphasizing both the outwardness of Christ and his divine and human natures, Baptists strongly defended his bodily presence in heaven. They argued that according to the testimony of the primitive church, Christ had risen from the dead with the same body of flesh that had been crucified, and with that body he had ascended to heaven. Grantham believed that this body was "of the proper dimension of Man's Body; or in respect of Stature, like other Mens," yet it differed from the bodies of other men not only in lacking "Sin, Corruption, and all things of that nature," but also in being glorified and not requiring earthly sustenance. If, however, in spite of all the biblical evidence and arguments presented by Baptists, Friends did not believe Christ's body to be in heaven, then where did they think it was? Grantham directed such a question to Ruckhill: "Sure he will not say, That that Body dwells in the fleshly Bodies of the Saints, otherwise than by Faith: if he will allow so much, he cannot deny but that Body was circumscriptible. He will not say that Visible Body is in Heaven; he dare not say it is on the Earth: Where now will Robert Ruckhill find this body?"[48]

Quakers did not answer this question or similar ones directly. Of course, they denied neither that Christ was in heaven nor that he was there with a body, but they could speak of Christ's body in more than one sense, and heaven could be other than "above the clouds." Burrough thought of Christ's body, the Church, in terms of resurrection and ascension, for he wrote:

> Members of his body we are (who thou enviously rails against) and witnesses
> of the body we are, whereof Christ Jesus is head: and because of the resurrec-
> tion of the dead body, which is ascended, we are called in question, and all
> Sects and opinions are troubled, and in an uproar concerning us; and I tell
> thee plainly, we are so far from denying the ascension and being of the body of
> Christ, that because of being called to witness it, as being members of it, we
> are persecuted and reviled.[49]

Further, Wolrich spoke of Christ dwelling in his saints "in whom he was
glorified with the same glory he had with the Father before the world
began." In addition, John Pitman and Jasper Batt, former Baptists in Somerset, affirmed that the "glorious God, at whose right hand Christ sits, fills
heaven and earth, and dwells in the Saints, whose conversation is in
heaven," and Fox declared that "the Apostle saith, They sate with Christ
in heavenly places: and the Saints are flesh of his flesh and bone of his
bone, and the Church which he is the head of is his body." However, as
Whitehead explained, Christ was not in heaven at God's right hand only
as he was in his saints on earth, "for his Exaltation and Glory (into which
he is ascended not only into the Heavens but far above the Heavens) Tran-
scends that Degree attained in these Suffering Earthly Tabernacles." Nevertheless, even when Friends spoke of Christ's body in heaven other than
within the saints, they were at least sometimes (*always*, Baptists feared) referring to his eternal spiritual body. Nayler, for example, declared, "The
body of Christ we own, and the ascension of it, and that it is the same that
came down from heaven, which became flesh, and is reall flesh and bone,
which flesh is our food to spiritual life." Thus, according to the Baptist report, at the Barbican meeting on 9 October 1674 Penn declared, "We own
the Man Jesus Christ," to which Hicks replied, "This Answer is not satisfactory: For by Man, you either intend, that once he was in the form of a
Man, but not that he is so now; or by Man, you mean something distinct
from and of another Nature than that which was taken of the Virgin."
Later at the same meeting, when Penn affirmed, "We do Believe the Holy
Manhood to be a member of the Christ of God," Ives retorted,"This is not
to the Question, which is, whether the Human Nature be part of the
Christ of God now in Heaven making Intercession for us? Whereunto, we
could gain no direct Answer."[50]

As previously shown, Friends could speak not only of Christ's body
as the Church and of his eternal spiritual body, but also of his earthly
body. Baptists were certain that the earthly body, glorified, was in heaven.
But did Quakers believe this? The question is not easily answered, for it is
difficult to determine in which sense the body of Christ is being considered in their arguments. Nevertheless, their many statements to the effect
that the Christ who ascended to heaven was the Christ who had come
down from heaven, and that Christ was in heaven with the same glory
that he had previously enjoyed with the Father make it seem likely they
did not. Thus Whitehead declared, "If your Christ doth consist of a
human or earthly Body of Flesh and Bone, our Christ who consisteth of

quickning spirit, and heavenly Body (of divine Life and Light, as spiritual and glorious body) is above you and yours."[51] Consequently, in White-head's view, for Baptists to speak of Christ's being in heaven with such a body of flesh was to commit the error of the Muggletonians, "who imagine God to be a personal or bodily Existence circumscribed as to place, denying him to be an infinite Spirit." Indeed, according to Ewins, on one occasion Hollister "did jeeringly ask one of this Congregation, to this effect: whether we did believe Christ to be an old man, sitting in a chair in heaven?" However, the basic Quaker objection was not primarily to anthropomorphic abuses or "denying him to be an infinite Spirit" but rather to relegating Christ to a remoteness from humanity unknown by New Testament Christians and thus by Friends also. The concern was illustrated by Whitehead's charge that those who believed Christ to be in heaven with a carnal body "endeavour to shut both God and Christ out of his People."[52]

With this statement of Whitehead we have come full circle, for the discussion began with the Quaker reaction against the remoteness of God in contemporary Christianity and their experience of the divine indwelling resulting from their zeal to encounter Christ directly as had the primitive Christians. As has been shown, that experience and the proclamation of it had a transforming influence on their doctrine of the person of Christ and on the development of their controversy with Baptists. Friends' close identification with primitive Christianity was accompanied by the internalization and spiritualization of outward, physical, historical events that in turn was reflected in the dichotomies of immediate and mediate, inward and outward, and spiritual and physical in their disputes. Thus, although members of the two groups agreed on the principle of divine indwelling, they disagreed on its mode and degree. They also concurred on the divinity of Christ but differed over his humanity, Baptists insisting that humanity was a part of Christ, and Quakers admitting that Christ had assumed a human body but not that it was part of him, and speaking of his body in spiritual terms.

The two groups further agreed that the Word was eternal, but Baptists, stressing Christ's humanity, considered only the incarnate Word to be Christ, whereas Quakers, maintaining that Christ was not human, held that he was both the pre-incarnate and the incarnate Word. Furthermore, in accord with their strong identification with New Testament Christianity, both Baptists and Quakers were reluctant to use the term *Trinity* and the trinitarian formula of the postbiblical theologians. However, Baptists insisted that certain distinctions be drawn between the members of the Godhead, whereas Friends blurred those differences and in doing so perhaps also came closer to the experiential, less rationalized life of the primitive church. Finally, while Baptists stressed the glorified earthly body of Christ in heaven, Friends emphasized the spiritual body of Christ in a heaven that seems not necessarily to have been a physical location outside of the saints or "above the clouds." To Baptists, the strong docetic overtones of the Quaker position, and to the Quakers, the spatial and temporal separation of Christ from humanity in the Baptist position, were also repugnant in the light of their respective conceptions of the soteriological process. To that process I now turn.

4

If there's salvation by the light within

Soteriology and Eschatology

[Quaker]
> *A Christ without friend clearly might I show thee,*
> *Stands in no stead at all, nor good can do thee;*
> *And therefore strive to witness Christ within,*
> *The light it is that doth redeem from sin;*

[Professor]
> *If Christ without, be wholly thus denied,*
> *How do you think for to be justified?*
> *If there's salvation by the light within,*
> *In vain hath Christ laid down his life for sin.*

Benjamin Keach, *The Grand Impostor Discovered*

John Bunyan, best known for *The Pilgrim's Progress* and three other major works, was also the author of more than fifty additional publications, the earliest of which were tracts of controversy directed against the Quakers. A number of face-to-face disputes took place between Bunyan and unnamed Quakers, including one at "Patnam" (now Pavenham) on 12 April 1656, and a second at "Paul's steeple-house" in Bedford on 23 May 1656, which also involved John Burton (Bunyan's pastor) and Richard Spencly, another member of the Bedford congregation. Two additional members, John Fenn and John Child, were engaged with Bunyan in a dispute with Friends on 23 October 1656, and Bunyan participated in yet another debate on 30 January 1657.[1] Such encounters launched Bunyan into print. In 1656, the first of his many works, *Some Gospel-truths Opened*, was published. It was answered by Edward Burrough's *The True Faith of the Gospel of Peace Contended For*, 1656, to which Bunyan replied with *A Vindication of the Book Called, Some Gospel-Truths Opened*, 1657. To this Burrough responded with *Truth (the Strongest of All) Witnessed Forth*, 1657. George Fox also replied to Bunyan's two tracts in his collection of polemical pieces, *The Great Mistery of the Great Whore Unfolded*, 1659.

In spite of Bunyan's oral and written attacks on Quaker doctrine and practice, the work of the First Publishers of Truth met with considerable success in Bedfordshire. By 1669, Quaker conventicles in the county numbered as many as those of Presbyterians, Independents, and Baptists combined. Fox ventured into Bedfordshire, most notably for a general meeting of as many as four thousand Friends in 1658. Nevertheless, Fox and Bunyan apparently never met. However, they both died in London and are buried in Bunhill Fields (Fox in the Quaker burial ground) within three hundred yards of each other.[2]

Bunyan, who had demanded in his first published work, "What Scripture have you to prove, that Christ is, or was crucified within you, dead within you, risen within you, & ascended within you?" added to the fifth edition (1680) of his spiritual autobiography, *Grace Abounding*, a list of eight Quaker errors, four of which dealt with soteriology and eschatology: "That Christ Jesus, as crucified, and dying 1600 years ago, did not satisfy divine justice for the sins of the people . . . That the bodies of the good and bad that are buried in the churchyard shall not arise again . . . That the resurrection is past with good men already . . . That he should not, even the same Jesus that died by the hands of the Jews, come again at the last day, and as man judge all nations, &c." Such charges by Bunyan and others were evoked by Friends' strong criticism of the emphasis on the objective, Godward side of the soteriological process and eschatological events that was so prevalent in the Puritan and Nonconformist tradition. This criticism was complemented by the strong Quaker emphasis on the experiential, subjective, human side that arose from their vigorous identification with primitive Christianity. Having entered the "Great Time" of the primitive church more fully than Baptists, Friends could claim as their authority that which the earliest Christians had before the New Testament was written, and also those Christians' immediate experience with Christ. However, as shown in the previous chapter, the latter required the internalization and spiritualization of major outward, physical, historical events in Christ's life. Those that were related to human salvation and future judgment produced in Friends' disputes with Baptists over soteriology and eschatology the same dichotomies of immediate/mediate, inward/outward, and spiritual/physical already observed in their debates concerning the Scripture and the person of Christ.[3]

The Work of Christ: Within and Without; the Extent

In taking up these subjects of controversy, it is again useful to examine the testimonies of former Baptists. Their stories of spiritual searching prior to joining with Quakers followed a similar pattern and resembled those of members of other religious groups who became Friends.[4] Their zeal to experience primitive Christianity included not only a "Cry of my Soul, . . . after spiritual Knowledge and Acquaintance with the Lord," as Howard described it, but also, in William Britten's words, a "true Hunger and

Thirst after Righteousness." They consulted various ministers and often joined successively with several different religious groups, but their cry was not answered nor was their hunger and thirst assuaged, for they found that in their religious experiences they still "fed on husks." Indeed, Bayly testified that he "knew not how to get out from under the power of sin and death." Ames acknowledged that even as a Baptist preacher he knew that "sin was alive in me, and that I was under the power of darkness," and that "I had only the forms of holiness, but power I wanted by which Sin might be overcome." Beevan expressed a common element in these testimonies when he lamented that "though we called ourselves the Saints of the Most High, yet I said in my self, if the Saints condition was thus, it was a miserable estate."[5]

From this state, they often proceeded to a period of "waiting," in which they eventually encountered the Christ within. Next came a time of severe inward and spiritual judgment, frequently described with such vivid apocalyptic imagery as "plague, and pestilence, and famine, and earthquake, and fear, and terror," and the wounding of Leviathan and slaying of "the Dragon that was in the Sea."[6] Enlightenment followed. Like other Friends who confessed they had previously lived contrary to the ways of Christ and his apostles, Howgill testified, "Then I saw the Crosse of Christ, and stood in it, . . . and the new man was made." "Here I came to witness a Disciples state," Ames declared, and, like other Friends who appear to have entered the primitive time of the earliest Christians, claimed to have found the peace, joy, and "power against Sin" he diligently sought.[7]

The Quakers' immediate experience of "a Disciples state" resulted in the internalization and spiritualization of the work as well as the person of Christ. Thus emphasizing the experiential, subjective, human facet of the soteriological process, Friends also criticized the emphasis on the objective, divine side that was characteristic of the Puritan and Nonconformist tradition. Baptists, on the other hand, like Presbyterians and Independents, thought of the saving work of Christ primarily in terms of the outward act of sacrifice he performed in the past. They pointed out that it was "the body of his flesh by which sin was purged," and that it was "the blood of Christ shed upon the Cross for man, that is the means or cause of the justification of man." The conviction that Christ's body slain was the sacrifice for sin was proclaimed by Grantham to be "a Truth so manifest, that he is more than ordinarily deluded that dares use a Pen or Tongue against it."[8]

Such an objective nature of Christ's work was usually described among Presbyterians and Independents in terms of Anselmic satisfaction, as developed by the Reformers into the penal theory.[9] In confessions prior to those of 1677, however, satisfaction and penal punishment were not mentioned by the General Baptists and were only briefly alluded to by Particular Baptists.[10] Nevertheless, in defending the necessity of Christ's human nature on soteriological grounds, some members of each group appealed to the concept of satisfaction. Burnet and Bunyan, for example, argued that only as a man could Christ gain humanity's acquittal and appease God's wrath, and Hicks and Russel declared that only with human nature could Christ die and thus satisfy divine justice.[11]

Quaker objections to the notion of satisfaction were not unique, being generally similar to those of English Socinians.[12] To persons such as Burnet and Bunyan, Quakers usually replied that Baptists were guilty of limiting God's power to save and his desire to forgive.[13] However, their basic objection did not arise primarily from belief in the divine attributes of omnipotence or love, but rather from their emphasis on the inward nature of Christ's work and its effect of actual righteousness. This objection was evident when, referring to Burnet's argument, Whitehead observed, "So by this he doth not mean Salvation to be a work wrought in man, as a saving and delivering from sin, or the offence within, but a satisfaction made to God that he may imbrace the Offender." It was also manifest when Penn rejected the concept of satisfaction because it was a denial "that Men may be Holy in Christ, by Virtue thereof, whilst not New, but Old Creatures, and so Unholy in themselves."[14]

Friends' rejection of satisfaction, however, did not in itself mean that they dismissed all objective explanations of the death of Christ. They did in exceptional cases use the terms *sacrifice, propitiation, offering for sin, the debt paid,* and *ransom.*[15] Nevertheless, they accompanied their strong emphasis on Christ's inward acts with a comparative silence concerning the outward work. Indeed, when pressed to justify the necessity of Christ's death, especially in regard to their claim that the light in all persons was soteriologically sufficient (see chapter 7), Friends seem to have experienced considerable difficulty.[16] Most often they asserted that Christ's coming into the world did not lessen or detract from the soteriological efficacy of the light within, but rather rendered the appearance of that light "more valid and effectual," and that Christ's death was a testimony or ratification of his love to humankind.[17] In the words of Penn, "And so well did he love the World, that, to testify the same, he gave up his Life not only to recommend his Love, but to Confirm his unchangeable Gospel of Remission of Sins, and Eternal Salvation to as many as believed, and followed him the Light of the World."[18]

Such explanations were unacceptable to Baptists, and thus Wright accused Friends of having the spirit of the Antichrist, because "in all thy Preaching, Teaching and Declaring, thou never makes mention of Christs dying for the sins of the World; nor that he tasted death for every man, thou art altogether silent in this Doctrine of Christs dying for man in the body of his flesh, and out of all other men, to Redeem men unto God, and so save him from his sins."[19] According to Bunyan, that light or conscience within them would never be able to get the Quakers "from under the guilt of one sinful thought the right way, which is to be done by believing what another man hath done by himselfe, *Heb.* 1. 2, 3. without us on the crosse, without the gates of *Jerusalem.*"[20]

The extent of Quaker striving to experience primitive Christianity lay beneath these disagreements. The internalization and spiritualization of the historical events overcame the obvious temporal impediments. Thus, in much the same way that the Christ "at a distance" became the Christ "within," the work and crucifixion of Christ came to be expressed in terms of spirituality and inwardness in order to be experienced with an immediacy like that of the disciples. Friends could speak of persons being guilty of spiritually crucifying Christ "as really as his Persecutors that pierced him outwardly" and declare, as Penn did to Hicks, that "he is crucified by such counterfeit Christians as thou art."[21] They were careful to distinguish between Christ's blood that fell to the ground and corrupted and his incorruptible blood that effected redemption, and they sometimes spoke of the latter being "shed abroad in their Souls." Martin Mason wrote that Christ "is a man of sorrows and suffers within thee, the just for the unjust, he is in the grave and not risen in thee, & did he not suffer for thee and within thee, thou shouldst soon feel that consuming fire which is not to be quenched." Whitehead declared, "That either all or any men are cleansed, or justified, or saved meerly by the outward Sufferings, Crucifixion, Death or Blood-shed of Christ, the Scripture proves not (but by Christ himself, and his Blood, Life, Spirit and Power)." Indeed, Penn warned, "Unless we come to know the Benefit of the Inward Life, answering to and expressed by that Outward Life he gave for the World, it will avail little."[22]

Baptists also advocated the importance of the inward application of Christ's outward sacrifice. Grigg declared, "We receive not the benefit of it, till by the help of the Spirit we are made able to apply it to our Souls," and Wigan warned his readers to "*minde his coming down in spirit into your hearts to manifest this redemption, and to live and work in you as a quickening spirit.*"[23] However, such inward work of the Spirit was neither to be confused with nor to be seen as detracting from Christ's outward work.[24] Given the Baptist emphasis, it is not surprising that disputes concerning the person of Christ often evolved into exchanges concerning his work. When Friends stressed the indwelling of Christ and denied that human nature was part of him, they appeared to be rejecting the historical Christ and thereby his death on the cross. Furthermore, as will be shown in chapter 7, when Quakers identified the inner light with Christ and argued for the soteriological sufficiency of that light, they seemed to Baptists such as Hicks to be establishing a different way of salvation than that provided by Christ's sacrifice and thereby to be rendering his sacrifice ineffectual and unnecessary. Again, when Quakers stressed the indwelling of Christ and denied that human nature was part of him, they appeared to be rejecting the historical Christ and thereby his crucifixion. Consequently, Grigg warned against "fixing thy Faith on a mysterious Sacrifice and Offering within, and not having dependency on that glorious Sacrifice of Christ's Crucified Body without, which was once offered to take away sin, Heb. 9.26."[25]

Quakers did not deny that the purpose of Christ's work was to take away humanity's sins, but they emphasized the fact that the method of this deliverance was by his inner work. Salthouse declared that it had pleased the Father "to reveal his Son in us; to destroy the works of the Devil," for, as Penn explained, "where the Devil hath Reigned and had Dominion to wit, in Man, there he must be defeated, and subdued."[26] A description Friends sometimes used for this inward soteriological process was the redemption of the "Seed," which was identified with Christ and the light. In the words of Penn, "the End of God's Manifesting himself in the Flesh was for the Redemption or Deliverance of his Holy Life that was in Man but as a small Seed, even the smallest of Seeds, that had been long vexed, grieved, bruised and pressed down by Sin and Iniquity."[27] The redemption of the Seed or "Holy Life" was sometimes described in terms of the Old Testament reference to the Seed that "bruiseth the Serpents Head" and at other times as "organic growth," illustrated by Whitehead's statement that the Seed was capable of being raised up in humans by the power of God and of growing up as a tender plant, as a root out of dry ground. Penn asserted that the task of Quakers was "to bring down, and humble the Mind of Man to it, that the Mind may be taught, and the Seed delivered from under the Pressure of Sin and Ignorance." To Baptists, Friends' association of Christ with an inward Seed seemed to deny the distinct and historical person of Christ without. In addition, the idea of the redemption of such an inward Seed was objectionable, for, as Wright argued, it was a doctrine directed to a supposed uncreated substance in all persons and reduced to a "blasphemous Riddle" the true gospel that offered salvation to the human creature. Further, as Hicks pointed out, "If then Redemption be of this Seed, and this Seed be Christ, either there must be more Christs then one, or else Christ came to redeem himself."[28]

An additional subject needs attention at this point, namely the extent of Christ's work. Among Presbyterians and Independents the generally accepted doctrine of predestination and reprobation limited the work of Christ to the elect. Baptists were divided in their views. Particular Baptists, even when demonstrating agreement with mainstream Nonconformists in the confession of 1677, omitted the Westminster Confession's section on reprobation.[29] General Baptists rejected predestinarian views and spoke of election in Christ, believing that Christ had died for all and that at some time all persons were put into a condition to be saved so that if they were to suffer damnation it would be as the result of their own unbelief.[30] With this Quakers agreed. However, the subject did arise in some arguments between General Baptists and Quakers, usually as the result of a misunderstanding of the difference between Christ's dying for all persons and their acceptance of his work.[31]

The disputes between Quakers and Particular Baptists on this point were rooted in fundamental differences. Bunyan stated the position of the latter group: "God seeing that we would transgresse, and break his commandment, did before chuse some of those that would fall, and give them to him, that should afterward purchase them actually." Friends, who believed that Christ died for all persons and that "God draws all men, though all men come not after him," reacted strongly. In the words of Whitehead, "His infinite Spirit is not tyed up to a few Predestinarian Electioners, who only conceit they are elected, and moving Grace only free for them."[32] However, this basic disagreement with Particular Baptists was not often discussed for its own sake but rather underlay the more frequent exchanges concerning the universality and sufficiency of the inner light.

Justification: Faith, Works, and the Law; Imputed and Inherent Righteousness; Sanctification and Perfection

One of the major points of controversy in the Protestant Reformation was the relative responsibility of God and humanity in the act of justification. The Protestant view emphasized divine action and the helplessness of humans, defining justification primarily as an act of God involving the imputation of Christ's righteousness. This position was held by most Puritans and mainstream Nonconformists of the seventeenth century, who, affirming the depravity of humankind, conceived of the act of faith primarily as divine and of good works as the fruit of that faith.[33] The position of Particular Baptists was similar. However, the Particular Baptist Thomas Collier spoke of *both* faith and works as the condition of justification and lamented the fact that Protestants "are too little for works."[34] General Baptists, while acknowledging the miserable state of fallen humanity, placed greater emphasis on the human role in justification by assigning to people an ability to accept or reject it. In this respect, they ascribed to individuals the responsibility for their own destruction and, by implication, their own justification, holding forth the possibility of "falling away" and stressing the importance of the life of holiness.[35] Nevertheless, to Baptists of both kinds, Quakers were clearly too much *for* works, seeming to advocate a covenant of works as opposed to a covenant of grace. Indeed, to Baptists, who underscored the placement of faith in the outward, historical work of Christ, the emphasis of Friends on the necessity of works seemed to threaten the sacrifice that Christ had performed for humanity.[36] Baptists did not deny good works to be important, but they maintained that they were the fruits of faith. In the words of Tombes, "We are saved by faith not by workes, that all might be of grace, and boasting might be excluded and Christ might be all in all." It appeared to Baptists that Quakers were guilty of just such "boasting," for, as Wright declared, "Laying low Self, and onely resting upon Christ by Faith thou canst not away with; therefore thou art in Self-exaltation in the highest degree."[37]

Quakers were much like General Baptists in underscoring the human role in justification, spurning predestination, and placing on individuals the responsibility for accepting or rejecting Christ's work. Contrary to the accusations of Baptists, however, Friends did not deny that justification was by faith, but, relying heavily on the epistle of James, they argued for the necessity of works.[38] Penn presented the logic of their argument when he wrote, "No man is justified without Faith. No man hath Faith without

Sanctification and Work; therefore the Works of Righteousness, by the Spirit, are necessary to Compleat Justification." People could not expect to be justified by faith when their lives brought forth only the fruits of unbelief. Indeed, unless faith "had that effectual Operation to subdue every beloved Lust, wean from every Dallila, and intirely to resign and sacrifice Isaak himself, [it] was a Fable, or as a Body without a Spirit."[39]

Closely related to the Baptist charge that Quakers sought to be justified by works was the accusation that Friends attempted to be justified by their fulfilment of the law. Baptists did not disavow the importance of the law and sometimes spoke of it in terms of light and inwardness. However, like Presbyterians and Independents, they could describe the law in at least two ways—as a natural law or law of works that all people possessed, or as a law of faith that they received as children of the new covenant. In both cases its function was to convince people of their sins.[40] However, individuals could not expect to obtain salvation by obedience to the law, for they could not fully satisify its demands. Christ had fulfilled the righteousness of the law, and people's deliverance came only by faith in him. Consequently, Bunyan charged that the law "is made an Idol of, and a Saviour" by those Quakers who sought to be justified by their obedience to it.[41] Indeed, according to Wigan, Friends were guilty of leading people "from Christ Jesus the true way, to the Law, that old deadly Gate, through which it is impossible for any of the sons of Adam to enter and live." However, the Baptist position was not antinomian, for, as Grigg explained, "We do not say, Christ fulfilled the Law so as to exclude our obedience"—but Baptists held that such obedience was the fruit of people's belief.[42]

Quakers emphasized the spiritual nature of the law, identifying it with the inner light. However, unlike Baptists, they did not draw a clear distinction between a law of works and a law of faith. Whitehead explained that people had the law within them before they entered into the new covenant, but it was "not as universally written or deeply engraven in their Hearts before."[43] They agreed with Baptists that Christ fulfilled the law, but in accordance with their emphasis on the indwelling Christ, they interpreted this fulfilment as occurring within. People were not acquitted by Christ's obedience on the cross unless the righteousness of the law was fulfilled in them.[44]

Although the arguments concerning works and the law may have been more dramatic, the discussion of imputed righteousness brought some of the basic points at issue into clearer focus. As noted, the general Puritan and Nonconformist view of justification involved the imputation of Christ's righteousness. However, references to imputation are not found in Baptist confessions prior to 1677. Nevertheless, when this concept was attacked by Quakers, members of both Baptist groups came to its defense. To them it was that righteousness that Christ fulfilled "in his own Person, wholly without us" (Russel), "in the body of his flesh wherein he also suffered on the Cross without the gates" (Bunyan), which was imputed to people. Indeed, Wigan declared that without this imputed righteousness none could be saved.[45]

Friends were not alone in their protests against such imputation, but their objections were perhaps more frequent than others'. Their criticisms included arguments that the concept was unscriptural and contrary to God's nature in considering people to be something they were not. Surely, Burrough reasoned, "the obedience of him without doth not justifie any; who are in the Nature of enmity against him." Penn argued that the condemnation or justification of individuals was based on their own actual performance, not on whether Christ's righteousness was imputed to them. Furthermore, it seemed to Quakers that the concept of imputation was an encouragement to sin. Indeed, Hollister charged Ewins with persuading his congregation in Bristol to believe lies in assuring them that their sins were pardoned and blotted out when in fact their lives revealed the contrary.[46] In the view of Friends, justification consisted of two parts: the remission of past sins and the new life of obedience. The former was the result of divine forgiveness as held forth in Christ's visible appearance, and the latter was the result of the work of Christ in human hearts. The mistake of Baptists was said to be the assumption that the former included the remission of sins present and future as well as past, and that the latter, therefore, was not necessary to justification. On the contrary, Penn declared, to exclude the latter, "and yet conclude men compleatly justified, by what Christ hath done wholly without, is a Doctrine of Devils; for it leaves men in an impure state and allows the Devils Kingdom to continue in being."[47]

To Baptists, human righteousness was, in biblical terms, only "as filthy rags," so that people "must flee to, and rely upon the Merits of Christ" and must have "that righteousness, which the Man Christ Jesus accomplished in his own person for sinners." This did not mean they denied the importance of inherent righteousness, for, Hicks declared, to emphasize an imputed righteousness did not overthrow the exercise of Christian virtues, and, Grigg explained, although he advocated imputed righteousness, "yet do I plead for spiritual Conformity to him, both in his Death and Resurrection; and that a man must die to sin, and rise to newness of life." However, such righteousness was said to be the result of salvation rather than its cause.[48] What Quakers referred to as the second stage of justification Baptists knew as sanctification. Baptists were aware of this confusion and accused Friends of placing "Sanctification in the stead and place of Justification." Baptists also emphasized the importance of sanctification, but they held that it followed rather than preceded justification. As Bunyan pointed out, having had the righteousness of Christ imputed to them, people were not to be "quiet" until "thou hast power over thy lusts and corruptions." From the perspective of the General Baptists, Caffyn cautioned that following their justification people had a good deal to do to maintain their justified state. Furthermore, the relative positions of justification and sanctification were not only temporal but causal, for just as good works and obedience to the law were the fruits of justification, so, in the opinion of Baptists, the process of sanctification, which included works and obedience, was the result of justification. The Quakers, they argued, were guilty of reversing this position, making justification dependent on sanctification and thereby abusing the work of Christ. As Collier explained, "If persons are justified no farther then they be sanctified and mortified, then their justification depends on their sanctification and mortification, and not on Christ crucified." To such charges, Friends made few replies except to reiterate the necessity of works and obedience for justification, a necessity linked with their emphasis on the experience of actual righteousness. According to Whitehead, justification was received only by those who truly departed from sin and evil. Indeed, as Burrough declared, "Justification is not without sanctification, as deceivers do falsly imagine a justification of men, when they are in the filth of the world."[49]

In light of the Quaker stress on the inward work of Christ, the importance of works, obedience to the law, the prominence of inherent righteousness, and sanctification, it is not surprising that their verbal exchanges with Baptists and others also took up the notion of perfection. Baptists could speak of saints being perfect in the sense of imputed perfection, whereby, in the words of Wright, "their sins shall not be remembered, and whereby their Persons shall be glorified for ever and ever." But in terms of moral infallibility experienced in daily lives, perfection was beyond human achievement. According to Collier, "God never had yet a Church in the world free from sin." This did not mean, Baptists explained, that they encouraged sin. On the contrary, they exhorted people to live in holiness and urged them, like Collier, "to be pressing forward after perfection." Nevertheless, they held, as Ewins put it, that the power and virtues of Christ were known only "in our measure," and that, in the words of Collier, perfection would not be attained "till Christ comes from Heaven."[50]

Baptists defended their position in two ways: by examining Scripture and by attacking the Quaker claim to perfection at the personal level. For example, they pointed out that in Scripture "perfect" often meant "sincere" and "upright," as when applied to Job and David.[51] Furthermore, they argued, even Paul admitted that sin dwelled in him and confessed that he was not perfect. According to the Apostle John, if people said they had no sin they deceived themselves.[52] That the Quakers fitted John's description, Baptists had little doubt.

Although Baptists stressed the importance of holiness, their sense of sin caused them to consider the Quaker claim to perfection to be evidence of pride and hypocrisy. They believed Friends had allowed their desire for righteousness to carry them to extremes. Caffyn explained:

> Certain men being somewhat troubled about their present conditions, and thereupon following after a more excellent estate, (though possibly not with that care and watchfulness as was meet should be) have on a sudden been greatly carried forth with inward Power and Zeal, and wonderful quicknings after some matters of holiness, so as scarce able to bear with the least appearance of Pride, Covetousness (or the like) in others, without reproof.[53]

However, that Quakers had any warrant to reprove others or consider themselves perfect or free from sin seemed absurd, for their lives indicated the opposite. Wigan, having quoted denunciatory statements directed against him by Margaret Fell, Thomas Curwen, and others, asked, "Whether any wise experienced Christian can judge this people to be in a perfect sinless estate, who appear with these open sinful revilings, cursings, judgings, in their mouths." In a more moderate tone, John Pendarves, Baptist minister at Abingdon, challenged Quakers to identify those among them who were without failings and imperfections. But Hicks, fully convinced of their sinful condition, proclaimed "That any Quaker can arrive to Perfection (in the way they are in) I believe is utterly impossible."[54]

Arriving at perfection did not seem to be impossibile to Friends. Although they could speak of perfection in terms of degrees and discounted suggestions that they thought themselves to be as perfect as Christ, they did believe that, in the words of Whitehead, "a perfect Freedom from all Sin in this Life is attainable." Such belief resulted from their emphasis on experienced righteousness and the intimate nature of the divine indwelling. Fox declared that it was Christ "who destroys the Devill and his works, and bindes the strong man, and spoyls his goods, and takes the possession of it to himselfe, and the creature is a perfect creature out of transgression." However, making such perfect creatures was, as Penn explained, a process that involved degeees. Eventually, as people subjected themselves to the Spirit, they experienced sanctification throughout the whole being, "which is that blessed state, wherein he that's born of God sins not." Quakers insisted that such perfection was to be enjoyed in this earthly life and declared that the Baptist attempt to postpone perfection until heaven was "repugnant to the Foundation of living and purifying Faith and Hope; and so excludes Holiness of Life."[55]

In support of their arguments on behalf of perfection Quakers made numerous appeals to the experience of the primitive church. They pointed out that in the New Testament Paul told the Romans they were free from sin and John declared that those who were born of God did not commit sin. They also drew attention to divine statements that people were to be holy and perfect, and they noted that it was the work of the ministry to bring this about.[56] They claimed it was in this work that Baptists, who believed that they could never be free of sin in their mortal lives, had failed. They were guilty of "pleading for sin and imperfection" and of keeping people in their sins. Their present state was viewed as apostasy by Friends, who affirmed that Baptists had once been a "tender" people but now betrayed the understanding God had given them.[57] Whitehead pointed out that in a letter to Baptist churches, Collier and others had admitted that a coldness, a deadness, a "Laodicean Spirit" had fallen on them. Referring to Collier, Salthouse asked, "What is become of all those desires and pressing after perfection that once appeared in him?"[58]

Eschatology: Second Advent, Resurrection, Judgment, and Future State

In exchanges concerning Christology and soteriology, the subject of eschatology also arose. The spiritualized events of Christ's life that Quakers experienced inwardly in the present (crucifixion, death, burial, resurrection, ascension) extended to the second advent and other eschatological occurrences that Baptists thought of as *future* events.[59] Although Friends also spoke of a future coming of Christ, they meant something very different. They claimed they had already experienced Christ's second advent as had the earliest Christians. Christ himself stated he would come again before many who heard him passed away, and in fact members of that generation had later witnessed he was in them and had saved them from sin, Quakers argued. Referring to occurrences that were to precede the second advent, including the coming of the man of sin (2 Thess. 2:3), Fox declared, "All this which Christ said should come, which the Apostles saw was come, and coming, before the coming of the just One: But the Just One is now come, who hath revealed it." Indeed, Fox and others often described their encounter with society as the Lamb's War, using the apocalyptic imagery of the Lamb (Christ) and his saints at war with the Beast.[60] Thus, in accord with their emphasis on the inward nature of Christ's presence and work, they alleged that Christ had already come a second time (although not with a body of flesh), that such an advent was experienced by each person who received Christ for salvation as in the New Testament church, and thus that for some it was still a future event. Whitehead explained, "The coming of Christ in the flesh, (wherein he was offered to bear the sins of many, Heb. 9.28) was one coming, and his appearance in Spirit, to save his people from sin, is another coming, which they that truly looked for Him receive; and they that yet have that his coming to look for, and waite for it, he shall so appear to their Salvation."[61]

Baptists, believing Christ to be in heaven physically, also held that his second coming was to be outward, physical, and visible. As Caffyn explained, "That Christ is a visible glorified man, leads us to expect his second coming as a distinct appearance from, and not in, his People." They argued that his return would be visible, as was his departure, and would be accompanied by marvellous events. Obviously, therefore, Christ was yet to come. Furthermore, Baptists thought Friends confused Christ and the Holy Spirit as they had done in arguments about the divine indwelling and the incarnation. Grigg pointed out that the saints "to whom Christ was Spiritually come, as gloriously as ever he came to any of the Saints, did, notwithstanding that, still expect, look and wait for his coming from heaven." Whatever factors were present in Friends' arguments, their error seemed profound, and led Bunyan to declare that the second advent must be imminent, for the prophecies of false Christs, deceptive prophets, and scoffers to precede that coming were surely being fulfilled in the Quakers. He also warned that, in dealing with those who, like Friends, mocked

Christ's second coming, God would "cut them asunder & appoint them their portion with hypocrites, and there shall be weeping and gnashing of teeth."[62]

Arising from exchanges on perfection and the second advent was the issue of the resurrection of humankind, which also was significant in relation to the resurrection of Christ. Baptists, like Presbyterians and Independents, believed in the future bodily resurrection of Christians.[63] Although Quakers also claimed to maintain this belief, they actually meant something different. In harmony with their emphasis on the inward, experiential nature of Christ's work, they interpreted the resurrection of believers as present deliverance from sin. Shewen, for example, complained that Ives had ideas about what God had done in the past and would do in the future, "but is ignorant and unacquainted with his Power at present, believes little of his Power and Ability in their own Particulars in this present time, wherein they are to know him by his Mighty Power to raise them out of the Grave of Sin, and give them Victory over it, and so to witness their part in the first Resurrection."[64] Burrough's position was similar, but also included references to the Seed of God that, having suffered by corruption in the bodies of persons, was then raised incorruptible in power and glory. Whitehead considered the term "resurrection" inapplicable to the dust of human bodies but rather a proper reference to the discarding of sin in the development of the "New Man." However, as he was careful to explain, this did not mean the resurrection was past, for the process of resurrection would not be complete until "our Labours and Sufferings are ended, and our Earthly House dissolved."[65]

The prospect of a future resurrection after the dissolution of the earthly body, not the concept of a present resurrection from sin, mainly occupied Friends' attention in these disputes, for it was to this point that Baptists directed their attacks. Quaker arguments aimed to prove that human bodies were not to be raised. Although Burrough appealed to Job's statement that he who goes down to Sheol does not come up, Quakers drew most of their prooftexts from 1 Corinthians 15. They argued that flesh and blood could not inherit the kingdom, that the earthly body was mortal and corruptible but the heavenly body immortal and incorruptible, and, therefore, that the natural body would not be raised.[66] As Penn declared, "The Scripture speaks of a Dissolution and no Resurrection of that which is destroyed, being Earthly, and Unfit for a Celestial Paradice." The bodies that people would receive were to be spiritual, heavenly bodies, bodies like Christ's.[67]

The temporal implications of these arguments were of further significance, for whereas the resurrection of earthly bodies that Baptists expected would occur at one future time for all persons, the reception of spiritual bodies that Quakers described could occur at the death of each individual. Penn argued that if people had to wait to be joined by their resurrected bodies then the joy of the saints in heaven was imperfect, and Whitehead pointed out that the discarding of "Earthly Cloathing" was "to our far greater Advantage & Glory, to be invested with that Spiritual Transcendent Cloathing." In addition, Burrough objected to the supposition that the saints had not attained the redemption of their bodies from the bondage of corruption, and Penn interpreted 1 Corinthians 15:53 to mean that

> We, who are Mortals respecting our Bodies, put off the Mortal Part and put on instead thereof Immortality; suitable to that weighty Passage of the Apostle Paul, For We know that if our Earthly House of this Tabernacle were disolved, we have a Building of God, an House not made with Hands, Eternal in [the] Heavens.[68]

Baptists sometimes described resurrection in terms of forgiveness and deliverance from sin, especially in relationship to baptism. However, they insisted that this was not synonymous with the future resurrection of the body. As Grantham pointed out, "It is one thing to rise with Christ to newness of Life (which I hope you have attained, but I beseech you abound more and more); and another thing to be raised from Mortality to a state of Glory." Baptists concentrated their attention on this resurrection of the body to the state of glory, appealing like the Quakers primarily to 1 Corinthians 15. They admitted that flesh could not inherit the kingdom but pointed out that this meant sinful flesh and such imperfection would be removed at the resurrection. The body at death suffered corruption but was raised incorruptible.[69] "Sinne, or bodily infirmities" and "all sorrows, miseries and imperfections" were removed, but it was, they insisted, the same body. As Grigg explained, it was "the same body, respecting the matter, substance, or essence of it." The change, he continued, was "touching the state, qualities, or condition of the body: the corruption and imperfection, and all manner of deformity shall be done away, and it shall rise more glorious then it was before."[70] Having been raised in this manner from the grave, the body would be reunited with the soul to experience either reward or punishment. In addition, Baptists argued, this resurrection was yet to come, and those who claimed that it was past were guilty of the error of Hymenaeus and Philetus, who had been condemned by Paul. In the eyes of Baptists such as Thomas Hicks, the Quaker position was a denial not only of the resurrection of humankind but of the resurrection of Christ as well.[71]

The subject of Judgment and the future state did not often arise in disputes between Baptists and Quakers. The former thought of heaven and hell in objective terms and of the Judgment as a future event.[72] However, Friends spoke of heaven in a subjective manner and emphasized the inward spiritual judgment they had already experienced. Such references sometimes provoked Baptist responses. When John Lawson referred to the Day of Judgment as past, Ives objected, insisting, like Caffyn, that it was yet to come. Again, when Lawson spoke of having experienced heaven and hell, Ives objected and questioned whether he had actually been there. On this occasion Fox and Nayler came to Lawson's defense, pointing out that primitive Christians had testified to these experiences.[73] Such statements led Wright to complain that Quakers "boast that Christ is come to them, neither look they for any other coming: That the world is ended with them, neither look they for any other end: That the Judgment is past with them, neither look they for any other Judgment." In fact, although Whitehead spoke of a final Day of Judgment and Fox referred to both a judgment in this life and an eternal judgment, the latter nevertheless declared, using the present tense, that the "Lamb is on the white Horse, who slayes with his Sword" and the Beast "is cast into the lake of fire." Fox accused Baptists of putting Christ and his Judgment far off. In a statement illustrating the differences between the two groups, Whitehead charged Baptists with imagining that

> the new Jerusalem (Prophesied of, that should come down from Heaven) must be some outward City or Place, consisting of fair buildings outwardly; and so might they not as well imagine of the Temple thereof, that it is some fair outward structure? Whereas the Lord God, and the Lamb, is the Temple and Light thereof; and the Nations of them that are saved, shall walk in the Light of this holy city.[74]

In some respects, the positions of Friends on these issues were similar to those of Seekers and Ranters, who were also at this extremity of the religious continuum. Seekers were believed by contemporaries to emphasize the law written within them and the divine indwelling with its authority and efficacy. Erbery reproved Baptists for their "fleshly apprehensions of Christ, and him crucified, of his coming and Kingdom, wich your carnal understandings mis-represent unto men." But Seekers themselves were reproached by the Quaker Edward Burrough, who warned that they were seeking at the wrong door and their seeking would end before they found eternal life. The common beliefs of Quakers and Ranters were in turn condemned by the Baptist Thomas Collier for including "No law but their lusts, no Heaven nor glory but here, no sin but what men fancied to be so, no condemnation for sin but in the consciences of ignorant ones." Ranters did reject a literal, external heaven and hell. Some also embraced an amorality like that of Abiezer Coppe, who, as noted, claimed, "I can if it be my will, kisse and hug Ladies and love my neighbours wife, as my selfe, without sin." As Bauthumley explained it, "The Sin lies not in these outward acts, for a man may do the self-same act, and yet not sin: that is, that a man drinks to excess, there is the sin, that a man drinks for necessity or delight, the same act and posture of body is put out in the one, as the other." Quakers vigorously distanced themselves from this aspect of Ranter thought. When Thomas Lawson wrote to Margaret Fell that Ranters south of London believed there was nothing different between the two groups except that Friends "did not see all things to be theirs," Fell denounced the notion as well as the fleshly liberty and licentiousness of the Ranters, declaring that Friends denied all Ranters and their principles.[75]

As in most other issues, Muggletonian beliefs contrasted with those of

Seekers, Ranters, and Quakers. Reeve and Muggleton thought that the body and soul died and were resurrected together. Hell involved torment in the body on earth, heaven was just above the clouds, and there all angels and other creatures in the presence of God were "spiritual male creatures," and fleshly pleasures were replaced by spiritual and heavenly joys. The way to heaven was described by John Gratton, a convert to Quakerism, who confessed that when he was a Muggletonian, "We had no more to do, but to believe *Muggleton*, and be saved." The path to hell might also be determined by Reeve and Muggleton, as in the case of the former Baptist Elizabeth Hooton, to whom Muggleton declared in 1668, "I do pronounce Elizabeth Hooton, Quaker, . . . cursed and damned, both in soul and body, from the presence of God, elect men and angels, to eternity."[76]

The testimonies of former Baptists reveal that their strong yearning for a New Testament "acquaintance with God" was accompanied by an ardent desire for actual righteousness. When their religious searching reached its culmination, their immediate experience of the New Testament Christ comprised internalized, spiritualized events of his life. Such internalization and spiritualization was extended to the soteriological significance of those occurrences and to eschatological events as well, raising again in their controversy with Baptists the dichotomies of immediate/mediate, inward/outward, and spiritual/physical. Thus, whereas the two groups agreed concerning the necessity of the inward application as well as the outward historical sacrifice of Christ, they were at odds over their relative importance. Whereas Baptists stressed the outward work of Christ and on occasion defended the notion of satisfaction, Quakers emphasized the inward work of Christ and rejected the outward satisfaction theory but then had difficulty explaining the necessity of Christ's historical sacrifice.

In some respects General Baptists were closer than Particulars to Quaker doctrines, for they had no quarrel with Quakers over the offering of salvation to all. Also, like Friends, they placed responsibility on the individual to accept or reject the divine offer, and believed in the possibility of "falling away." However, in their disputes with Friends, members of both Baptist groups opposed Quaker views on works as a part of justification, the fulfilling of the law by Christ within, inherent as opposed to imputed righteousness, sanctification, and the possibility of sinless perfection in the earthly life. Baptists recognized the importance of works, the law, inherent righteousness, and sanctification, but contended that these were the results of justification and not such an integral part of it as Quakers thought. They also held that perfection was to be sought but not realized in the life of this world. Finally, in accord with their experiential approach, Friends emphasized a spiritualized and realized eschatology, whereas Baptists, in keeping with their more outward, historical approach to soteriology, stressed an objective eschatology yet to occur.

Quakers appeared to Baptists to deny the outward work of Christ, both past and future, and to rely on their own efforts to achieve salvation.

To Friends, Baptists seemed to depend on an outward act of another person in the past for salvation, and by postponing its completion until the future to separate salvation from righteousness and thus to allow for, and even encourage, sin. To such Baptists Fox pleaded, "Come on to perfection; to his who doth increase; Not laying againe the foundation of Repentence from dead workes, & Baptismes; but come into the Covenant which connot be altered, nor doth not wax old."[77] Such "Baptismes" that Quakers thought *had* waxed old are examined in the following chapter.

5

Fleshly forms we utterly deny

Baptism and the Lord's Supper

[Quaker]
Your fleshy forms we utterly deny,
The light within us is a full supply;

[Professor]
You do pretend to lay all Forms aside,
Saying, none shall by Forms be justifi'd,
Yet must make use of Forms, your own invention.

Benjamin Keach, *The Grand Impostor Discovered*

The temporary relaxation of restrictions on Nonconformist activity result-ing from Charles II's Declaration of Indulgence in 1672 freed many Non-conformists from prison and also provided opportunity for further disputes between Quakers and Baptists. Even in more repressive times, imprison-ment could not always inhibit such controversy. In 1664 Fox and the Bap-tist John Wigan, who had disputed in London six years earlier, found themselves in Lancaster prison with Margaret Fell and others.[1] A vigorous debate ensued in the prison hall. Wigan first contended with Margaret Fell, who later denounced his "blasphemies" and "lyes," then turned to Fox, who got "up to a seat with one foot, and to the table with the other, whereas I and others were standing on the ground about the Table." But the Quaker report maintained that Wigan did "stand upon the Table be-fore *George Fox*, and was so unruly not as to be gotten off the Table," and that he "cockt up thy Hat, more like a Ranter and a Player in a Tavern, then one imployed in the service of God." Fox also recounted that in ad-dition to debating, Wigan had a collection taken up in the area for prisoner relief, which many donors thought was to include the Quakers, but that Wigan intended it only for himself and "another drunken preacher of his, that would be so drunk that he lost his breeches." Finally, Fox reported that the following year in London Wigan and his wife were "cut off by the plague." "The judgements of God came upon them," Fox said. Among the

vehemently debated topics in the Lancaster prison encounter were the ordinances of baptism and the Lord's Supper, and materials from the dispute
are among those examined in this chapter.[2]

We have previously seen that Quakers spiritually entered the time of
the primitive church so fully as to assert as their own the authority primitive Christians had before the writing of the New Testament. They also
claimed to have immediately experienced Christ and the events of his life,
albeit in an internalized and spiritualized fashion. They extended such
qualities to baptism and the Lord's Supper. Thus, Friends abandoned the
outward ordinances entirely while emphasizing their immediate, inward,
spiritual administration. Although Baptists discarded baptism as it had
been practiced for centuries, they retained its outward physical observance.
They also retained the physical administration of the Lord's Supper and
thus maintained continuity with the practices of Presbyterians and Independents. Nevertheless, Quakers and Baptists had more in common with
each other in these doctrines than might at first be expected.

The Nature of the Ordinances: Outward
and Physical, Inward and Spiritual

Among Presbyterians and Independents the two sacraments were considered signs and seals of the covenant of grace. By their proper use the grace
exhibited was conferred by the Holy Spirit and the benefits were sealed to
the believer.[3] Baptists preferred to use the term *ordinances* (a word they
also employed for other divine commandments) rather than *sacraments*.[4]
They gave the subject little consideration in their early confessions.[5] Furthermore, they generally took a more Zwinglian view of the ordinances
than these other groups, preferring to consider them "signs" rather than
"seals" and sometimes objecting strongly to the latter Calvinist concept.[6]
Tombes declared that Scripture did not mention sealing as their end or
use, and Bunyan referred to them as "shadowish or figurative ordinances,"
which were "representations" and neither the fundamentals of Christianity
nor the grounds of communion.[7] Nevertheless, Baptists attached considerable importance to their observance because it was commanded by
Christ, and when they were discontinued and their use assailed by Quakers, Baptists came to their defense.

Friends claimed they did not deny the ordinances of Christ, but only
a practice of them that was empty of the divine power. Burrough declared
that ordinances "as they are performed in the Power of God by the leadings of his Spirit we own, but where such things are done out of the power
or leadings of that Spirit in mans wills, they are but formal, dead and
empty, and as such to be denied." Contrasting the outward and the inward, the physical and the spiritual, they drew an emphatic distinction between outward form and inward substance. The former Baptist Humphrey
Wolrich warned against those who were "setting up the shadow instead of
the substance, and things that are seen with a carnal and visible eye above

those things that are eternal, everlasting but not seen." Here too, the dichotomy of mediacy and immediacy was involved, as seen in Burrough's
protest against those who, in practicing water baptism, "have in your own
wills thrust in your selves, and acted without, and not having received the
command from Christ into your selves."[8] Were one to have received such
a command and to have performed such outward acts with the power of
the Spirit as the Baptists believed they did, would the outward observance
of the ordinances have been acceptable in the Quaker view? Although
Wolrich did claim that under these circumstances at least water baptism
was permissible, to most Friends it was not a question of permission but of
possibility. They severed outward form from inward substance and replaced the former with the latter. In doing so they appealed both to their
own experience and to primitive Christianity.

From their earlier experiences, Quakers testified that the inward substance was simply not to be found in the outward ordinances. In the words
of Wolrich, they formerly had been "in those carnal Ordinances," but
"could never find the pearl in them, where it was not to be found." With
respect to Scripture, they considered New Testament ordinances to be of
the same nature as Old Testament rites, arguing that such outward figurative ordinances were now obsolete, having been replaced by the actual
substance. As Penn pointed out, "they were in the beginning used as Figures and Shadows of a more Hidden and Spiritual Substance," but the
coming of the gospel terminated them. Christ had come, he argued, "to
remove, change and abolish the very Nature of such Ordinances," which
were by their outward nature unable to give eternal life. That Christ had
established such a change was evident in the New Testament, for, as Fox
contended, "Doth not the Apostle bring off of those things that are seen?
And is not outward water, and outward bread the things that are seen?"
Thus Friends found no basis for the continuing use of outward ordinances.
In fact, the Quakers' primitivism evoked revulsion in them toward practices that were humanly constructed in postbiblical times. Appealing to the
authority of primitive church practice, Hollister asserted, "Invented and
carnal observations used in and about the worship of your God, for which
no ground being in the Scriptures, ye and others have by tradition received
it from Popes, Cardinals and Priests, and other Heathens that know not
God."[9] Furthermore, these "observations" were of no effect, for such
"Baptists Shells, Husks and Shadows," declared Whitehead, "are both dry
and empty, and the Lord is departed from them, so as neither Life nor
Substance is to be found in them." They were, according to Robert Wastfield, "the ordinances of the Man of Sin."[10]

Baptists did not believe in a close relationship between outward form
and inward substance either. However, unlike Friends, they did not find
the two incongruous. Justification was not the result of submission to such
outward ordinances, they admitted. Nor was it enough to engage in their
observance, for as Grigg pointed out, "a Person may find the Shell, and

have no kernel in it." Nevertheless, outward observance was not necessarily devoid of spirituality. In fact, Baptists advocated the "spiritual practice" of ordinances. The importance of such practice, Pendarves claimed, was not diminished by Quaker arguments against a "carnall formall practice." In justifying their position Baptists were not primarily concerned with relationships between form and substance, but rather with primitive Christianity. The ordinances, they claimed, were to be observed because this had been commanded by God and practiced by the New Testament church. Such observance was an indication of faith in God and God's authority over believers. Like the whole of the primitive faith, the ordinances had been delivered for the use of the churches of the present as well as the past, and those who rejected them denied the faith as well.[11]

Wigan attributed the Quaker refusal to practice the ordinances to Friends' denial of Scripture as the rule of faith. Others thought it was also evidence of the rejection of additional basic doctrines. Because the ordinances were appointed by Christ to declare his having come in the flesh, it followed that rejecting them was a denial of his advent and thus also a clear demonstration of the spirit of the Antichrist.[12] The gravity of all this caused Griffith to warn his readers:

> The more perverse speakers do arise saying, In vain have we kept his Ordinances, the more do you love them, and contend for them, meeting often together, the Lord will take notice of it, there shall be a Book of Remembrance written, yea, and you be his in the day the Lord shall make up his Jewels.[13]

Although Quakers rejected the observance of outward ordinances, they professed not to deny them as performed in the power of God, in their "spiritual practice," and "in life and power" as they were in primitive Christianity. They contrasted the ordinances practiced in this way, said to be "living, spiritual and true," with those observed in an outward manner, which they claimed were humanly constructed in postbiblical times and thus "traditional, invented, and carnal."[14] According to Nayler, it was the true ordinances established by God that

> we worship in, for those Ordinances are spiritual and have life in them, wherein God dwells, and in them by him we shall be kept. And the clear water we know, wherein our bodies are washed: and the blood of cleansing, and the bread of life, which was broken for us and is given to us, by which we live.[15]

Baptists found such a fully internalized and spiritualized interpretation unacceptable. To them, the outward physical nature of the ordinances as first practiced by the primitive church was obvious. The fact that their observance was commanded by Christ was unquestionable ground for continuing such practice. As Pendarves declared, "the Saints have the footsteps of the flock in primitive times going before them, and the appointment of Christ for the continuance of these till his coming." Quakers, by refusing to observe them and by reproaching those who did, were said

by Collier to be guilty of leaving "the weighty things of faith and obedience to the Laws and Ordinances of Christ undone, as vile and con-
temptible."[16]

Baptism: The Water Without and the Spirit Within

Although baptism might at first appear to be the doctrine that separated
Quakers more widely from Baptists than from Presbyterians and Independents, in fact there was some affinity between the views of the two groups.
Whereas the Baptists' usual practice of believers' baptism by immersion
was the characteristic that most easily distinguished them from the latter
groups, their doctrine of baptism was weaker in its initiatory, outward, and
Godward qualities. For example, although the initiatory aspect of baptism
was significant for General Baptists, it was of less importance to Particular
Baptists.[17] Their confession of 1644 made no mention of it, and although
their confession of 1656 noted that baptism signified becoming a part of
the visible church, their confession of 1677, modeled after the Westminster Confession, omitted the latter's statement concerning the necessity of
baptism for admission to the church and referred only to its signifying an
ingrafting into Christ.[18] Indeed, among the Particular Baptists, there were
ministers like Jessey, Bunyan, and Ewins whose churches did not require
believers' baptism as a condition of membership at all. The existence of
strong disagreement over such open membership was admitted by Particular Baptists in the appendix to their confession of 1677, which said that
for the sake of unity all mention of the subject had been omitted.[19] Furthermore, even though General Baptists affirmed its initiatory significance,
baptism was apparently to many of them of no greater importance than
the laying on of hands, which they also required for admission to their
churches.[20]

The Baptist doctrine of baptism was also not as strong in its outward
aspect as might be expected. The practice of baptism by immersion, which
was not introduced among Baptists until 1641, arose not primarily from
concern over form per se, but rather from preoccupation with fidelity to
the primitive model. Furthermore, as an outward act it was usually considered to have only the importance of a sign rather than a seal.[21] In emphasizing the inward quality of baptism, Bunyan declared that the believer
who is dead to sin and lives to God has something better than that outward physical act: "he hath the heart, power and doctrine of baptism." He
further explained, "The best of Baptisms he hath; he is Baptized by that
one spirit; he hath the heart of Water-baptism, he wanteth only the outward shew, which if he had would not prove him a truly visible Saint; it
would not tell me he had grace in his heart."[22]

The Baptist doctrine was also weak with respect to divine efficacy. References in the Westminster Confession to such efficacy, conferring of
grace, and a seal of the covenant in baptism were omitted from the 1677
and 1679 confessions of the two Baptist groups. Further, in the appendix

to their confession of 1677, Particular Baptists openly objected to the opinion that baptism was a seal of the covenant and claimed that the true seal was the indwelling of the Spirit of Christ in the individual.[23] Indeed, the primary emphasis of Baptists in water baptism was not on the divine but the human. It was essentially an act of the baptized, a profession of faith by the individual. Its chief end was, according to Tombes, "To testi-fie the Repentance, Faith, Hope, Love, and Resolution of the Baptized to follow Christ." The signification in baptism most often stated was the bap-tized's affinity with the death, burial, and resurrection of Christ, which, ac-cording to Bunyan, assisted them to see "that they have professed them-selves, dead, and buryed, and risen with him to newness of life."[24]

It is clear then that the practice of believers' baptism did not arise pri-marily from Baptists' interest in it as an initiatory rite, an outward form, or an act of God, but rather from concern for primitive Christianity and zeal for following the New Testament pattern. This zeal resulted not only in the administration of believers' baptism by immersion, but also among some Baptists of the observance of such other primitive church practices as the laying on of hands, the love feast, footwashing, anointing with oil, casting lots, and the holy kiss.[25] Given the relative weakness of its initia-tory, outward, and Godward qualities, the Baptist doctrine was closer than that of Presbyterians and Independents to the experiential emphasis of Quakers. Nevertheless, Baptists and Quakers, who shared a devotion to the primitive model of Christianity, differed significantly in their percep-tion of that model and thus engaged in vigorous debates like the one in Lancaster prison.

In their disputes with Baptists, Friends were often careful to point out that they believed in the ordinance of baptism and objected only to the practice of baptism by water. Sometimes their arguments focused on the nature and efficacy of the outward act, claiming that either the act in itself accomplished the washing away of sins or the plunging into Christ's spirit, or it was simply a sign or figure. In the latter case, the only acceptable one to Baptists, it seemed to Friends that the outward act was therefore of lit-tle importance. As Whitehead argued, the power of God "baptised his people into his death, and raiseth them up in the likeness of his Resurrec-tion, and not outward water."[26] Quakers also believed they had ample ex-periential evidence that the use of water was insignificant. Those who were formerly Baptists had found it deficient. Luke Howard, who had been baptized by the Particular Baptist William Kiffin in London, testified, "We were dipped in Water in Hope of Life and Peace, and call'd Brothers and sisters by Waterdipping: but that Formality satisfied not the Cry of my Soul," and William Bayly declared that after his baptism in water "I was the same every way as before, no more better nor satisfied by the water." Friends could also point out baptism's ineffectiveness in the lives of others. Nayler charged, "You that go into the water come out as full of pride, envy, covetousness and all manner of wickedness as you go in, and the Devil hardened in many of you in lying against the truth, onely thereby

being conceited that your sins are washed away." That Baptists, being satisfied with an outward form, had stopped short of the power of righteousness caused Whitehead to exclaim, "Oh ignorant Men! how do you lead
silly Women Captive blindfold, and in darkness into your Water-Baptism[;]
you never knew the Nature of true Repentance (nor the Spirit's Baptism)
through which the Mind is changed from Darkness and Sin to Light and
Righteousness."[27]

On other occasions Friends appealed directly to the primitive model.
Raising again the dichotomy of mediacy and immediacy, Quakers charged
that John the Baptist had received a commission from God to practice
water baptism, but that Baptists had not. According to Burrough, Baptists
practiced it "without either immediate command from Heaven, or motion
of Gods Spirit for it." Although in such statements they may have implied
it, Quakers were not willing to claim explicitly that their abandonment of
water baptism was by immediate divine command. Instead, they sought
vigorously to justify their action on biblical grounds. Here they struck at
the heart of the Baptist position. Daring to attack the very text that Baptists held as the unquestionable foundation of their doctrine, Parnell asked
to be shown "where Christ ever commanded water Baptisme." The great
commission of Christ did not warrant such a practice, he argued. Furthermore, there was no evidence that Matthew, Mark, Luke, John, or any of
the apostles were baptized in this manner. Boldly sweeping aside all biblical claims that Baptists used, Nayler declared to Ives, "You cannot find one
Scripture that doth command it with water."[28] The baptism with water
used by John, Friends argued, had been replaced by the baptism of the
Spirit as commanded by Christ. As Penn explained, "The time of the Baptism of the Holy Ghost, Christ's only Baptism, therefore called the One
Baptism, has been long since come; Consequently the other, which was
John's, was fulfilled, and as becomes a Fore-runner, ought to cease." That
baptism with water had ceased was clear from Scripture, which declared
that there is now only one baptism. Quakers admitted that certain of the
disciples had on occasion baptized with water, but this was done, as Whitehead claimed, "for the sake of some that were weak or young in the truth,
and not wholly redeemed out of the state that such carnall or weak ordinances related to, which were upheld in the time of the Churches infancy."
Thus it appeared to Friends that Baptists were clearly wrong in their practice, even by their own admission, for as Fox reported of his dispute at
Dorchester in 1655, "They fell into discourse about their water-baptism,
and I asked them whether they could say they were sent of God to baptize
people, as John was, and whether they had the same power and spirit the
apostles had, and they said they had not."[29]

Such occasional acts of water baptism in the primitive church had been
done by permission, not by commission, argued the former Baptist
Humphrey Wolrich. He also explained that as a Quaker he was no longer
"feeding upon the Wind, and eating that which died of itself, and that did
not satisfy" but had now found the way wherein "the shadows flee away."

As the Church matured, such outward acts had become unnecessary and were terminated. In the words of Whitehead, "As people (who had a zeal for these outward Figures) grew into the Substance and Life wherein they ended, that they were able to bear the denying of them; the Apostles Preached the end of them, and refused to be in bondage to them again." The Apostle Paul, for example, testified that Christ had not sent him to baptize and expressed his thankfulness that he had baptized only a few.[30] In fact, true believers had progressed beyond outward signs or figures, for, according to Burrough, "they are come to be baptized into his death, and to be raised in his life by that Spirit which hath baptized them, which is the Substance wherein the signes and shadows are ended." The Quakers, the former Baptist John Perrot maintained, were "in the true Water," which, he claimed, "Baptiseth, Dippeth, & Plungeth the Conscience, and cleanseth it from sin." Baptists who were guilty of practicing water baptism not as in primitive times but "by tradition and imitation" were in reality using only a "carnal empty shadow or low things that God is gone out of," Burrough declared. Nevertheless, Wolrich as a Quaker no longer "feeding upon the Wind" administered water baptism to a woman who requested it. Claiming that, like Paul, he had not a commission but permission from God, Wolrich appealed to the unlimited nature of the Spirit and declared that the woman had been led "not from the Baptists rule and leader, which is the Letter, and kills, but by the Spirit."[31]

The Baptists' distinctive doctrine of baptism arose from their strong desire to observe the primitive church pattern. As Grigg declared, "We plead for Baptism as it was dispensed and administered in the Primitive time."[32] Thus their defense against the Quakers' attacks consisted primarily of biblical arguments designed to expose Friends' misinterpretations of the Scripture. Like the Quakers, Baptists distinguished between water baptism and the baptism of the Holy Spirit, but they insisted that the latter was administered only by Christ. Baptism in water was to be administered by and to believers. Christ had submitted to such a baptism, and believers were required to follow his example. In addition, Baptists argued, the disciples had understood Christ's commandment to have been for baptism by water, for there was abundant evidence that they practiced it.[33] Philip, for example, had baptized the Ethiopian eunuch, and Peter had commanded Cornelius and several others who had already received the baptism of the Spirit to be baptized with water. Peter had preached that baptism was a duty for all believers. Baptists admitted that Paul had declared he had been sent by Christ to preach, not to baptize, but, they argued, this meant only that Paul's chief work was to preach. They pointed out that he did in fact baptize.[34] Furthermore, as Caffyn explained, "Paul had baptized but few of the Corinthians, for which he gave God thanks, not from a low esteem thereto, but because they thereby had no show, to say that he baptized in his own name, as they were apt to say." Baptists also admitted that Christ had ended the shadows and services of the Mosaic law, but they held that he had not ended the gospel ordinance of baptism. Rather he had commanded its use. In a letter addressed to "those deluded soules called Quakers," Thomas Tillam argued that persons who experienced the Spirit's baptism "were by the same led to Water Baptisme, and the rest of Christs ordinances." According to Grantham, for Quakers to claim that the practice had been terminated was to speak as if time could decay the divine commandments when God had not actually abrogated them.[35]

Although Baptist arguments were primarily centered on the foundation of water baptism in the primitive time, on rare occasions they appealed to their own experience. Randall Roper, objecting to Perrot's claim that those who practiced water baptism had not come to Christ the substance, declared, "It is a Lie, for many with my self can experience his coming by his Spirit into our hearts, and yet we dare not let go the Ordinances of Christ." Roper admitted that some Baptists had fallen away from the faith. However, he argued that this did not undermine the importance of baptism, for their apostasy was a result of not having received the truth initially, having been baptized only because it was fashionable, and now preferring to live in unrighteousness. These persons, like all others who denied water baptism, were guilty of disobedience to Christ.[36]

The Quaker rejection of water baptism was complemented by their emphasis on the baptism of the Spirit within. According to Fox, "Who comes into the baptisme of the spirit, they come into the one, in which all the other ends, the greater." The true Christian, wrote Penn, "*is one Inwardly.*" His baptism, he continued, "*is of the HOLY GHOST and FIRE.*" That this was the baptism intended in the great commission of Christ, Friends were thoroughly convinced. They went on to point out that in that commission, baptizing εἰζ τὸ ὄνομα was baptizing into the divine Spirit or power. "Is not his Name Spiritual, representing his Nature, yea, Spirit, Power, and Life?" asked Taylor. Insisting on actual righteousness, Wolrich declared that the divine name consisted not in words but in purity, righteousness, and holiness. Furthermore, Penn argued, the fact that the great commission intended a spiritual baptism was evident not only from its own form of statement but also from the sequence of events leading up to it. John, who baptized with water, was to decrease but Christ was to increase. Later Christ reminded the disciples that John had baptized with water but that they would be baptized with the Holy Ghost. Then, Penn concluded, "comes the Commission in Force, Go, Teach, Baptizing &c. How? With the Holy Ghost, turning People from Darkness to Light, and from the Power of Satan unto God."[37] That the disciples had understood this and had carried out Christ's command was also evident. On one occasion when Peter witnessed the coming of the Holy Spirit on those to whom he was speaking, he was reminded of Christ's statement contrasting John's baptism with that of the Holy Spirit. On additional occasions Paul and others had baptized with the Holy Spirit. Consequently, the Baptist doctrine of outward baptism by water was said by Wolrich to be "a Doctrine of Devils." Inward baptism saved. Indeed, warned Perrot, "If you tye yourselves to the strength of the Water, into which you are dived, and will not leave that as an insufficient thing, for your Souls cleansing, and come to the other which is alsufficient to perfect the work: the Evil will be yours."[38]

Although most General Baptists associated receiving the Spirit with the laying on of hands, in their arguments against Friends they insisted, as did Jeremiah Ives, that the baptism of the Spirit was exercised only by Christ. Further, Caffyn declared, the disciples could not baptize with the Spirit, for Christ had reserved that act for himself. It was evident to Baptists that the baptism given to humanity to exercise was water baptism. That Quakers ceased to practice such baptism was attributed to their rejection of the Scripture as the rule of faith and to their being led by a light other than that of Christ, for to disobey the commandment of water baptism was to condemn the one who gave that commandment. Such flagrant disobedience seemed to Baptists to entail other doctrinal errors as well, for, as Wright asked, "What esteem have they of the Person of Christ, that have none of his Commandment? Of what value is the Coming of Christ in the flesh, his Death, Burial, and Resurrection, with those that despise his Doctrine, and that blessed Appointment of his?"[39]

The Lord's Supper: The Physical Without, the Spiritual Within

As with baptism, the Baptist view of the Lord's Supper was more Zwinglian and weaker in its outward aspects and divine efficacy than that of Presbyterians and Independents. The Particular Baptist confession of 1644 omitted discussion of the Lord's Supper, and that of 1656 mentioned it only as the "Breaking of bread" in a list of twenty-one commandments to be observed. Although modeled after the Westminster Confession, the confession of 1677 gave evidence of a resistance to the Calvinistic view of the ordinance by omitting the older confession's use of "sealing" and by substituting "figuratively" for "sacramentally" with reference to the relationship between the outward elements and the body and blood of Christ. Bunyan referred to the ordinance only rarely, and then simply as a memorial.[40]

The General Baptist confession of 1651 considered the Lord's Supper "a memorial of his suffering," and that of 1660 referred to it merely as the "breaking of Bread" and a duty to be observed.[41] Although the confession of 1679, also modeled on the Westminster Confession, included the latter's reference to the sealing quality of the ordinance, it omitted the section concerning the nature and the relationship of the inward and outward partaking.[42] This concept of "memorial" or "remembrance" taken from Christ's words of institution (Luke 22:19 and 1 Cor. 11:25) was the primary characteristic of the view of General Baptists who, like many Particular Baptists, preferred not to go beyond the simple ideas, language, and practices of the New Testament church in their strong desire to adhere to the primitive pattern. As Grantham explained, "It was our Saviours design by this Holy Rite, to keep himself the better in the remembrance of his chosen Disciples," and thus it was to be regarded essentially as a memorial service.[43] As in the case of baptism, the Baptists' weaker view of the outward and divinely active qualities of the Lord's Supper rendered its observance closer than that of Presbyterians and Independents to the experiential emphasis of Friends. Here again, however, their controversy revealed a difference in their perception of the New Testament practice.

In their attacks on Baptist doctrine, Friends were careful to point out that they did not deny the observance of the Lord's Supper but objected only to the outward practice. Sometimes their arguments focused on the nature and efficacy of the ordinance. Perrot reasoned that the outward bread and wine must either be the real body and blood of Christ or a figure and shadow. Discerning the relative nearness of Baptists and Quakers on this issue, he argued that Baptists did not believe in transubstantiation but rather that the elements were "shadows" and concluded that such shadows could not possibly be thought of as an everlasting ordinance. In fact, that the elements *were* only shadows, the partaking of which was of little value, Quakers could affirm from their own experience. The former Baptist Hester Bird Andrews testified, "Your outward Bread and Wine satisfies not the Soul; I have had more peace when I did not touch your Shadows, than when I did."[44]

Although Burrough claimed that the abandonment of the outward figure of the Lord's Supper was made evident "in the eternal light by the Spiritual eye of God opened in us," Friends did not usually appeal to an immediate divine command to justify cessation of the ordinance. Instead, they sought to support their action by appealing to the experience of the primitive church. Striking once more at the very passages on which Baptists based their practice, Friends admitted that Christ had commanded his disciples to partake of visible bread and wine but claimed this was only to be done for a short time. That the practice was meant to be discontinued, argued Whitehead, was demonstrated by Christ's statement that he would not eat or drink with the disciples until what it signified had been fulfilled in the kingdom.[45] However, in interpreting the Pauline presentation of the ordinance, Quakers may not have been in complete harmony. Penn, for example, admitted that breaking bread had been practiced in New Testament times and that Paul had received the practice from God, although he had not enjoined it on all. Whitehead, on the other hand, while admitting that Paul had received a description of the former outward administration of bread and wine, insisted that he had also been given "the Communication of the Mystery, viz. the Body and Blood of Christ" that was the bread and cup of which believers were to partake. Nevertheless, Friends were in agreement that the outward observance was but a sign, a shadow, "a carnal figure of a spiritual thing," which ought to have continued only until the substance, the "One Bread" had come.[46] That Baptists continued to observe the outward ordinance led Perrot to charge:

> You eat Bread & drink wine as the Israelites did Manna & Water, and yet in unbelief dyed in the Wilderness; you rest in shadows like the unbelieving Jews,

though you know that in them you are but in the teaching, tasting, and handling, of the things which perish with the using.[47]

According to Humphrey Wolrich, Baptists had lost "the Spirit which the true Jew, and they that had the one Baptism into the one spirit, and the new wine in the Fathers Kingdom, and the living Bread which came down from Heaven had."[48]

Most Baptist counterarguments were designed to expose Quaker misinterpretations of the practices of the primitive Christians. Although they concurred with Quakers that the coming of Christ had put an end to the Mosaic law, they insisted that the Lord's Supper was not such a law, but a gospel ordinance. There could be no doubt that Christ had instructed his disciples to practice it or that Paul had followed this instruction. According to Ives, Scripture plainly indicated "that bread and wine was instituted by Christ, and practised by the Primitive Christians, in remembrance of the dying of the Lord Jesus."[49] Furthermore, the spiritual presence of Christ with his disciples after his ascension had not ended such observance, for it continued to be practiced long afterward. It was evident to Baptists that the Lord's Supper had been plainly established in Scripture and, therefore, as Wigan pointed out to Fox in their Lancaster prison debate, the Quakers' abandonment of that ordinance was a result of their rejection of the Scripture as the rule of faith.[50]

However, Baptists were convinced that the Quakers' action was related not only to their doctrine of authority but also to other fundamental beliefs. Wright asserted that the abandonment of the outward Lord's Supper was a result of their denial of Christ's having come in the flesh, his death, and his continued existence as a person distinct from other individuals, and Grigg thought that it was also related to their heretical doctrine of the second advent. Friends' discontinuation of the Lord's Supper, with all its implications, led Bunyan to compare Friends with Ranters and to ask, "Are you not the same?"[51] Collier thought they were. In fact, in contrast with other issues, Quakers, along with the Ranters, Muggletonians, and Seekers who shared the radical edge of the religious continuum, were all in basic agreement on the doctrine of ordinances. They concluded that the outward practice of baptism and the Lord's Supper should cease, since they were only signs or shadows of spiritual things and "are to the *Spirit* in the *New Testament* as the *shadowes* of the *Old* were to the *flesh* of *Christ.*" Like the Quakers, Erbery chided Baptists for opposing God with their empty forms, and Abiezer Coppe denounced them for "damning all those that are not of thy Sect." Nevertheless, there was still room for criticism. Edward Burrough reproached Seekers for substituting an inward form for an outward one. "Your chiefest Idoll is in your heart," he declared.[52]

The Quaker abandonment of the outward observance was complemented by their emphasis on a spiritual, inward partaking of Christ's body and blood. But their statements did not always make their position clear, as when Nayler declared, "the Supper of the Lord we own, and the bread we breake is the Communion of Christ's body, and the Cup we drink is the Communion of his blood." A Quaker participant in the Lancaster prison dispute declared, "We do drink of the Vine, and eat of the Bread that comes down from Heaven." Ewins and others expressed the frustration of Friends' adversaries with such declarations, exclaiming, "Oh! how darst you to publish such equivocation to the World, when in your consciences you know, you own neither of those two Ordinances, neither Baptism by Water, nor Breaking of Bread; why then do you use such mental reservations? deal plainly that men may know what you are."[53] Most often Friends *did* deal plainly, as when Fox argued that those outward visible elements of bread and wine as used by Baptists were temporal, whereas the unseen things were eternal. In a manuscript addressed to Baptists, he further explained that the light "brings to drinke into the one spirit, into the one faith, & into the one bread, which hee that eates of, lives for ever, it leads to the cupp which is the blood of Christ." Christ's eternal flesh and blood were communicated spiritually to his Church and were to be enjoyed inwardly. The true supper of the Lord, Penn wrote, was that supper "which is of the Bread that cometh down from above, which gives Eternal Life to as many as eat thereof, and that is of the wine which is to be drunk new with Christ in the Kingdom of God within."[54] Therefore, there was no need of an outward memorial of Christ's death, for divine light gave Quakers a living memorial within them. Thomas Curwen, a disputant in the Lancaster prison confrontation, asked John Wigan, "Doth thou think to come any nearer to Christs death then to take Bread & Wine in Remembrance of his death, and so keep alive in the old nature; and is not this the deceiver?" According to Burrough, to those who like Baptists were "doating about outward shadows, as bread, and wine," the Lord's Supper was a mystery of which they "never came to eat or drink." What is visible is natural, and what unites to Christ is eternal, Fox argued, "& you I know, who have the forme, & not the power, soe with it you are to be condemned." Wolrich alleged, "You are eating and discern not the Lords Body, and ye are drinking Condemnation to your selves." The table of the Baptists, he concluded, was "a table of Devils."[55]

To Baptists, the Quakers' spiritualized and internalized interpretation of the Lord's Supper was wholly unacceptable, for it was obvious that the outward physical nature of that ordinance was practiced by the primitive church. Indeed, Grigg strongly protested against the assumption of Friends that the Spirit was to accomplish the ends of the Lord's Supper "without making use of the meanes God in his Word doth direct." However, as Grigg's statement implied, Baptists were not concerned primarily with the inward spiritual quality that Quakers advocated, but rather with its superseding quality and the relationship of that quality to other more fundamental doctrines. To them, the Quaker doctrine involved not only a denial of all that the outward ordinance represented but also an act of deliberate disobedience to Christ's commandment. With those who held this erroneous doctrine, Roper pleaded, "Have respect unto all the Commandements of the Lord, and be not led by the errour of the wicked, be no longer deceived by false Teachers, who as much as in them lies makes the Commandments of God of none effect."[56]

The influence that the religious experience of Quakers seeking to embrace primitive Christianity had on their attitude to outward forms in general and their doctrines of baptism and the Lord's Supper in particular has been observed in this chapter. As also noted, in certain respects the Baptist doctrine of these two ordinances was weaker than that of Presbyterians and Independents, and Baptists were therefore closer than those groups to the position held by Friends. However, to Baptists, whose zealous desire to follow the New Testament model resulted in their strong emphasis on fidelity to the Scripture, which stood between them and the primitive church, it seemed that Quakers were abandoning the faith and practice initiated by Christ and observed by the New Testament church. For their part, apparently having entered the "Great Time" of the Christian "beginnings" more fully, Friends stated or implied that their authority for not practicing the outward ordinances was the Spirit, the same authority that the earliest Christians had, and they appealed to the primitive model to justify their position, interpreting the ordinances in terms of spirituality and inwardness. They admitted that water baptism was administered by permission in some cases in the early church and that the Lord's Supper was originally an outward physical event, but they argued that as the church matured, such outward practices ceased, as Christ intended. Thus to Friends it seemed that Baptists were adhering to empty, outward forms that were more a part of the Old Testament than the New and were more closely related to the practice of the Roman Church than the usage of the primitive church. As Fox declared to Ewins, "And for Baptisme, and Ordinances, and the Lords Supper, and the bread that the Saints broke, ye have all been ignorant of in this night of apostacy since the dayes of the Apostles."[57] Other notions and practices that Quakers believed were part of that apostasy are analyzed next.

6

From his Fold we will not turn aside

The Church

[Quaker]
> Is it not possible the Lord may still,
> As he hath done, reveal his holy will
> Unto his Prophets in the holy day?
> Mark well thou formal Christian what I say.

[Professor]
> Many by you, we know, have been deceiv'd,
> And many have your feigned words receiv'd,
> But our true shepherd is our onely Guide,
> And from his Fold we will not turn aside.

Benjamin Keach, *The Grand Impostor Discovered*

Jeremiah Ives (fl. 1646–74), boxmaker and cheesemonger, was minister of a General Baptist congregation in Old Jewry, London, for more than thirty years. He supported Leveller and perhaps Fifth Monarchist views, and was also an active disputant, contending against Seventh Day Baptists as well as Quakers. He was involved in the egregious Baptist-Quaker London debates of the 1670s, but began disputing Quaker doctrines as early as 1656, when he had at least three encounters with James Nayler in London. The first was at the home of the Quaker Gerrard Roberts.[1] The two then engaged in debate in Beech-lane in May and again on 22 June at the Bull and Mouth meetinghouse in Aldersgate. Their conflict gave rise to Ives's *The Quakers Quaking*, Nayler's reply, *Weakness Above Wickedness*, and Ives's response, *Innocency Above Impudency*, all published in the same year. Four months after their last encounter, Nayler made his "triumphal entry" into Bristol—the replication of an episode from the primitive time—with which Ives may have had something to do, for he strongly challenged the genuineness of Nayler's call to the ministry.[2]

Disputes over the nature of the ministerial call were one of the practical ramifications of the Baptist-Quaker theological differences. The determined effort to erect the "Holy Community," which characterized Puritanism and Nonconformity, was fraught with a number of divisive issues for Baptists and Quakers concerning the work of the ministry, the church's relation to the state, and the nature, authority and worship of the church. What call and preparation was required for the ministry? What was the role of women? Should tithes be paid and oaths taken? What constituted the "true Church," and how was authority to be exercised within it? What forms of worship were to be followed? We have observed that their zeal to experience primitive Christianity led Quakers to claim as their own the same authority the primitive church had before the writing of the New Testament, as well as the immediate experience of Christ along with the soteriological events of his life, albeit in an inward and spiritual manner. They also extended these characteristics of immediacy, inwardness, and spirituality to include eschatological events and the ordinances. With respect to some of the topics in this chapter, Quakers and Baptists agreed in several of their criticisms of the religious tradition from which they had separated, but disagreed in their perceptions of the primitive pattern. Thus Quakers, who may be seen as having entered the time of Christian "beginnings" more fully than Baptists, criticized the latter for not having come further out of the night of apostasy and cast off their empty outward doctrines and practices. Baptists, on the other hand, believed that the false doctrines and practices of the Quakers had separated them entirely from the true Church.

The Nature and Authority of the Church: Separatism and Unity

The establishment of a holy community in the Puritan and Nonconformist tradition was in one respect carried further by Baptists such as Ives. Like Presbyterians and Independents, Baptists described the Church as the body of Christ, which in its visible form consisted of persons called out and separated from the world to walk in fellowship with each other and in obedience to God. However, in their ardor for duplicating primitive Christianity, Baptists drew more limited boundaries for the visible church, emphasizing the church's regenerate quality and limiting its membership to those who were of sufficient age to experience the faith, repentance, and baptism required for entrance. This was especially true of the General Baptists, who placed considerable importance on the human response in the soteriological process and on the initiatory significance of baptism.[3]

Baptists approached along the path of separatism the goal of erecting such a holy community. Although they warned against separation that was hasty or concerned with matters not fundamental, they were convinced that it was sometimes necessary. Grantham probably expressed the opinion of most Baptists when he wrote:

> If after all endeavours used, and patience extended, some part of those professing Christian Religion, remain wholly averse to Reformation, . . . it cannot

then be reasonable, nor is it scriptural, that those whom God hath enlightned, should be bound to walk with the obstinate (who often are the greater number) in their by paths.[4]

Friends were in full agreement with Grantham's statement, and his further declaration that God "commands the faithful ones to withdraw from such as have a form of godliness, when they deny the power thereof," might easily have come from the pen of a Quaker.[5]

Just as many Baptists had separated from various separatist congregations, so numbers of Friends separated from the Baptists. Luke Howard, for example, confessed that as a Baptist he realized "we were not in the Gospel-Faith, which we so much professed; and that we were not Baptized by the One Spirit into the One Body." He continued, "Then I became very much dissatisfied, and constrained to forsake those things & People in their observations." Quakers were convinced that although Baptists had reformed certain practices, they had not gone far enough. They had only made another "likeness" rather than *becoming* the primitive church. Howgill testified that as a Baptist, "I saw the ground was the same, and their [Baptist] doctrine out of the life with the rest of the Teachers of the world, and had separated themselves [from other Protestant groups], and made another likeness."[6] Baptists were still concerned with the mediate, the physical, and the outward. According to Salthouse, they continued to cling to "a word without: Christ without; A Church without; ordinances and administrations all without." Their reputed churches, Hollister declared, were only "fleshly Forms and Sects." If by his use of a "Church without," Salthouse was protesting against Baptist utilization of physical buildings or their reference to them as "churches," his protest was unusual. Baptists generally were not associated with what Fox often called the "steeplehouses," but, like Quakers, met in homes or in buildings rented or purchased for the purpose. In addition, some Baptists had misgivings about referring to a building as a church. Perhaps for these reasons they generally escaped such charges as that Fox directed against Baxter: "Was it not the papists game to set up your Masse-houses which you call Churches [?]"[7]

Friends believed that Baptists were still in the "night of Apostacy" and proclaimed to them the coming of Christ the light and the gathering of the true Church. "The light is come, the night is gone," cried Fox, "the Lamb and the Saints are going on conquering, and to conquer." This coming meant not only the gathering of the Quakers as the "true church," a "Church without sin," God's "spiritual house," but also the destruction of the false church. The church of "fleshly Forms" was that which "Christ comes in Spirit to destroy, and therefore must fall and be broken, routed and scattered."[8] Those who were the "Teachers and gatherers into Sects, and Names, and Heaps" were the prophesied wolves in sheep's clothing. Indeed, Hollister declared to the Broadmead church, "You are no Church of Christ, neither know the name of Christ, but a synagogue of Satan, and a Cage of unclean and hateful Spirits."[9] Baptists, who thought of the Church as the spiritual body of Christ, could speak of it like Friends as "the habitation of God." But the numerous and serious alleged doctrinal errors of Quakers made it seem absurd to Baptists that they should claim to be members of the true Church who were to deliver the Baptists or anyone else from a state of apostasy. Surely the Quakers were not destroying the "false Church-State, except it be by bringing them from that, to a worse condition," asserted Wright. Baptists were certain that Friends were the people spoken of by Jude when he foretold the coming of those "Cursed children who separate themselves (from the true Church) who are sensual, not having the spirit."[10]

As separatists themselves, both Friends and Baptists were confronted with the challenge of preventing further separation within their own groups. In Quakerism's earliest years, the strong charismatic qualities of its leaders, the excitement of conversion and mission, and the consolidating influence of surrounding opposition perhaps left relatively little room for strong disagreement internally. Further, Fox's concept of the light within included its power to bring a person into unity with other Christians.[11] Nevertheless, the discarding of scriptural authority for the authority of the Spirit in every person may have contributed to the fact that as the movement spread and membership increased, controversy over the imposition of outward authority arose. In addition to the Nayler-Fox dispute, one of the more serious challenges came from the former Baptist John Perrot, who, when he returned to England from Rome in 1661, became a focal point of dissension and division. Although he protested against the "form" of removing the hat during prayer and other customary Quaker practices, the primary significance of his position was the advocacy of the right of individuals to follow their own leading by the Spirit within. Commenting on this controversy and revealing something of its coloring, the former Baptist Rebecca Travers declared, "I testify against [the] spirit of pride and exhaltation when joined to hat on or off." Perrot left England the following year never to return, but others continued to promote his views. To provide authority for meeting such challenges and determining "orthodoxy," leading Friends established a more elaborate organization, similar to Presbyterianism, with monthly, quarterly, and yearly meetings, and with meeting clerks and "weighty" Friends exercising significant influence. However, resentment against the imposition of such authority continued to smoulder and in the 1670s burst into flame with the Wilkinson-Story separation. John Wilkinson (d. c. 1683) and John Story (d. 1681), who stressed the leading of the Spirit in each individual, objected to the control over such leading that was exercised within the new organization. A schism followed between the majority of Friends' meetings and those in several counties that supported the Wilkinson-Story position. Fox had maligned Perrot's followers with the charge that they were reviving "the Rotten principle of the old Ranters." Robert Barclay treated Wilkinson-Story supporters in a similar fashion. In governance, as in other areas, Friends encountered the dilemma described by Geoffrey Nuttall: "All forms are dangerous; yet some form is necessary."[12]

As is shown more fully in the next chapter, Baptists were well aware of the danger of individualism and subjectivism inherent in the Quaker position on the authority of Christ or the light within. If two Quakers disagreed, asked Keach, who could decide the case? Among Baptists the congregation could resolve such a dispute and could admonish or even excommunicate an erring member, but according to Hicks, the Quakers could not take such action. As he explained, "For Christians to plead this, who own the Scriptures for their rule, and not the meer light within, the argument may safely be allowed." But, he continued, "I see not how you can urge this, and yet consist with your selves," for "how can you impose that on another as his duty, which the light in him discovers not so to be?"[13] In fact, Friends did not believe that every person was led by the light of Christ who claimed to be, and in such cases as Keach described, the Spirit of Truth in the elders and members of the congregation was to render judgment. Indeed, in reply to Hicks, Penn pointed that certain Baptists censured those who differed from them on points of Scripture, and asked, "Why may not we also by the Light of Christ judge those to be deluded, who notwithstanding pretend to be ruled by it?" Further turning the question back on Baptists, the former Reading Baptist William Loddington declared that they must consider Presbyterians and Independents to be antichristian for denying baptism, "and some Baptized Churches must be Antichristian for denying Laying on of Hands on all, and others for not keeping *Saturday*-Sabbath."[14]

The Call and Work of the Ministry: Immediacy and Prophecy, Learning, Women, and Maintenance

In their urgent mission to proclaim the message of deliverance of people from the night of apostasy and the gathering of them into the true Church, Quakers identified themselves with the prophets and apostles of biblical times. Like them, they had been called immediately by God to their task and continued to receive God's immediate direction in their performance of it. The resistance of Baptist ministers to their message and their reliance on the Scripture in doing so caused Friends to question the immediacy of their opponents' calling and to doubt their possession of the immediate guidance of the Spirit. Fox complained of ministers "tellinge people what the prophets said and did and what ye Apostles saide and did, and so to be aproved on in ye sight of men, but such are aproved on in the sight of god as be in ye life, yt they were in yt gave forth scriptures," and he asked, "Whether you Baptisers cast out Devils, and Drink any deadly thing, and it not Hurt you, and whether ye house was ever shaken where you met and where did He give ye Holy Ghost." "This is to show that you are not beleevers, nor in the power yt the Apostles was in," Fox concluded.[15] Experiencing such apostolic power himself, Fox performed "miracles," many of which were recorded in his "Book of Miracles." (The unpublished manuscript was "lost," and some other references to Fox's "miracles" were suppressed, but it has been partially reconstructed by Henry J. Cadbury.)[16]

Baptists did not reject the notion of immediacy in the call to the ministry. As reported by Kaye, when John Whitehead questioned the immediacy of his call, Kaye testified that he had heard the voice of Christ and had received the teaching of the Spirit, so that "I can witness an Immediate Call."[17] But Baptists seriously questioned the claims of Quakers to such a call and demanded proof. Jeremiah Ives directed the strongest and most extensive attack on this subject, assailing James Nayler at Beech-lane and the Bull and Mouth in 1656. Nayler's contention with Fox over primacy of leadership in the movement made this an especially stressful period for him. On the one hand, he had the strong support of certain followers, some of whom addressed him with such extravagant phrases as "only begotten Son of God." On the other hand, George Fox, in asserting his own primacy, berated him and would in a remarkable incident in September slight him by offering him his foot to kiss.[18] Now this forceful and relentless Baptist disputant was pressing such disturbing questions as "Whether ever any was immediately sent of God to preach the Gospel, but either God did bear witness to them from heaven, or else he did enable them to work Miracles, by which they might evince the truth of their authority upon earth?" According to Ives, when Nayler responded by appealing to the sacrifice of his own farming for the sake of his ministry, to other Quakers having left their homes to preach throughout the country, and to their successes in having made many proselytes, Ives retorted that this was nothing more than the Catholics had done. "I therefore did tell them all," Ives related, "that it was horrible presumption for such as they, to proclaim both in City and Country, that they were sent of God, when indeed the Pope can say as much for his Infallible Chair, the Turk for his Alcaron, and the Jew for his Talmud, and a great deal more."

Ives continued to exhort Nayler to provide evidence of *his* calling. Could he speak in tongues? As reported by Ives, when Nayler answered that he could speak in tongues his antagonist could not understand, Ives scoffed at his "canting dialect" and finally laid down this dramatic challenge: "If he could shew as good a Sign for his immediate Call, as Christ did shew that generation, to prove he was the *Messiah*, we would believe all he told us." In a letter to Fox, Nayler reported that London Baptists were pressing him to "prove my Call by a miracle there."[19] According to William G. Bittle, one of his modern biographers, in early October Nayler decided on a sign that would validate his calling. The sign would have additional meaning within the Quaker movement with respect to primacy, for his followers had persuaded him that the inner light of Christ burned more brightly in him than in others. On 24 October his procession entered Bristol and reenacted a dramatic event from the "Great Time." In a letter to Margaret Fell in November, Hubberthorn reported that Quakers

and others who observed the imprisoned Nayler still saw women supporters "exceeding filthy in acting in Imitations . . . and wonders at ye Imitation which is Acted Among them, as often they will kneel before him &c."
Friends distanced themselves from Nayler's actions. But given the extravagant language sometimes used by and about Fox (chapter 3) and the
"miracles" he performed, one wonders whether such a triumphal entry
would have been less objectionable to Friends had it been acted out by
Fox, or less objectionable even as enacted by Nayler, had there not been
the struggle for leadership within the movement and the widespread no-
toriety attached to Nayler's act.[20]

That Baptists for their part allowed Scripture to stand between them
and primitive Christianity, depending on the Bible in their various disputations and in their ministry as a whole, led Friends to attack the Baptist
ministry as nonapostolic. The apostles of the primitive church, Quakers
maintained, were ministers of the Spirit, not of the letter. Those who de-
spised the Spirit and relied on "Paper and Inke" were "Ministers of their
brain-imaginations, from the letter," declared Farnworth. "They are false
Apostles and false teachers." Indeed, Lawson accused Caffyn of "taking
upon thee to teach others, and art untaught thy self, only hast treasured up
the letter in thy corrupt minde, and ministers it forth to others, as thou
imagines of it, so steals the word from others, as the false Prophets did."[21]
Quakers were convinced that Baptist ministers carried out their work without the immediate guidance of the Spirit. Dennis Hollister complained
that the preaching of Thomas Ewins, minister of the Broadmead church,
was dry and empty. Burrough warned against a ministry that was carried
forth by the human will rather than the will of God, and Taylor declared
that such false apostles were "not to be owned or received, but to be denied and judged by all."[22]

That Friends should accuse them of lacking the immediate guidance
of God because they used "means" in their ministry angered Baptists. Did
not the Quakers do the same? Wright charged, "Thou cryest down the letter, and Scriptures of Truth; and yet makest use of Letter, and writest many
Books, thereby to disperse thy false Doctrine." Furthermore, if the Spirit
within was sufficient for salvation, why did the Quakers need to preach at
all? According to Tombes, they had failed to consider "that if their hearers
may be guided by their own light to God, that they need not look at man
more, they need not look at themselves, nor to hear them, nor entertain
them to teach them."[23]

Friends did, of course, employ preaching, teaching, printing, and
other "means" in the cause of truth. As Fisher declared, "We deny not
Preaching without by such as are sent, as Paul was." Such preaching, Penn
explained, was the means to lead people to the immediate experience of
the Spirit. Nor did they deny the use of teaching among the saints for their
edification. According to Shewen, such exhortation and edification was the
purpose they had in publishing and preaching. Burrough explained that
the immediate teaching of Christ within and the outward edification by

persons were not contrary to each other, and Fisher declared that "If we do hear men speak that are moved by the Spirit, its not in vain, it being all one whether that holy Spirit speak in me, or in another to me." What Quakers objected to was the use of such means by Baptist ministers in denying their message and clinging to the traditional doctrines of the apostate church. According to Nayler, Friends did not "deny instrumentall, but Traditional Teaching."[24]

If Quakers considered Baptists to be false prophets because they lacked the call and guidance of the Spirit, Baptists believed Friends to be delusive guides because they were led by a spirit other than that of God. Reputed evidence for this was found in various Quaker acts of extravagance. One of the two editions of Ralph James's *A True and Impartial Narrative* (both issued in 1672), for example, included a section entitled *A True and Impartial Relation of Some Remarkable passages of Charles Bayley a Quaker, Who Profest Himself a Prophet, and that he was sent of God*, written by Richard Hobbs and others. According to this account, Hobbs was visiting prisoners in Dover jail when Bayley accosted him. Bayley, who was an ardent supporter of Perrot, was said to have prophesied that a divine public rebuke would strike Hobbs because he had resisted the Spirit. To this Hobbs replied, "I am persuaded thou art not sent of God, and that God will Manifest thee a False Prophet."[25] A short time later, when Bayley announced to the prisoners that the rebuke had occurred, Hobbs returned to the jail and was found to be normal. In Quaker replies to this tract, Howard averred that the incident had occurred some ten years earlier and that the Quakers had "deny'd" Bayley "for many years." Thus disowned, declared Rudyard, "he shall certainly bear his Burden, and Answer for his own Iniquity."[26]

More frequent than mention of such inaccurate prophesying were references to Quakers going naked in public. Baptists found such acts highly offensive. Wright, in characterizing a typical Quaker leader, wrote:

> So unclean are his commands, that he requireth some of them, men and women, to strip off all their clothes, and as naked as they were born, to stand sometimes upon a Marker Crosse in the time of Market, and sometimes at a Grave, while the dead is burying, in their naked bodies, and there to tell the People they are for a sign of their destruction.[27]

The former Baptist Solomon Eccles seemed especially inclined toward such overt expressions of prophecy. Burnet complained that he not only had gone naked but on one occasion dared to enter "befouled with mans dung into a publick Assembly." This type of incident was clear evidence to Baptists that Quakers were not prophets of God but rather led by a "Spirit of delusion." Stung by such charges at a dispute in Surrey between George Whitehead and the Baptists Burnet, Ives, and Caffyn, Eccles, who was not present, later challenged his accusers. "I do Challeng," he wrote,

> *Matthew Caffyn, Jeremy Ives, William Burnet*, or any of the Teachers amongst the *Baptists*, or *Jesuits high Priests, and low Priests*, for these are all blind

Guides, . . . *To Fast seven daies and seven nights and not to Eat nor to Drink* . . . [and] *To Wake seven daies and seven nights,* . . . and he that the Lord shall carry through this fiery Tryal, shall be counted a worshiper of the true God, . . . But he that tyres by the way shall be counted a member *of a false Church, and a Heretick.*[28]

Quakers considered going naked to be a prophetic "sign" in the tradition of Old Testament prophets. They argued that Isaiah had gone naked as a sign to Egypt, and Saul had done the same in prophesying before Samuel. Their strong biblical primitivism meant that the unlimited Spirit of God might require some persons to do the same in the present. Indeed, declared Hollister, the holy men of old "wandered up and down, and to the voice of God were obedient in so doing, and some of them to the going naked, though you be so blind and ignorant, as to oppose the same in them, who witness it a sign to such as you."[29]

Believing they followed the primitive pattern, members of both groups also addressed the issue of the education of ministers. Although Baptists maintained an ordained and separated ministry, few ministers held university degrees or had formal theological training. Some, like Keach, believed such training to be beneficial but not of ultimate importance. Bunyan, although probably exaggerating the lowliness of his own social and educational background, shared this distrust of university learning, professed that he was unfamiliar with the Hebrew language or the use of syllogisms, and denounced "Sophistical arguings." His own minister, John Burton, said Bunyan came from a "heavenly University."[30] Others expressed a more negative view of such education, strongly denying any to be ministers who had not truly repented but had been "brought up in the Schools of humane learning, to the attaining humane arts, and variety of languages, with many vain curiosities of speech." In addition, like the Independents, Baptists encouraged lay preaching. Thus, the Baptist Henry Denne came to the defense of both John Bunyan and George Whitehead when they were criticized by Cambridge University librarian Thomas Smith for preaching without a commission like Smith's own.[31] Nevertheless, Baptists were criticized by Quakers, who, as a rule, were more outspoken on the subject.

In keeping with their strong identification with primitive Christianity and emphasis on the immediacy and the Spirit in the call and work of the ministry, Friends often asserted that ministers were made by the Spirit, not by a university education, and sometimes referred to the latter in deprecatory terms. The former Baptist Elizabeth Hooton and others, perhaps ignoring or unaware of the anachronism, declared, "You do not read in all the Holy Scriptures, that any of the Holy men of God were *Cambridge* or *Oxford* Schollers." Fox himself argued that Paul had been made an apostle not by men but by the revelation of Christ, and the Oxford-educated Samuel Fisher, referring to the work of the Quaker ministry, declared, "We own All Teachers set forth by God for the work of the Ministry (which are such only as are made Ministers by gifts of God from above, and not such as buy their gifts at University, that they may sell them again) to be both needful, useful, and profitable."[32]

One characteristic of the university-educated that was especially irritating to Quakers was their use of Greek and Hebrew. Yet Friends were not above utilizing the biblical languages for their own purposes. Fisher expertly employed them in *Rusticus ad Academicos* and in his work with Jewish groups in the Netherlands. George Fox's own rather ostentatious use of Greek and Hebrew led Quaker historian William Charles Braithwaite to conclude that "A Certain parade of learning was indeed one of his weaknesses."[33] Still, Quakers were suspicious and resentful of the use of these languages by others. When, as reported by Hubberthorn, Tombes employed a Greek word in argument, for example, Hubberthorn replied, "This is the long and thick mist of darkness which hath been long kept over the understandings of people, that when the plain Scripture will not prove their ends and intents, then they will tell people it is otherwise in the Greek, or Hebrew."[34] In a more moderate fashion Shewen asked Ives, Whether the knowledge of natural tongues made persons infallible? Did not the unlettered Peter and John know the meaning of Scripture? Tombes drew most of the criticism from Quakers. Not unusual in its tone was the assertion of Hubberthorn and Fisher that "whereas Jo. Tombes writes himself B.D. yet he is read among such as are truly wise, by the name of *Blinde Divine*, rather then *Batchelor of Divinity.*"[35]

The role of women in the church was another disputed topic. Diane Willen has argued that the interaction between Puritanism and gender changed both and that within this interaction the pursuit of godliness provided greater moral authority as well as an improved status for "elect ladies." Furthermore, the presence of such godly women "does much to explain subsequent developments in Puritanism, including the emergence of radical sectarian women in the 1640s." Whatever its origins, an enhanced religious role did develop for sectarian women. Among some Independent churches women participated in the period of prophesying after the sermon even in the presence of men in a mixed congregation. The heresiographer Robert Baillie described such practices of the Independents, but also noted that among the Baptists "many more of their women do venture to preach."[36] However, most Baptists actually seem to have been conservative on this issue. In their confession of 1656, Particular Baptists exhorted women in the church to learn in silence, and both the Western Association in 1654 and the Abingdon Association in 1658 expressed the same view. Bunyan, who thought that Eve "at one clap" had overthrown women's reputation forever as well as "her Soul, her Husband, and the whole World besides," overturned his congregation's practice of allowing women to meet separately for prayer and worship without the leadership of men. He also believed that women should not minister in prayer before the whole church, noting that otherwise he would be a Ranter or a Quaker. In this he reflected the Baptists' attempt to distance themselves from radical movements and to be seen as moderate. The subject was not mentioned in the confessions of the General Baptists, but in 1678 Grantham, although admitting that the promise of the Spirit had been made to women as well as men, argued against their preaching, preferring that they exercise their gifts more privately, especially among those of their own gender.[37]

Among the Friends, it was thought that women could and did possess and exercise the gifts of the Spirit, just as they had done in the primitive church. Thus some Quaker women preached and even went naked as a sign. One of Fox's earliest converts was the Baptist Elizabeth Hooton, whose name among the Quakers "heads the noble roll of women-ministers," according to Braithwaite. Some Baptists came into direct conflict with such women Friends, who refused to remain silent in the church. As reported by Ewins, a Quaker woman interrupted a service of the Broadmead church, and a women's prayer meeting of the same congregation was also broken up by two Quaker women who walked up and down the room, humming and making loud noises. Ives complained that in his debate at the Bull and Mouth, he was unable to answer fully one of Nayler's arguments because he was interrupted by the Quaker women preachers. Conflicts such as these may have sharpened any opposition to preaching by women that Baptists already felt. In any case, several Baptists protested against this Quaker practice. Caffyn and Hicks did so in typical fashion, appealing to Paul's injunction that women remain silent in the church.[38] Grantham went beyond commands and invoked the ideal of primitive Christianity:

> We read not that those of that Sex which were extraordinarily gifted, did preach openly as the Gifted-Brethren did in the Primitive Times; and therefore it seems to be the greater Arrogency for Women of ordinary Gifts, to appear so openly in mix'd Assemblies, as those among the Quakers frequently do.[39]

Wigan, the most vehement of the Baptists on this subject, alleged after the Lancaster prison debate against Margaret Fell and George Fox that among the Quakers one "may hear not onely men, but women-teachers, . . . Teaching lyes in the name of the Lord, and causing their weak captivated disciples to erre by their lyes, as that woman Jezebel did, Rev. 2.20."[40]

Friends rarely answered such charges. When they did, they usually appealed to biblical experience, where important contributions of women were not difficult to find. Occasionally Quakers defended their position by claiming that the woman who was to keep silent in the church was the flesh, an interpretation that Baptists like Caffyn summarily dismissed. Friends also distinguished, as they did in response to Wigan, between those forbidden to speak and those encouraged to do so. Further exhibiting their close identification with the New Testament church was the Quaker appeal to the fulfillment in the primitive church (Acts 2: 17-18) of Joel's prophecy (Joel 2: 28) that the Spirit would be poured out on all flesh and that daughters as well as sons would prophesy. This argument and others were employed in one of the most spirited defenses of the practice, Margaret Fell's best-known printed work, *Womens Speaking Justified* (1666). Indeed, she, Elizabeth Hooton, and others did much to establish a strongly enhanced *religious* role for women Friends, although they accepted a secondary one in family and society.[41] On the other hand, Christopher Hill has argued that George Fox's view of women's religious role changed between 1656 and 1680 just as his marital status did. Fox is said to have expounded the traditional Pauline position on women being silent and submissive and learning from their husbands at home in his tract *The Woman Learning in Silence* (1656). In this case Fox's statement has been taken too literally and out of context, for he went on to describe this position as the law from which Christians were freed by Christ who "in the Male, and in the Female is one." Fox also identified the "unlearned" as persons who were to "learn of their husband at home, Christ, who makes free from the Law." Finally, like Margaret Fell, he argued that Joel's prophecy was being fulfilled in the pouring out of God's spirit upon all flesh with sons and daughters prophesying.[42]

The maintenance of ministers was also a point of dispute. Although Baptist churches provided some voluntary maintenance, most ministers worked at a traditional occupation in order to support themselves. The General Baptist confession of 1651 and the Particular Baptist confession of 1656 actually required them to do so in an attempt to duplicate the primitive church pattern. But as the decades passed and the Baptist movement became more institutionalized and more like mainstream Nonconformity, both groups discarded this requirement and instead urged fuller support of ministers in their confessions of 1677 and 1679.[43] Friends, like Baptists, approved of a voluntary provision for those whose work among them hindered their earning a livelihood. The Quaker William Britten confessed that as a minister in the national church he preached "for hire, selling my Sermons as my best Marker" but in turning Baptist he engaged in "preaching freely without selling." However, Friends disapproved of any ministering for a "set wage" at all, and several times attacked the practice of some Baptists on this point. For example, addressing himself to Howet, Nayler criticized those who were guilty of taking tithes and set wages, and he challenged Collier to minister as the apostles had done, "freely without hire." Burrough asked Bunyan whether "to Preach for hire, for gifts and rewards, and to Divine for money, and to make Merchandize of people for so much a year for preaching to them, is not true marks and signes of a false Prophet." Only Bunyan responded to such charges. He agreed with Burrough that some ministers in the nation sought to profit from their work, but noted that wolves in sheeps' clothing were also present and added pointedly, "Therefore examine your selves."[44] The aspect of maintenance that was of greater concern to Friends, however, was tithes, an issue discussed later.

The Worship of the Church: Silence, Quaking, and Singing

The Quaker identification with the primitive church and its immediate experience of Christ was strongly evident in their approach to worship and
consequently in their disagreements with Baptists on this subject. Friends'
worship included periods of silence in which there was direct communion
with the Spirit, and they rejected human actions that might interfere with
such immediate experience. As Penn explained, the Quaker

> silently waits to feel the Heavenly Substance brought into his Soul, by the Im-
> mediate Hand of the Lord, for it is not fetching in this Thought, or remem-
> bering the other Passage in Scripture, or calling to Mind what has been for-
> merly known, but every Immediate Word that proceeds from out of the
> Mouth of God, that can satisfie him.[45]

Baptists criticized the Quaker use of such silent worship or "silent meetings." Burnet, appealing to the pattern set by the primitive church, considered such meetings to be "contrary to the practice of the Saints in the
Apostolical days; for their coming together was to exhort one another, and
not to be silent, Heb. 10.24, 25." Wright alluded to a sinister aspect of the
practice when he asked, "By what else are you inabled at your meetings,
when you have nothing to say, but by a spirit that comes into some of you
[?]" In defense, Quakers drew examples from New Testament Christianity. Thus Whitehead, replying to Burnet, appealed to the "waiting" of the
disciples in Jerusalem to justify the practice.[46]

What Baptists objected to more strenuously than silence was the out-
burst of emotion in the form of groaning, trembling, and the like that
sometimes accompanied Quaker meetings. Wigan described such gather-
ings as including "a company of worshippers, in great confusion, praying
and singing, or teaching and singing, all or many together with loud
voices." Wright complained of their "humming, blowing, and hollow sigh-
ing," Howet of "muttering and uncouth howling," Hicks of "Quakings,
foamings at the mouth, with dreadful roarings," and Griffith of their "rav-
ing like mad men." Howet attributed such acts to the work of a spirit that
Wright described as unclean and cruel.[47] Friends, however, insisted that
the spirit that moved them was the Spirit of God and justified their actions
by appealing again to the experience of the earliest Christians. Burrough
pointed out to Wright, for example, that Paul referred to groans and sighs
experienced by godly men. Indeed, Fox asserted, Paul also exhorted people to work out their salvation with fear and trembling, so that whoever
"denyes trembling, denyes salvation as is wrought out by it."[48]

When that immediate Word from God did come to one of the Quakers in their meetings or elsewhere, it was often shared. Even then, as
Richard Bauman has argued, all outward speaking was thought to be sus-
ceptible to carnal impulses, which thus had to be neutralized by "mini-
mizing speaking as much as possible: 'Let your words be few.'" The strong
emphasis on the immediacy of the Word also led Friends to deprecate

means ordinarily used by others in preaching. According to Burrough, "There is no such thing amongst us as brain-study or knowledge before-hand that we shall speak, or what we shall say, like the Diviners of this age." Thus Wolrich rejected any dependence by Baptists on written sermons, and Nayler repudiated their "preaching from a text." These were seen, along with their "hour-glass preaching" and use of appointed speakers, as forms that restricted the movement of the Holy Spirit. To most of these objections Baptists made no reply. However, Hicks did point out that Quakers also appointed ministers to speak at certain meetings, and he asked: "How know you, Such a one shall be Immediately moved then, and not another instead of him? And when you invite others to your silent meetings, telling us, they will be such, How are you assured that those you invite may not be moved to speak in that meeting?"[49]

A further question that arose in connection with worship was the role of singing. Baptists were not in agreement among themselves on this issue. Most General Baptists opposed singing psalms, at least when done con-jointly and in rhyme and meter, partly because of the formalism they be-lieved it introduced into worship. However, the use of unaltered psalms sung by a solo voice seems to have been permissible. Among the Particu-lar Baptists, psalm singing was more acceptable. Keach's introduction of the congregational singing of hymns of human composition, however, caused considerable controversy among both groups of Baptists and re-sulted in several resignations from his congregation.[50] Quakers also ob-jected sometimes to singing psalms in rhyme and meter, because David's words had been altered and because they were sung without the power of the Spirit that David had. However, singing induced by the Spirit was ap-proved by George Fox, and early Friends sang psalms and hymns in their meetings and elsewhere. In Carlisle in 1653, Fox's singing in prison so in-furiated the jailer that he brought in a fiddler to try to force Fox to dance also. Fox reported: "I was moved in the everlasting power of the Lord God to sing; and my voice drowned them and struck them and confounded them." After his arrest at Swarthmoor in 1660, Fox was also "moved to sing praises unto the Lord in his triumphing power over all." In the 1670s, however, there was a sharp decline of singing among Friends, apparently as a result of its unseemly use by some Quakers and its association with Ranter behavior.[51]

Because of the similarity of views and the secondary importance of the subject, arguments over singing occurred infrequently. Nayler, however, did protest to Howet concerning "singing Davids words in time," and, ac-cording to Kaye, John Whitehead made a similar complaint to him. Only Kaye responded, arguing that the Spirit was obviously not hindered by the use of syllables in the vernacular, and that therefore the Spirit was not ham-pered by the use of measured syllables in singing either. The primary con-cern of Friends in this issue, as in preaching and silent meetings, was the replacement of empty forms by the immediate experience of the Spirit like that known by the primitive church. It was Fox's call "to bring them off from all the world's fellowships, and prayings, and singings, which stood in forms without power; that their fellowship might be in the Holy Ghost." Burrough published a letter to Baptists at Newcastle in which he averred that the Lord "is appearing in his power, to utter his thunders, and all Flesh shall tremble at his presence; and all Formes of Worship will he dash to pieces at his appearance."[52]

Church and State: Tithes, Oaths, and the Rendering of Honor

Baptists and Quakers held similar views on the relationship of church and state. Both approved of magistracy as ordained of God, supported religious toleration, and disapproved of the concept of a national church. However, the two groups disagreed over tithes. Quakers, not wanting to contribute to the support of false worship, objected to tithes, and many of their number suffered imprisonment for refusal to pay them. However, some did remit them or arranged for non-Quaker acquaintances to do so on their behalf.[53] Baptists, on the other hand, as Whitley has pointed out, "were not generally reluctant to pay the accustomed tithe," although they found the acceptance of such tithes by Baptist ministers to be objectionable. Nevertheless, a few Baptists received such maintenance (six were ejected at the Restoration), and it is not surprising that two of them came into conflict with Friends as a result.[54]

The Quakers' major line of attack was to show that tithing was contrary to the primitive Christians' experience. Kaye, who served as vicar and later rector at Stokesley, Yorkshire, was challenged by John Whitehead to give New Testament evidence for receiving tithes. Appealing to Acts 28:10, Kaye declared: "The light of the Apostles, that took whatsoever was given them, satisfies my conscience to praise God for the Magistrate that doth freely give me it." In his account of his 1657 debate with Tombes in Leominster, Fox told of a man who "stood up and told him how he [Tombes] had sued him for tithe eggs."[55] Fox also referred to the incident in attacking Tombes in *The Great Mistery*, declaring, "And Esa. 56. doth judge thee, for thou are one that seekes thy gain from thy Quarter, a greedy dumb dog, can never never have enough, as witness thy Eggs, and how thou didst hale before the Justice for not paying of them."[56] Tombes's defense of the practice was like Kaye's, but he added the practical observation that voluntary contribution "in most places is so scant, that persons of worth are necessitated to live in a sordid manner, or people are necessitated to take persons of little worth, and thereby the Ministry is debased, the people untaught or ill taught."[57]

The taking of oaths was a second question regarding church and state debated by members of the two groups. Baptists, however, were not in agreement among themselves on this question. The General Baptist confession of 1679 and the Particular Baptist confession of 1677 as well as the second edition (1646) of their 1644 confession noted the legality of oath-taking. However, a number of Baptists opposed oaths and, like Quakers, suffered imprisonment for refusing them.[58] Not until the Restoration, when the problem of oath-taking became acute, did the subject surface in the pamphlet war waged by the two groups.[59] The basic argument used by Friends was a simple appeal to the instructions to the earliest Christians (Matt. 5:34 and James 5:12), which they interpreted literally as forbidding any kind of oath. On the other hand, Baptists such as Tombes argued that these passages had to be understood in the light of other biblical passages, and from such a comparison concluded that the prohibitions applied only to "frequent, vain, light, profane, unnecessary, customary passionate swearing." Passages that Baptists employed in this comparison included those referring to swearing by Abraham, Moses, and Paul. Although Henry Denne came to the defense of George Whitehead when the latter was accused of being a papist for refusing to take oaths, he pointed out on another occasion that even God swore.[60]

Quakers did not accept such precedents from the Old Testament, for they believed that in instructing people not to swear, Christ had terminated oaths, as he had sacrifices and the two ordinances. Nor did they accept the affirmations of Paul as oaths, for, as Fisher declared, although they were willing to do as Paul had done, simple affirmations were not acceptable to the magistrates. On the contrary, the oaths against which they objected were rituals and forms belonging to the "Ceremonious Customs of the Nations, which are vain, so as to swear upon a Bible, and kiss the Book, and lay one Finger at least upon it, and to be sworn by So help me God, and the Holy Evangelist, and his Holy Gospel."[61] Baptists who had submitted to any such oaths had obviously broken Christ's command. However, the Baptists for whom Quakers such as Burrough reserved the harshest condemnation were those who had refused the oath, had been imprisoned along with Quakers, and then had changed their minds and taken it. Said Fisher, such "do chuse rather to purchase their liberty by Swearing, then either to come into, or continue in prison." Hubberthorn and Fisher alleged that Tombes "will deny and break any of Christ's commands, (and teach people so) rather then suffer persecution." Tombes, at least, did not regret having saved himself and others from what he considered unnecessary hardship. Referring to his work, *A Serious Consideration*, he wrote, "I know my self of many, and am told of more hundreds, yea thousands, who have had their liberty and their families, saved from ruine, by reason of the clearing of the point to them in that book."[62]

Speaking the truth was an integral part of the actual righteousness that was such an important factor in the Quaker understanding of salvation. The insistence on honesty in speech, in their view, rendered an oath unnecessary, but it was a view that led to fines and imprisonment for many. Prosecution for refusing oaths, as for refusal of tithing, unauthorized meetings for worship, and other offenses, was not accepted passively, however. Among other things, Friends sent letters and petitions to authorities, practiced noncooperation, sought expert legal advice, and hired lawyers.

They also tried to persuade grand jury members that punishments had been intended for Catholic recusants and seditious conventicles rather than the peaceful conventicles and religious practices of Protestant dissenters. In addition, they sought to delay trials by lodging numerous appeals, thereby also delaying payment to informers, thus discouraging them. Such efforts became more focused and centralized with the establishment of the Meeting for Sufferings in 1676.[63]

Replacing the formal with what Friends considered spiritual reality led them to abandon other conventional practices, in actions that, although less serious in their consequences than the refusal of oaths, set them apart from the rest of society and exacerbated the frictions already existing between them and others. Three of these practices, all associated with the rendering of honor, arose in disputes between Baptists and Quakers. To Baptists, showing deference to persons of superior position was an accepted practice. It was founded on scriptural precedents, they argued. Howet pointed out that Scripture exhorted people to honor their fathers and mothers, and Ives noted that Paul had shown respect to Festus and had also instructed servants to give homage to their masters. Friends did not deny the extending of esteem "wherein every one is bound to honor one another without respect of persons," but, as Nayler declared to Howet, "If it be that honor that stands in the pride or riches, or respect of persons, we deny it, and thee in it." Most conventional practices, they believed, fell into the latter category, and consequently they refused to use "flattering Titles," to employ the polite "you" instead of "thee" and "thou" when addressing persons of superior position, and, as Burrough said, to "put off our Hats in Honour to any mans person."[64]

Baptists generally distinguished between the proper and the vain use of such acts. Ives opposed giving flattering titles to those to whom it was not due but believed it was a duty to give them where they were in fact appropriate. In a similar manner, Haggar maintained that the use of "you" for a single person was not "improper speech, and therefore the people of God may and ought to use it upon occasion." The removal of one's hat also had its proper place, and the fact that Quakers refused this practice led Kaye to ask John Whitehead to "examine thine own heart, whether thou dost not, Pope-like as farre as thou canst, exalt thy self above, or Contemn all, in that thou Cryest down all, and wilt not put off thy Hat to the Magistrate, &c."[65] Indeed, the Quaker refusal to render honor to others in these ways, like their claim to perfection, convinced Baptists that they were not, as Wright said, "more Humble, but more Proud rather than others."[66]

On some of the issues of this chapter, others at this far edge of the spiritual spectrum—Seekers, Ranters, and Muggletonians—were in agreement with Quakers and each other. All rejected the traditional organized church and its ministry and forms of worship, and objected to tithes, although Muggletonians were willing to pay them to avoid imprisonment. Muggletonians also objected to most oaths.[67] There remained room for controversy, however. Reeve's claim to have literally heard the voice of

God appointing him as divine prophet was dismissed by Penn as similar to a case in Ireland in which an army commander was tricked by his men, who spoke through a hollow tube under his bed and pretended to be the voice of God. Muggleton reproved Friends for preaching "ninnny-nonies & senseless words" and finding fault "with a piece of Ribbon or Gold-button" in their use of plain dress. Further, in a statement echoing Quaker criticism of Baptists, Muggleton reproached Penn for having no more proof for his arguments than what he read in old books at the university, whereas Muggleton's own knowledge of spiritual things came "from the University of Heaven." Fox, however, thought Muggleton "hath made himself a Pope."[68]

As I have demonstrated, Quakers entered the "Great Time" of primitive Christianity so extensively as to claim to have experienced immediately Christ and certain events of his life. The resulting emphases on immediacy, inwardness, and spirituality in their religious beliefs was also evident in their views on the church. As shown, Baptists and Quakers sometimes generally agreed on basic issues, but disputed over particular points or as a result of other doctrinal differences or personal conflicts. With respect to the relationship of church and state, the two groups held many similar views but disagreed on tithes and oaths. Baptists were themselves not of a single mind concerning the latter. On the subject of worship, both groups generally opposed the use of "empty" forms, but whereas Friends discarded a number of traditional practices that they thought devoid or restrictive of the Spirit, Baptists retained them, believing that the practices were not in their own experience the way Quakers negatively described them. With regard to the ministry, although the groups disagreed concerning the role of women, they concurred on a number of other points, including the immediate nature of the call, the use of means, and the nonessential nature of formal education. At the same time, each doubted the true call of the other, Friends believing Baptists to be false prophets because they resisted the doctrine of the Christ within, and Baptists considering Quakers to be delusive guides *because* of their doctrine of the inner light of Christ as well as other offensive doctrines and practices.

The two groups were also in general agreement concerning the nature and authority of the church, and the principle of separation. However, Baptists believed that because of Quakers' doctrinal errors they had separated themselves from the true Church, whereas Friends maintained that Baptists were still in the "night of apostasy" because they had failed to cast off the "outwardness" of their doctrines and practices in their act of separation. Perhaps the basic attitude of Quakers toward Baptists in these matters was best summarized by Salthouse when, with reference to the reputedly erroneous doctrines of the times, he declared,

> The people call'd Anabaptists are as chiefly concerned herein as many of those
> whom they themselves have formerly pretended to differ from and declare

against as Anti-Christian both in call, practice, maintainance, doctrine and worship, with whom they are joyned and confederate to fight against the truth.[69]

In turn, the fundamental Baptist attitude to Friends was probably best expressed by Wigan when he asked:

Do they bear a witness against hyreling priests and teachers, against tythes, against superstitious, carnal, formal worship, against swearing, against corrupt worldly customs in any part of our conversation? herein I joyne with them. Are they, at least in shew and pretence, for the power of godliness as well as form, for worshipping in spirit and truth, for justice, for righteousness, sobriety, modesty, gravity, and whatsoever is excellent in life and conversation? all these I allow, and am really for.

However, referring to Quaker *doctrine*, he added, "All these fair pretences, and high expressions, are found to be a covering too short to hide their nakedness and deceit."[70] To one of those doctrines, the inner light, I now turn.

7

A Guide within to lead all Men to Heav'n

The Light Within

[Quaker]

    Turn to the Light within, for that's the thing
    Which will thee strait to rest in Canaan *bring,*
    All others Guides thou wholly must forsake,
    If thou this Journey dost resolve to make:

[Professor]

    Prophets, Apostle, and Christ Jesus too
    Did never such a Doctrine Preach, nor shew
    That God in Man hath plac'd a Light, or given
    A Guide within to lead all Men to Heav'n.

        Benjamin Keach, *The Grand Impostor Discovered*

True Old Light Exalted Above Pretended New Light was the title John Tombes chose for his tract published in 1660 against "the Quaker, Arminian, and other Assertors of Universal Grace" and "Commended to publick view By Mr. *Richard Baxter.*" Educated at Magdalen College, Oxford, Tombes (1603–76) became vicar of Leominster, Herefordshire, in 1630, but during the civil war moved to Bristol and then London to avoid Royalist forces. He adopted Baptist views in the early 1640s and was one of the few Baptists to be ejected in 1662, after which he seems to have become a lay conformist. An active disputant, he debated with Richard Baxter on infant baptism in 1650 and with the Quaker Alexander Parker at Leominster in 1656. The following year he contended with Fox himself. In his journal Fox described Tombes as "an Anabaptist priest" who "yet had the parsonage at Leominster" and thus considered his status to be one in which "his wife was the baptized people and his concubine was the world."[1] The dispute described hereafter between Fox and Tombes over the inner light was one of many taking up this doctrine.[2]

    Members of the two groups were in wide disagreement on nearly every point of this Quaker principle. Friends' zeal for primitive Christianity, as we have seen, led them to enter the "Great Time" and to experience the New Testament Christ immediately but, of necessity, in a spiritual and inward fashion. In describing this experience Quakers came to employ Christ's own claim to be the light of the world (John 8:12) with the Johanine declaration (as Friends understood it) that Christ was the true light that enlightens every person coming into the world (John 1:9). Using the terms *Christ, light, God, Holy Spirit, Spirit of Christ,* and *Spirit of God* interchangeably, they fashioned the doctrine of the inner light for which they became so widely known. Thus in their conflicts with Baptists, Friends asserted that the light within all persons was supernatural and therefore sufficient for authority and salvation. Baptists subscribed to the opposite view and were alarmed at the behavior of Friends that they believed was invoked by this Quaker tenet.

The Natural Light: A Created Light, Reason, and the Conscience

Presbyterians, Independents, and Baptists generally spoke of "the light" as supernatural or natural. In the former sense the term was used with reference to Christ or God, and in the latter with regard to the light of nature, that is, the external light of creation and the internal light of reason. The light of reason, however, was reputedly corrupted by the fall of humanity and consequently incapable of leading people to salvation.[3] In this context, some Baptists occasionally spoke of Christ as "the light" ("I am the light of the world," John 8:12), or of Christ enlightening every human, or even of a light within all persons. In a work printed in 1646, the General Baptist Henry Denne, who was to defend the Quakers on at least one occasion (see chapter 6), wrote, with reference to John 1:9, "*Christ is the true light, which lighteth every man that commeth into the world.* Now, *God is Light,* and *God is a Spirit:* If then Christ lighteth every man, God lighteth every man; and if God lighteth every man, the Spirit lighteth every man that commeth into the world."[4] However, the light described by Denne and other Baptists was very different from the light revered by Quakers. Although John Wigan admitted that the light considered abstractly or with respect to its author was spiritual, he insisted that it was a natural light when regarded as united to its subject or placed within human nature.[5] This emphasis on the light as natural was basic to most Baptist reasoning. The light, they argued, was a divine creation and therefore separate from God. It was thus in the same category as other created, natural lights, such as the sun, moon, and stars. Baptists thought it absurd for Quakers to believe that the light was divine simply because it was divinely bestowed. If, as Whitehead claimed, God was the cause and the light was the effect and therefore divine, then, declared Hicks, "We may conclude not onely the light within, but every creature, both Beasts and Trees are God." To this Penn retorted, "Is there no Effect of Power, besides that of Nature? Did the Father of T. Hicks get a Beast or a Man when he begat him?"[6]

Quakers did not believe that beasts, trees, or heavenly bodies were supernatural, of course, but they insisted that the light within was. Thus when Baptists spoke of it as natural or created, Whitehead condemned them for their "gross Error."[7] In the 1657 debate with Tombes in Leominster, Fox attacked this alleged misconception. According to his own account, in preaching and disputing with several ministers and priests in the town Fox convinced at least one Baptist, who subsequently asked why Tombes did not appear to debate with Fox. "And then some went and told the priest and up comes he with the bailiffs of the town and magistrates and officers." Tombes took his place on a stool near Fox as the latter expounded the doctrine of the light.

> This Priest Tombes cries out, "That is a natural light and a made light."
> And then I desired all the people to take out their Bibles; for I would make the Scriptures bend him, and I asked them whether he did affirm that was a created, natural, made light that John, a man that was sent from God to bear witness to it, did speak of who said, "In him was life," to wit the Word, "and this life was the light of men." John i. 4. And I asked him whether this light was that created, natural, made light he meant.
> And he said, "Yes."
> Then said I, "Before I have done with thee I will make thee bend to the Scriptures. The natural, created, made light is the sun, moon, and stars and this outward light. And dost thou say that God sent John to bear wittness to the sun, moon, and stars which are the made lights?"[8]

Fox's insistence on the supernatural quality of the light is examined later. It need only be noted here that he and others believed, as Penn said, that "the Light must be superadded, that is over and above Man's Composition," and therefore that God "enlightened Man with a Supernatural Light."[9]

Baptists spoke of the natural light in humanity in various ways. Wigan seems to have given it its broadest application and most thorough treatment, associating it with the entire soul: the will, the affections, and the reason. However, except for some charges that Quakers were following their own wills and impulses, their disputes did not involve the first two elements of the soul. Baptists sometimes employed in their arguments what Wigan distinguished as the third element, the way of considering the light in every person "with respect to the intellectual powers." According to Burnet, this light of reason or nature was what "every man hath bestowed upon him above a beast." It was the mind, understanding, and spirit of the human, the "candle which the Lord hath set up in him to see by." It could be used for good or evil, but in any case it was a created or natural light.[10]

Friends did not deny that the reason or spirit of people was natural, and in reply to Baptists were generally content to point out that this was not the light to which they referred. The true light was not mere human spirit or reason, but was far superior to the human intellectual or rational faculty, Penn said. It was, in Whitehead's opinion, "an Immediate Divine Light of God and Christ in every Man (to which their Minds, Reason, and

Understandings are to be directed)." Quakers not only relegated reason to a position secondary to the divine light but also were actively suspicious of it. Such suspicion was shared by Baptists but was more pronounced among Friends, in accordance with their strong emphasis on immediate revelation. When Ives, who was fond of presenting his arguments syllogistically, challenged Quakers to a debate in which he claimed he would prove that they were not Christians, Shewen replied,

> Neither are all thy Syllogistical Arguments able to prove thy self a Christian, nor them none; that ancient Christian Evidence recorded in the 8th Chapter to the Romans, Verse 16. *The Spirit it self beareth witness with our spirit, that we are the Children of God,* accompanied and demonstrated with a Holy Life, and Righteous Conversation would stand thee in more stead than thy crafty Art of Reasoning.[11]

Despite accusations to the contrary, Friends did not reject the use of reason in matters of religion. Obviously they employed it against their antagonists. What they did object to, according to Burrough, was the use of ungodly or carnal reason, by Baptists and others, that resulted in "Scripture torn asunder, and strife, and contention, and endless disputes." Burrough declared that Howet would be unable to enter the Kingdom of God "till thou lay down thy contending in thy carnal wisdom, and striving, and resisting."[12]

Baptists such as Tombes also could consider the inner light as the conscience, a part of the soul and, more particularly, of human reason. Given by Christ to all persons at birth, conscience could show people that there was a God, and in the words of John Bunyan, a key spokesperson for the Baptists on this point, it could function "as a Judge to discerne of things good or bad." Frequent Quaker references to the light in the conscience and to the light's convincing people of sin made it seem to Baptists that the conscience was the light of which Friends spoke. It was wrong, they believed, to consider human conscience as supernatural or divine simply because it could convict of sin. That Quakers committed this error caused Bunyan to comment, "Now this Conscience, this nature it selfe, because it can controule, and chide them for sin, who give ear unto it, therefore must it be Idolized, and made a God of."[13]

Friends agreed with Baptists that the conscience was not supernatural. Like Baptists, they believed it was "that computure of knowledge and understanding which God has placed in the mind and spirit of man" and could be directed by either light or darkness. But, they insisted, the conscience was not the light of which they spoke. They could describe the conscience as a location of the light, but the two were not to be confused. Whitehead most clearly defined their relationship: "That Light in Man, which we contend for, and direct to, is an Immediate In-Shining of Divine Light upon Man's Conscience, that kindleth and lighteth Man's Spirit, and maketh it become the Candle of the Lord, which shews him Good and Evil, and moves him to decline Evil, and excites him to Good."[14]

The Supernatural Light: Christ, the
Holy Spirit, and God the Father

The light that was within all persons, that shined in their consciences, that was uncreated and supernatural, Quakers indentified primarily with Christ. Their evidence for this came mostly from the fourth gospel, especially the first nine verses. As already observed, Friends emphasized the divine nature of the Word and insisted that the term be applied only to Christ, who according to John was the Word that was with God in the beginning. Penn presented the rest of the Quaker interpretation of this passage: "He then tells us that *The Word had Life*, and from thence descends to inform us, what the Word was with respect to Man; *In Him, the Word was Life, and the Light of Man*: as such, He was that true Light . . . which inlightens all Mankind coming into the World."[15] Penn's last phrase, taken from John 1:9, was typically linked by Friends with Christ's declaration "I am the light of the world" (John 8:12) to form the core of their doctrine. In slightly varied forms but with the same meaning and unyielding conviction, Quakers repeated this statement often in their disputes with others. Burrough declared to Bunyan, "The same which saith I am the light of the world, is he, and no other, which lighteth every man that comes in to the world." Farnworth, in reply to Haggar, asserted, "The light we own and follow, else we should deny Christ, who is the light of the world, that lighteth every man that commeth into the world." Addressing himself to all Baptists, their former compatriot Humphrey Wolrich proclaimed, "Christ is the true Light that lighteth every man that cometh into the World, John 1:9, John 8.12."[16]

In his debate with Tombes, Fox extended his scriptural references to render even more explicit the identification of Christ with the light in all persons, concluding:

> So all natural created lights were made by Christ the Word. And Christ saith he is the light of the world, and bids them believe in the light, John xii. 36. And God saith, "I will give thee for a light to the gentiles that thou mayest be my salvation to the ends of the earth," Isa. xlix. 6. So Christ in his life is saving. And the Apostle said, the light that shined in their hearts was to give them the knowledge of the glory of God in the face of Jesus Christ, and that was their treasure in their earthen vessels, 2 Cor. iv. 6, 7.[17]

Nayler expressed the same idea in a staccato association of short biblical passages:

> Christ saith, I am the Light of the World; and the kingdome of God is within you; and the Apostle saith, By the light that shined in their hearts, did they come to the knowledge of the glory of God in the face of Jesus; and Christ in you the hope of glory.[18]

The Quakers' light in all persons, therefore, was supernatural, for, as Whitehead explained, "The Life which is the Light of Men (that true Light wherewith every man is enlightened, Joh. 1.4.9.) in its own Being is

God and Christ, and not a meer Effect of Power, as a made or created Thing, but Divine and Increated."[19]

Baptists and Quakers concurred that Christ was the Light spoken of in John 1:9, but they disagreed over the nature of his enlightening of humanity. In interpreting this verse Baptists did not make a point of the position of the participle ἐρχόμενον as John Owen did, nor did they, like him, restrict this illumination to a limited number. Neither did they, like Baxter, rely on a "two worlds" dichotomy: nature and grace. Instead, Baptists spoke of two enlightenings, that of all persons by Christ as creator, and that of believers by Christ as the Savior.[20] Tombes, Wigan, Bunyan, and Henry Grigg argued the point vigorously.[21] But Collier put the main thrust of their position most succinctly when he declared that Christ "is the light of the world, . . . but not so the light of the world, as he is a light to believers." Their arguments dealt with the universality of the light, a subject addressed later in this chapter. It will suffice here to note that Baptists, and Owen and Baxter as well, were agreed that the light *in all persons* was *not* Christ. To declare the opposite was to Grigg "a vile and wicked thing," and to Wigan the act of "a deceiver, and an Antichrist."[22]

Friends also identified the inner light with the Spirit of Christ, the Holy Spirit, and God the Father. In the exchanges between Bunyan and Burrough, for example, the former feared that because both conscience and the Spirit of Christ could convince people of sin, the Quakers were confusing the two. He argued that although Christ as he was God had given all individuals a light that was the conscience, it did not follow that the conscience was the Spirit of Christ, which Spirit, he pointed out elsewhere, "he gives not to all." Burrough, who held that the light in all humans was not the conscience, in typical Quaker fashion saw no reason to draw a rigid distinction between the light of Christ and the Spirit of Christ. He argued that "the light of Christ, given to every man, is not contrary to the spirit of Christ, and to the grace of God, but one in their nature." They were, he added, "one in union, leading in the same way unto the same end."[23]

Burrough thought the same of the light and the Holy Spirit. Penn also spoke of "Faith wrought by the Light and Spirit of God in the Heart," and of the work of the "Light and Spirit of Truth" and the "Divine Light and Spirit." Farnworth declared that the light and Spirit was the convincer that guided the obedient into all truth, and when Hicks, arguing about biblical authority, insisted that he did not oppose the Scripture to the Holy Spirit but rather to the inner light, Whitehead asked why he implied such a difference between the two. At other times the close functional association of light and Spirit was accompanied by an actual equating of the two *in esse*. Penn quoted Genesis 6:3: "My Spirit shall not always strive with men," which he said proved that humanity was not destitute of the Spirit or divine light. In response to criticism by Caffyn, Nayler replied, "Is this the doctrine of Christ, that men are not led into all truth by a light within them, John 16.13 Rom. 8.14?" but his biblical references mentioned only the Spirit and not a light.[24]

A similar difficulty arose when Friends appeared to Baptists to equate the light in all persons with God the Father or creator. When Grigg attempted to distinguish between the lights of Christ and the creator, Whitehead retorted, "No such distinction nor contraiety between the Light of God and the Light of his Son is owned in Scripture." Fisher spoke of "the Light of God in the Conscience," and Farnworth, referring to the work of Christ, maintained, "There was great worke done by others, from the same light and power, or working of the Father in them." According to Scripture, God was light, and thus Penn concluded that the light that Thomas Hicks called common was actually God, who, according to the Bible, enlightened all people. Such statements were to Hicks and other Baptists as blasphemous as the assertions that the light was the Holy Spirit, the Spirit of Christ, or Christ himself. According to Grigg, the light was never bestowed to be made an idol by people or set up in the place of God.[25]

Adding to the Baptists' perplexity was the Quaker practice of describing the light sometimes as distinct from Christ, the Holy Spirit, or God and at other times as measures or degrees of them. Penn provided some insight into the seemingly interchangeable use of these terms when he explained,

> Whatever is to be obtained and enjoyed within, is originally and chiefly ascribable to the Discoveries, Convictions and Leadings of the blessed Light of Christ within through every Generation, however variously the Principle may have been denominated; as, the Word of God nigh, Wisdom, Light, Spirit, &c. under the Old Testament; and Light, Grace, Truth, Christ, Spirit, Anointing, Gift of God, &c. under the New Testament.[26]

Such explanations were unacceptable to Baptists, who insisted on a clear distinction between the light that God or Christ had created in all persons and the light that constituted God and Christ themselves. Hicks, using the reductionist argument of which he was fond, declared, "Either the Light within in the least measure is God, a Creature, or nothing. Thou wilt not say, 'Tis a Creature. It must then be nothing. Might not thy time and abilities have been better improved than in contending for that which is neither God nor a Creature?"[27]

The Inwardness and Universality of the Light: The Inner Light, the Old Testament, Gentiles, and Sinners

The notions of "within" and "all" were pivotal in disputes over the nature of the light. Whereas Baptists acknowledged that Christ was the light and that a light existed in all persons, the Quaker insistence that the supernatural light was *within* and especially that it was within *all* people made their doctrine repugnant to Baptists, who held that Christ the light was *without* and that the Spirit of Christ or the Holy Spirit that could be said to dwell within did not dwell in *all* persons. Apart from the issue of the indwelling Christ, Baptists assailed Friends on the question of the light's inwardness. The major thrust of their attack was exhibited in interrogative form by John Pendarves, who asked whether the Quaker doctrine of the inner light was the same as the gospel preached by Christ and his apostles.[28] Baptists cited numerous examples from the experience of the primitive church to show that various apostles neither were converted themselves by a light within nor exhorted others to turn to the inner light. In fact, Christ himself condemned the idea of such a light. According to Haggar,

> When Christ had to deal with those that boasted of the light within them, He answered, that *if the light within them were darkness, how great was that darkness?* from whence we may observe, that those that pretend to walk by the light within them, were in the greatest darkness.[29]

Friends experienced some difficulty in countering this attack, for although numerous references to light appeared in the New Testament, few could be cited in defense of its inward quality. Appeals were sometimes made to the Word in the heart and to the kingdom within. Another passage employed was 2 Corinthians 4:6. Salthouse's reply to Collier was typical: "We labour to turn people to the true light of Christ *in them*: *in* for God who commanded the light to shine out of darkness hath shined in our hearts." Fox added the second part of the verse when he pointed out to Ives that Paul told people the light that shined in their hearts would give them the light of the knowledge of the glory of God in the face of Christ Jesus.[30]

The arguments used by members of the two groups concerning the universality of the light usually focused on one of three areas: the light in Old Testament characters, the light in Gentiles, or the light in sinners. The breadth of the Quaker concept of the light made it not too difficult a task to show that Old Testament persons had possessed it. Moses or the prophets were sometimes employed as illustrations. David, however, was the favorite example used by Quakers, who, like nearly all Christians of their time, accepted the Davidic authorship of the Psalms. Having quoted several such references to the light, Penn concluded it should be evident to all that David had this inner light or Spirit of God present with him.[31] Direct replies of Baptists to such assertions were relatively few, perhaps because their position was implicit in arguments concerning such subjects as Scripture, the natural character of the light, and Christology. To them, the light spoken of in the Old Testament was God's Word or commandments, not a supernatural inner light that all people possessed. All persons had a light within them, but it was only the light of nature, they argued.[32]

The Quaker defense of universality also included arguments concerning Gentiles in both the pre-Christian and Christian eras. They employed Isaiah's references to the light that was sent to the Gentiles to be God's salvation to the ends of the earth, and, like the former Baptist Samuel Fisher, cited Colossians 1:23 to prove that "That light, which is Gods Gospel in them [the Gentiles] . . . is preached in every creature under Heaven." However, their evidence was not limited to the Bible, for Penn, who contributed a philosophical undergirding to Quakerism during the Restoration, presented what he considered clear proof that ancient "heathen philosophers" possessed the light. Several, he claimed, believed in a supreme God who was the omnipotent and omnipresent Creator, and objected to heathen gods. Some actually witnessed against the practice of swearing years before Christ had advised people not to swear at all, and Virgil foretold the coming of Christ, whom he said would be born of a virgin for the salvation of humankind. Who could doubt that these heathen philosophers had been enlightened by the divine light? Furthermore, bringing the subject into an ethical context, he declared, "Not a Nation in the world ever knew an Age, in which it was destitute of such a Discovery of Internal Light, as gave to discern Evil from Good."[33]

Baptists did not deny that certain ancient philosophers and others had some knowledge of divinity and morality, but they maintained like Ives that these persons derived it from a natural light. Such light, however, was dim and imperfect. As Tombes asserted, although "No light which is truly such is to be rejected, yet in comparison of the light of Christ, it was but darkness. Philosophers guided men well in some things, in most did lead men into crooked and dangerous wayes: in the true worship of God they were wholly dark."[34]

The question of whether the supernatural light was in people of the Old Testament or in the Gentiles, although germane to the argument, was remote from the present, for the great leaders of Israel and the classical philosophers were long since dead and the present heathen populations were far removed. To ask whether this light was in sinners, however, was to raise a very pertinent question, for Quakers and Baptists agreed that sinners were still to be found in abundance and could be as close as one's neighbors. Not surprisingly, therefore, this aspect of the dispute drew the most attention. Quakers boldly claimed that all persons, including sinners, had the inner light, and they chastised Baptists for thinking otherwise. Nayler declared to Collier, "You have an imagination that Christ is the light onely to inlighten you that call your selves believers; but who must inlighten the rest? Christ saith, *I am the light of the world*, he doth not say, *I am the light of such a form, or such a people*, who are of a self-separation."[35]

In maintaining this position, Friends had to explain how people could be sinners if they had the supernatural light in them, a difficulty related to the one Calvinists attempted to resolve with the concept of predestination and Arminians tried to meet with the idea of modified free will. The solution of Quakers, akin to that of the latter group, lay in a distinction between "giving" and "receiving." In the enlightening of humanity, it was said, all were offered the light but not all received it. As Burrough explained to Bunyan, "It is given to men, though every man received it not; and it strives with the wicked man, though he follow it not." Fisher used the imagery of inwardness when he pointed out to Tombes the distinction between the light being in persons and persons being in the light.[36]

Apart from this distinction, however, Friends had difficulty when pressed on the subject. When Ives declared that according to John 11:10 the man who walked in darkness had no light in him, Nayler, ignoring "in him," replied:

> The words hath relation to his way; which is true, in the way of the wicked there is no light, yet in the heart of the wicked there is a light which condemns his wicked wayes, who is gone out of the light into the darkness, and so being in the night, stumbles, because the light is not in that way.[37]

Ives was offended by this response and declared, "For shame man, leave off thy adding to Scriptures! Dost not thou adde to the words of the book? doth not the Text say, *There is no light in him*, and thou sayest, *there is no light in his way?*" To similar challenges by Ives, replies by Fox published three years later (1659) and by Shewen some eighteen years later (1674) were hardly more satisfactory.[38]

As we have seen, Friends could identify the light with the several manifestations of the Godhead and could speak of the light itself, however identified, in terms of measures or degrees. Although they were usually consistent in claiming that sinners had the light within them, they did not unequivocally maintain that such sinners *always* had the Spirit of Christ or the Holy Spirit or even the light within. When Wigan used Jude 11 and 19 to show that some persons did not have the Spirit, Curwen explained, "They that went in his [Cain's] way from the Christians, err'd from the spirit, the righteous way, and so became natural, and sensual, in the self separation from the spirit where thou art." When Bunyan inquired whether Judas had the Spirit of Christ in him, Burrough replied, "If I should say the spirit of Christ was not in him, yet was the worke of the righteous law of God written in his heart which is spirituall, and Christ Jesus was not without his owne testimony in Judas, which is light, by which Judas was and is Condemned eternally." Answering the use of Jude 19 by Tombes, Samuel Fisher seemed to admit that people could cease to have not only the Spirit but the light as well, when he wrote:

> Every man that hath not so long resisted, grieved, quenched the motions of the Spirit of God striving in him, that it thereupon is taken from him, as it was from those sensual ones Jude speaks of, whom God had given over to their lusts, hath the Spirit striving within him, and that's enough to our purpose, who own such a state, that some may be given over to, for not using what they had, while they had it, as wherein to have wisdom (at whose reproof they would not turn) withdraw and leave them to the way of folly, and the good Spirit depart from them (as he did from Saul, Judas, the Jews, and others) and leave the house, even their hearts wholly desolate and destitute of his presence, for the evil Spirit that lusteth in men to envy, to enter and wholly to possess them, and the talent or measure of Gods Light within (sith they would not trade with it) taken away from them, . . . but all this proves not, but that

once they had it, or else Christ would not have said to such as yet walk't not in it, *Walk in the light while ye have it, least darkness come upon you.*[39]

In the Quaker view, then, although people could refuse the light, turn from it, and perhaps even cease to possess it, yet *at some time* at least they did have it and, therefore, at some time had the opportunity to turn to it and to experience salvation. In this Quakers obviously had much in common with General Baptists. However, the dispute over the universality of the light did not draw out any theological differences between General and Particular Baptists, for the Baptist concern was not primarily with the extension of the opportunity of salvation to all persons by means of a supernatural inner light, but rather with the existence of such a light regardless of people's status as believers or unbelievers. In their rejection of the Quaker position, disputants from the two groups of Baptists were in full agreement. They appealed to primitive Christianity to show that a supernatural light, however the Quakers defined it, did not reside in sinners. They also concluded that Friends who advocated the existence of such a light stood in opposition to Jesus, who had declared that those who walked in darkness had no light in them. If by "the light within," Quakers meant the Spirit of Christ, they were again mistaken, for according to Paul those who were not Christ's did not have his Spirit. If by "the light within" Friends meant the Holy Spirit, then they were once more in error, for according to Jesus the world could not receive the Holy Spirit because it did not see it or know it. Nor did Baptists accept the Quaker distinction between the giving and receiving of the light, for they claimed that people either had this light within them or they did not. Burnet provided the best summary of the Baptists' adamant rejection of this Quaker doctrine when he wrote, with reference to Ephesians 5:8,

> If there were a time when the best of Saints were in darkness, even in the time of their unregenerate state, then there is a time, when every man may be said to be in darkness; And if so, that every man while unregenerated, is in darkness, then no man, no not any man, can be said to have, either God, Christ, or the Spirit in him in that estate; for if God were in man, he is Light; and if Christ were there, he is Light, and the man that had either, could not be said to be in darkness: but these people were in darkness: to what then shall such turn within for Light, that have there nothing but darkness?[40]

The Sufficiency of the Light for Salvation: The Natures of the Light, Salvation, and God

In addition to "within" and "all," the notion of "sufficiency" was significant in disputes over the nature of the light. Burrough voiced a basic tenet of Friends when he declared that the light within was sufficient to lead to repentance from sin, and pardon of sin, and to comfort in God for the soul. Such belief in the soteriological sufficiency of the light followed from the Quaker certainty about its supernatural quality. When, according to

Fox, Collier attacked the idea that the only way to bring people to God was by means of the inner light, Fox retorted that this light was Christ the way to God and salvation for believers but a basis for condemnation for those who rejected it. Likewise, when Friends identified the light with the Holy Spirit or with God the creator, it was seen to be the way to salvation. Even when the light was considered only in terms of a measure or degree of the Divine Being, it was sufficient, as Whitehead pointed out. Penn stated the case most clearly when he wrote, "If God be Divine and sufficient to Salvation, and the Word be God, and the Life of the Word, the Light of Men, then is the Light of Men Divine and Sufficient to Salvation."[41]

The sufficiency of the light was far more than the result of such reasoning, however, for Friends believed they had directly experienced it. George Fox's call to evangelize was a directive to turn people from darkness to the light that they might receive Christ and be saved just as he himself had been. Francis Howgill, converted by Fox, confessed that as a Baptist he was ignorant of true religion but was led to righteousness when he turned to the inner light. Another former Baptist, William Ames, testified that it was not until he obeyed the light of Christ within him that he was reconciled to God. Baptists also believed they had experienced the work of the light that they thought all persons had within them. This light could teach people their duty, could assist them to live morally, and could even lead them to know that there was a God. They also believed that Christ the light was sufficient for salvation and that he gave to believers a saving light. However, as Wigan pointed out in speaking of the Lancaster prison debate, the question was not whether there was a light in every person or whether Christ enlightened true believers with a saving light, but whether the two lights were the same. Baptists were convinced they were not and thus insisted that Christ did not enlighten every person with a saving light. As Burnet noted, "There is a vast difference between a created light, that man by the favour of God in Creation bringeth into the world with him, and the saving Light of Christ or his Spirit, that the Saints receive as the effects of regeneration, Ga. 4.5.6."[42]

The Baptists' aversion to the Quaker claim for sufficiency was intensified by the apparent threat it posed to Christ's historical work. If the light were sufficient for salvation, Christ need not have come into the world, his sacrifice was without purpose, and consequently God had cruelly asked him to suffer a needless death. Such a notion was viewed with horror. To Baptists, Christ lived, died, and rose from the dead for the purpose of providing salvation. The light could not accomplish this nor could it make known to humanity all that Christ had done. As Grantham contended,

> That Man's salvation must depend upon the Death of the Son of God: that he to that end should be born of a Woman, even the blessed Virgin, Mary by Name: that he should arise from the Dead, and ascend the Heavens: or, that he shall come again to raise the Dead, and Judg the World, are things wholly beyond the reach of the Universal Principle of Light in Man.[43]

Evidence of this insufficiency of the light within all persons was given in Keach's allegorical *The Progress of Sin* during the court trial of Sin. In the witness box a pagan from a distant land testified: "as for him you call Christ, none of us, who are called Pagans, ever heard of him."[44]

As already noted, external historical events were of less importance soteriologically to Quakers than to Baptists. Whitehead, when referring to the light that all persons had to teach them, observed, "The Question is, whether all that are so taught, and are such, be they called Heathens, or others, be not in Reality Christians?" When asked if the name of Christ could be known to the world without the Scripture or tradition, Nayler further clarified the Quaker position by replying in the affirmative and adding that the name of Christ consisted not of letters or syllables but of righteousness, mercy, and judgment. However, as Friends were careful to point out, it did not follow that because the light within was sufficient, the shedding of Christ's blood was needless. To suggest otherwise was the same as to say that "If God makes manifest any thing in Man that's Saving, then all the outward Testimonies of his Love to Man were needless."[45] Quakers encountered difficulty in convincing Baptists that Christ's death was only such a "testimony," however.

The most telling arguments that Friends used to support their claim for sufficiency were based on their concept of the nature of God, who because of love and mercy was unwilling that people should live or die in sin. Here the Quakers reacted strongly against the Calvinist doctrine of predestination. How could a God of love condemn the major portion of humankind to destruction? How could the ancient Gentiles or the heathen of today be left without excuse in not honoring God if they did not possess the knowledge to do so? How could sinners be condemned for disobedience if God did not give them the opportunity to obey? Such fundamental questions rose to the surface of debate in various forms. Shewen declared to Ives, "We say and affirm, That God affords to all men a Day of Visitation, and puts them into a Possibility of being saved; else, how would he be clear when he judgeth?" Burrough asked, more dramatically, "Is not the Lord clear from the blood of all men, even though they goe to distruction[?]" Fisher further defended divine justice by claiming that God did not command people to worship him without giving them the knowledge to do so. Focusing more on the human side of the issue, Whitehead implored, "And why must the wisest of the Heathen be Excluded from the Sufficiency of such an Obligation or Rule, as Man was always under? Are they No Men? and have they no Souls to be Saved?" He added the caustic observation that divers heathen were more moral, pious, and Christian in behavior than many Baptist preachers![46] For Baptists to assert that the light in all persons was natural and insufficient for salvation therefore, according to Friends, was an affront to the righteousness of the Gentiles or heathens and, more importantly, was "Unjust to God."[47]

To charges such as these there were very few replies, and then only from Particular Baptists. Tombes presented their position when he argued that the light within was sufficient to render persons who sinned against it inexcusable and therefore made God justified in condemning them, but it was not sufficient to direct them to salvation. To Friends this was not an answer but a statement of the problem. Calvinistic Baptists, however, asked, If God had predestined some to salvation and had left the others to the just rewards of their evil, what more could be said? The ways of God could not be questioned. As Bunyan declared to Burrough, "O vain man! what is that to thee if God should make some vessels to dishonour: hath not the Potter power over the clay, of the same lump to do therewith as he please[?]"[48] Obviously, General Baptists were of a different opinion, and their lack of comment on such charges may be the result. However, with regard to the sufficiency of the light for salvation, it was not a question of extent but of means, and although General Baptists did not describe a specific method by which salvation was offered to all, they were certain that it was not by means of the light within all persons, for that was only a created and natural light.

The Light and Authority: Scripture, the Rule and Touchstone, and Intellectual Infallibility

As shown in chapter 2, Baptists insisted on the primacy of Scripture as authority but assigned a significant place to the Holy Spirit in discussing the relationship of the Spirit with the Scripture. The dispute over the connection of Scripture with the light within all people in regard to authority, however, was a different matter, since to Baptists the light within was not the Spirit or in any way supernatural. It seemed absurd to them that Friends should oppose the authority of this light to that of Scripture. Haggar, for example, referring to the New Testament, asked "Whether is it not folly and madness for any man now to refuse that light of the glorious Gospel of Jesus Christ, to walk by the light and dictates of his own heart, which is deceitful and desperately wicked[?]" True believers were taught by the light of Christ to obey the Word of Christ in the Bible, and thus those who opposed the authority of Scripture had no light in them. Consequently, Tombes warned people to be very diligent in using the Scripture to examine what they heard, for there were those who wanted to replace biblical authority with the authority of the church, or a council, or a Pope, or an inner light in all persons.[49]

Unlike their opponents, Quakers closely identified the light with the Holy Spirit and therefore found the relationship between the light and the Scripture as authority no different from that between the Holy Spirit and the Scripture as authority. However, in debating this question they generally chose to speak of the Holy Spirit, and their position has in effect already been dealt with. On the few occasions when they directly opposed the authority of the light to that of the written Word, their arguments followed the previously observed pattern. Penn, speaking of the light, and linking it as he often did with the Spirit, argued that there must be "a more Inward Spiritual and deep grounded Faith of those things recorded in Scripture, of Christ's Appearance &c. then the meer Letter is able to give. And therefore that Light and Spirit which gives that discerning and works that deep Sence and Faith must needs be as well the Rule as Author of it, and not the Scriptures." Furthermore, people were to use the light rather than the Bible to test persons' claims of religious truth, for as Fisher declared, "No man need (to trouble himself so much as) to try other mens spirits, or prove all things, lest he be deceived, for that is but labour in vain, sith if he have not a measure of Gods Infallible Light and Spirit in him where by to judge of things." That Baptists believed these functions belonged to the Scripture caused Parnell to complain in 1655 that they tried to direct people away from the inner light to the dead letter of Scripture that they wrongly called the light.[50] The following year in a manuscript addressed to Baptists at Sunderland, Durham, William Ames criticized those "whose God was without, & Christ & word without & light without" and complained that at their Baptist meeting the minister "laying hands on mee sought violently to thrust me out of the roome."[51]

Whereas the Baptist discussion of the Holy Spirit as the rule and touchstone was somewhat hypothetical (perhaps because Baptists did not consider the real question to involve Quakers being led by the Spirit), their treatment of the authority of the light was more tangible. They were convinced that Friends were led by a light and they believed they had ample evidence to show that this light was not only insufficient but dangerous. Such evidence was of two types. One illustrated the hazard of extreme individualism, the other the risk of satanic influences. Both dangers, Baptists believed, were inherent in the Quaker doctrine. Grantham best described the peril of the former when he wrote, "If every Man have this Judg of all Debates in himself, and he aver, that what he saith and doth is according to the Voice of this Judg, (or that of God in him) no Man can take in hand to judg contrary thereunto, without becoming the Judge's Judg, and so violate the Rule proposed." Hicks brought the problem into a more personal perspective when he complained that if the light were the guide, he would have no other proof that the Quakers' doctrine and practice were correct than that William Penn declared them to be so. Tombes further illustrated this difficulty by turning the tables and asserting, "If every man is to follow that light, then I am to follow my light in me: Now my light within me shews me, that the Quakers opinion about the light in them is errour." Tombes also pointed out the implications of disagreements among Friends themselves, noting with some satisfaction the estrangement between Fox and Nayler. The problem of satanic influence that Baptists also believed inherent in the Quaker stance on this issue was raised by Pendarves, who wondered whether Satan, who often changed his appearance, might now have come as an angel of light. Those who ascribed so much importance to the inner light gave Satan the advantage of being able to impress various things upon them as their light, and by this means, Tombes concluded, Satan had drawn persons to commit horrible acts that they judged to be necessary duties. One such act was described by William Kaye, whose neighbors "in obedience to the lights thats in them, that they were taught to be Christ, as most horribly deluded, did sacrifice or kill their own Mother."[52]

Considering the widespread belief in witches, the vituperative nature of religious conflict, and the extravagant behavior of some Quakers, it is not surprising that they were sometimes accused of witchcraft.[53] John Bunyan may have been involved in one such episode, for in 1659, James Blackley, a Quaker of Cambridge, rebutted a story printed in an anonymous tract and repeated in a second tract (not extant), which he claimed Bunyan wrote. The story was of a Quaker widow, who, it was charged in court, changed a woman into a mare one night and rode her some four miles to attend a feast. In refuting the report, Blackey pointed out that the judge had dismissed the charges, but the author of the anonymous tract had no doubt achieved his aim in warning readers against "adhering to Sorcerers, which like so many Mushrooms (in this Age) spring up in an instant, deviating from the Truth, and fancy a New Light, preceeding onely from the Prince of Darkness."[54] Of course, if adversity could befall an innocent person as the result of an evil one's witchcraft, it could also occur to an evil individual as the consequence of divine judgment. Such a case was reported in 1672 by Ralph James, a Baptist minister at North Willingham, Lincolnshire, who described the main points in the title of his tract:

> *A True and Impartial Narrative of the Eminent Hand of God that Befell a Quaker and His Family, at the Town of Panton in Lincolnshire: Who Affirmed He Was Commanded of God to Pronounce Mr. Ralph James Preacher of the Gospel a Leper from the Crown of His Head to the Sole of the Foot: the Same Judgment of Leprosie Shortly After Falling Upon One of His Chrildren: Himself, Wife, and the Rest of His Children, Being Also Afflicted With a Painful Distemper.*[55]

However untrue and unfair, reports like these were related with great seriousness and illustrate in a dramatic way the problem of authority that Baptists believed inherent in the Quaker position. If, as Friends claimed, Scripture was not their authority, how could conflicting claims be settled? And how could one distinguish the light of Christ from that of Satan?

Such questions, of course, applied not just to Quakers but to others at this radical end of the religious spectrum as well. As shown in chapter 2, Seekers and Ranters also appealed to an inward spiritual authority. Indeed, William Erbery, emphasizing the immediate experience of the divine indwelling, criticized Baptists for their "fleshly apprehensions" of the divine, but John Jackson also warned Christians of the danger of the devil posing as an angel of light and asked James Nayler and the Quakers to consider whether the devil might be "making use of them as he once did *Eve.*" However, Quakers were convinced that these other inward authorities, not their own, were erroneous. Edward Burrough condemned both Seekers and Ranters for not having the *true* light. Richard Farnworth reminded Ranters that Satan sometimes appeared as an angel of light, and James Nayler denounced them for serving their own lusts and choosing deceit rather than truth. Margaret Fell, having criticized Ranters for their swearing, lying, and drunkenness, concluded that their light was really darkness. The intensity of such denunciations may have partly reflected reaction to Cromwell's statement reported by Anthony Pearson to Fox, that "ye light within had ledd ye Ranters & all yt followed it into all manner of wickednesses." In any case, unlike these others, Muggletonians appealed to an outward authority. Lodowick Muggleton wrote to his own followers, "You all ought to be taught of me, . . . else you cannot be taught of God." Muggleton's animosity toward Friends (among other things, he described the Quakers' shaking as "witchcraft fits") was so strong, Isaac Penington explained, "because we stand most in his way . . . because we have received the true Light."[56]

Although Friends acted promptly to reveal the discrepancies and falsities in such bizarre stories as those just related, they had some difficulty in disputes over this basic issue of authority. Their reaction was often simply to declare that the person involved had not been led by the true light. On rare occasions they claimed a self-evidencing quality for the light.[57] In practice, however, their criterion for distinguishing the light of Christ from that of Satan was their knowledge of the nature of God and Christ as it accorded with the primitive church's experience. In addition, with the development of an organizational structure following the Restoration, the power to judge in cases of disagreement between members was more clearly seen to lie in the elders and members of the church.

One final point requires attention. If, as Quakers claimed, they had a divine light in them, then it seemed to Baptists that they should also possess intellectual infallibility. Friends' own references to "Gods Infallible Light and Spirit" within them and their adherence to the possibility of perfection may have contributed to Baptist calls for demonstrations of such ability. As previously noted, they demanded that Quakers supply facts about the life of Jesus that the Scripture did not include. In a more sweeping challenge, Russel asked, "Pray tell me, how it's possible for any Quaker (admitting their Notions to be true) to be ignorant of any thing that is knowable, and necessary to be known?" Not content with unanswered queries, Baptists cited specific cases when Friends had displayed their fallibility. Thomas Hicks supplied the most dramatic stories, including one of a Baptist who spoke to Quakers from inside a trunk and discovered that they could not distinguish his voice from the immediate voice of God. In response to such tales Quakers followed their normal practice of refutation. At the same time, however, they pointed out that the light was infallible, not those who possessed it. According to Penn, Hicks, in assuming the opposite, was guilty of "confounding the Light and Creature together, and concluding Imbecilility, Insufficiency and Ignorance in the Light, which are the Imperfections of the Creature."[58]

As has been shown, Friends entered the "Great Time" to experience immediately, but also inwardly and spiritually, the Christ of the earliest Christians.
Using John 1:9 and 8:12, they subsequently described the Christ they experienced as well as other members of the Godhead in terms of a divine light
dwelling in all persons that was sufficient for authority and salvation. Given
their respective emphases, as previously related, it is not suprising that Baptists and Quakers intensely disagreed in their debates over this Quaker doctrine. The former held that the supernatural light of Christ was the possession of believers only and that the light in all persons, which they identified
with reason or conscience, was natural and therefore insufficient either to
lead to salvation or to function as the authority for faith and practice.
Friends, on the other hand, believed that the light within all people was supernatural, identified it with Christ, the Holy Spirit, and God, and insisted
that it was therefore sufficient both to lead to salvation and to be the au-
thoritative guide for Christian belief and action. For Baptists to claim this
sufficiency for the Scripture instead, according to Whitehead, was to mistake

> a litteral Notion and Historical Faith, for the divine Light within (which is
> given to all) which is a pure, Incorruptible and Unchangeable Principle of Life
> and Truth, immediately given, and shining from Christ the Eternal Word; and
> not mans acquired Notions from the History of Christs outward manifestation
> in the Flesh.[59]

Here again the Scripture stood between Baptists and the primitive church
and was their authority. In contrast, Quakers claimed for themselves the
authority primitive Christians had *before the Scriptures were written*. That
authority—God, Christ, the Holy Spirit, the light—was also sufficient for
salvation. Furthermore, that Friends used these terms interchangeably was
also significant. Whereas the Baptists' zeal to duplicate New Testament
Christianity often made them more reluctant than Presbyterians and Independents to go beyond the basic experiential notions and language of the
Bible, they were surpassed in this regard by the Quakers' strong aversion
to drawing theological distinctions between various divine manifestations
and the inner light of Christ.

This chapter ends where it began, with Fox's 1657 dispute with John
Tombes in Leominster. At the conclusion of his journal account of the
episode Fox reported that "The Lord's power came over them all and his
everlasting Truth was declared that day, and many were turned by it to the
Lord Jesus Christ . . . And of great service that meeting was in those parts."
The next day, according to Fox, Thomas Taylor went to reason further
with Tombes "and came over him by the power of the Lord." Such reports
of "overcoming" were not unusual in these conflicts. Nevertheless, at the
end of another such confrontation—and characteristic of the tone of the
Lancaster prison dispute, the London debates of the 1670s, and most of
the controversy between Baptists and Quakers in seventeenth-century
England—Tombes reportedly concluded, "When I mean to Go to Hell, I
will go among the Quakers."[60]

8

And by his Word, I've put them to flight

Conclusion

[Professor]
> The Old Apostate, Papist, Atheist, all
> His Factors, he has set to work my fall:
> But thank my Heav'nly Father, (whose strong Arm
> Hath hitherto protected me from harm,)
> His Grace has been sufficient; in his might,
> And by his Word, I've put them to flight:
>
> .   .   .   .
>
> Thy case is sadder than thou wilt believe,
> I can but pity thee, alas, and grieve,
> Truly desiring that I might implore
> The Lord in thy behalf, and say no more.
> Quakers must dye, all flesh is Transitory,
> And I must leave them in themselves to glory.

Benjamin Keach, *The Grand Impostor Discovered*

Baptists and Quakers have been set against a background of Puritan and Nonconformist tradition that showed interest in millenarianism, encouraged the re-creation of biblical experiences through dramatic imagination in the present, and, most important, stressed primitive Christianity as the model for faith and practice—"Quod primum id optimum," Baxter declared. It is hoped that the paradigm of primitivism employed here will prove useful in the analysis of the life of other religious groups and perhaps of movements in secular spheres of human activity as well. In any case, the present study has shown that both Baptists and Quakers possessed a passionate desire to recover the life of the New Testament church. This yearning among Baptists induced a strong emphasis on the human, experiential side of Christianity—faith and practice as it had been before the church's rationalization and extensive development of theology took place. Thus Baptists, especially in their earlier years, were wary of theological constructs and preferred not to go beyond simple biblical language in points of doctrine. In their views on salvation, this emphasis placed them near the Quaker position, and although the Arminianism of General Baptists brought them closer than Particular Baptists to Friends, the Calvinism of Particular Baptists was itself of a more moderate nature, thus was also nearer to Quakerism than that expressed in the Westminster Confession and the Savoy Declaration. Perhaps most noticeably to their contemporaries, the Baptists' zeal for primitive Christianity evoked their adoption of believers' baptism by immersion and thus their abandonment of what had for centuries been regarded as Christian baptismal practice. At the same time, their doctrine of Baptism was weaker in its initiatory, Godward, and outward qualities than that held by Presbyterians and Independents. Here again Baptists and Quakers were closer. Indeed, additional points of affinity have been shown between the two groups, and the religious road that extended from the Baptist position to Quakerism was shorter than the paths leading there from Presbyterianism and Independency. Baptists stood between Presbyterians and Independents on one side and Friends on the other.

As has also been demonstrated, with respect to authority in faith and practice, Baptists and Quakers agreed in principle that the Spirit led neither contrary to nor beyond the Scripture, and members of both groups regularly appealed to biblical accounts to support their arguments. Yet Baptists were aghast that Quakers claiming to be guided by the Spirit in conjunction with Scripture could adopt such radical views on Christology, soteriology, and other doctrines. The explanation lay in the extent to which Friends were willing to go to satisfy their fervent desire to experience New Testament Christianity. Just as this urge took Baptists in some ways beyond Presbyterians and Independents, so it took Friends beyond Baptists. Perhaps stimulated by the contemporary interest in the dramatic, imaginative re-creation of biblical experiences and in millenarianism, Quakers in the height of their enthusiasm seemingly believed they lived in biblical times, *were* the primitive church, and waged the Lamb's War against the Antichrist. As previously observed, this phenomenon was similar to that described by Mircea Eliade as "the rejection of profane time" and the "recovery of the Great Time, *illud tempus* of 'the beginings.'"[1] The obvious historical difficulties that resulted for Quakers were mitigated by the internalization and spiritualization of outward, physical, historical events. That they had not witnessed the physical crucifixion or resurrection of Christ as had the disciples was transcended by Quakers' present inward experience of these events spiritually. Or again, that seventeenth-century Friends had not observed the second advent and the resurrection of the saints in the future was overcome by Christ's spiritual second coming and the spiritual resurrection of the saints, both of which events were experienced inwardly in the present. The Quaker identification with primitive Christianity contrasted with the views of others at this radical end of the religious spectrum: Seekers were said to be waiting for the true Church and ministry to be restored by divine initiative, Muggletonians believed that the apostolic age had ended and the new age begun in 1652, and Ranters thought, according to Nigel Smith, "that the inspiration which they [now] felt was the first manifestation of the new age" of the Spirit.[2]

Baxter had complained that "We set God and Heaven so far from us," and admonished readers to "put Christ no further from you, then he hath put himself, lest the Divine Nature be again inaccessible."[3] The Quaker response to such concerns was not to allow themselves or others to put Christ "far off"—neither in the past as "crucified, and dying 1600 years ago" . . . "on this crosse, without the gates of *Jerusalem*," nor in the future "coming from heaven," nor at a distance "in Heaven above the Skies."[4] From their immediate experience of Christ in the "Great Time" of primitive Christianity arose the Quaker emphases on the immediate, inward, spiritual elements that in turn shaped their view of the primitive model, as described in chapter 1. The model included the perception of the major events of Christ's life, both past and future, in an internalized and spiritualized form that could be experienced in the present. Those emphases also molded Friends' views on the Scripture, Christology, soteriology, eschatology, and other doctrines and practices that were so highly offensive to Baptists. In contrast, Baptists, although going beyond Independents and Presbyterians in this regard, refused to enter the primitive time as fully as Quakers, but rather retained a sense of difference between their own age and the extraordinary age of the primitive church. They continued to stress the physical, outward, and mediate elements in Christianity and its objective events, both past and future, according to their own literal perception of the primitive model.

To Quakers, therefore, Baptists seemed to be engaging in hollow imitations, vain traditions, and empty forms lacking the Spirit and power that the primitive Christians had. But they had not always been thus. Fox remembered the Baptists of the 1640s as "tender then," for they emphasized the role of the Spirit in Christian life. William Penn and Thomas Ellwood said much the same.[5] Ellwood was more specific, citing Baptist writings that gave evidence of such tenderness, including William Kiffin's postscript to Samuel Howe's *Sufficiency of the Spirits Teaching Without Humane Learning* (1639, reprinted 1655), the General Baptist Edward Barber's *A True Discovery of the Ministry of the Gospel* (1645), and Thomas Collier's *A General Epistle to the Universal Church* (1649). Kiffin had described Howe's book as advancing "the Teachings of the Spirit of Christ in the unfolding of the mystery of the Gospel to the hearts of men, as the choice Revealer of that glory of truth to the soul," and Barber had said that a minister "must be one converted to the Faith, by the Spirit inwardly," and was "to be experimentally acquainted with the misteries of the Gospell." Collier had written that "*external actings* according to a rule without, is nothing, if not flowing from a principle and power of *life* and *love* within," and that the Spirit "will be in thee not only a *light* discovering, but a fire consuming fleshliness." Fox had a copy of Collier's book, and from additional

sources and experience, he and other Friends knew of further evidence of
Baptist emphasis on the Spirit.[6] But, according to Fox, when Baptists and
others "were got up and got many members, they began to make laws and
orders and said, 'Hitherto shalt thou go.'"[7] This "once tender people"
ceased to be so.

As the century went on, Baptists accused Quakers of much the same,
for they as well as Baptists experienced that process described by sociolo-
gists of religion as institutionalization and routinization.[8] In addition, the
early radicalism of both groups was tempered by the defeat of the Good
Old Cause and by a Restoration that encouraged accommodation and adjustment in order to minimize persecution and ensure survival. Thus, as
has been shown, Baptists codified belief and practice and projected a more
moderate image by aligning themselves with mainstream Nonconformity.
But it was the more radical of the two groups that made the greater
changes through the development of a hierarchical organization, control
of publication, curtailment of their earlier more extravagant views and behavior, and even suppression of the evidence of some of those extravagances. A few resisted, such as the former Baptist John Perrot, as well as
John Wilkinson and John Story.[9] Furthermore, although it is better to describe Restoration Quakerism in terms of vigorous engagement than of
withdrawal and quiescence, by the time of the Act of Toleration, Quaker
quietism was already in evidence.[10] Yet there remained some of the old
practices at least, although in an occasionally fossilized form. As early as
1661, the Welsh Baptist Vavasor Powell had protested that "their chiefest
Godliness doth stand in the least things of Religion, (as in *thouing, keeping
on the hat*, &c.)." A decade later, the anonymous R. H. complained that
Friends were marked with "a *sullen meagre look*, and this Characteristick
Thou; A Fox in a *Lambskin Coat*, that retains his *subtlety* though not his
colour, a *dough-baked* piece of formality that decries *Superstition*, yet idol-
izes *Garb* and *Phrases.*" Indeed, by the end of the century certain Quaker
practices became so formalized and institutionalized that Margaret Fell,
who had provided such strong leadership in the movement, found it necessary to criticize as "a silly poor Gospel" the notion of some Friends that
"We must be all in one dress, and one colour." She also warned, "It's a
dangerous thing to lead young Friends much into observation of outward
things, for . . . this will not make them true Christians." "It's the Spirit that
gives life," she reminded Friends.[11] Quakers as well as Baptists had been
more "tender" in their earlier history.

The words from *The Grand Impostor Discovered* with which this chapter begins were ascribed by Benjamin Keach to the Professor, but they
might well have represented the attitude of both Quakers and Baptists to
the other later in the century. Both had fended off the "Old Apostate," disputed vehemently with each other, and by the time of the Act of Toleration could leave their antagonists to the judgment of God. The acrimony
of the earlier disputes perhaps partly reflected the religious character of the
times, the fact that they were competing for some of the same social and

religious groupings, and the pressures of communicating their identity and gaining respect within society in the midst of political turmoil and uncertainty as well as religious persecution. In the great London debates of the 1670s, for example, Baptists were communicating to the broader audience that they were not radical but part of the Nonconformist mainstream and were defending Christianity against the heresies of Quakerism. At the same time, Friends were denying that they were radical and were claiming to be not only Christian but adherents of the purest form of primitive Christianity. The titles of Thomas Hicks's *A Dialogue Between a Christian and a Quaker* and William Penn's and George Whitehead's *The Christian-Quaker* reflected these contrasting views.

To what extent either group benefited from the disputes is difficult to determine. In describing the tumultuous Barbican debate of 1674, the writer of *The Quakers Ballad* pessimistically concluded:

> Thus in brief a strange clutter we kept, and a stir
> But what good came on't, if I know I'm a cur,
> Only people went home, some sick, and some lame,
> But all of them just as wise as they came.

Perhaps closer to the mark was the opinion of the Baptist Henry Grigg, who acknowledged that to some, such controversies seemed fruitless and wearisome, but argued that he had "some good ground to judge that God hath blessed some former undertakings of this nature, to the great benefit and advantage of some poor Souls." "And let none blame us," he went on, "for standing up in the defence of Christ and the Gospel, where the Foundation of true Religion and Godliness is thus struck at." Ann Hughes has concluded that "Radicals and orthodox disputants both believed that the truth would emerge inevitably through honest debate although they differed over what that truth was, and over who to blame when disputations were not fruitful."[12]

Public debates and printed exchanges no doubt attracted attention and perhaps converts. They also forced disputants to prepare, think through, and sharpen their theological positions, thus enhancing the practical edification of their adherents. Finally, the setting forth of accusations, rebuttals, and clarifications shed much light on the beliefs and perceptions of the adversaries and has allowed this study to conclude that the fundamental link between Quakers, Baptists, and the Puritan and Nonconformist tradition was an emphasis on primitive Christianity. Whereas both groups amplified and extended that emphasis, Quakers went significantly further in entering rather than imitating the "Great Time." As a result, the basic religious element connecting Quakers to the Puritan and Nonconformist tradition also served to separate them in a significant way from that tradition. Theirs was a major advance beyond the positions of Presbyterians, Independents, and Baptists. By experientially extending to its furthest point *Quod primum id optimum,* early Quakers made one of the most original lasting contributions to the history of Christianity in England.

Notes

Chapter 1

Place of publication is London unless otherwise stated. For seventeenth-century works not abbreviated, publication dates are repeated in the notes to facilitate placement in historical context. Only dates, not spelling and punctuation, are modernized. Citations of Scripture are selected from those provided by the seventeenth-century authors unless otherwise noted. William Penn's *The Christian-Quaker*, 1674, and George Whitehead's *The Christian-Quaker*, 1673, were bound together (the book said to be in two parts), but separately paginated and bearing different publication dates. Thus they are cited separately.

1 Among them was Benjamin Keach's *The Grand Impostor Discovered*, 1675 (quoted in the epigraph to this chapter), which in rhymed dialogue depicted and criticized the beliefs and practices of Quakers. Benjamin Keach, *The Grand Impostor Discovered*, 1675, p. 194. Benjamin Keach was baptized as an infant but joined with General (Arminian) Baptists in 1658, and in 1660 became a minister in Buckinghamshire. In 1668 he moved to London, where he came in contact with leading Particular (Calvinistic) Baptists, and within four years he adopted Particular Baptist views. By the end of his life Keach had published more than fifty works. Part of the foldout illustration that is bound in the copies of *The Grand Impostor Discovered* at the Folger Shakespeare Library, Washington, D.C., and the Bodleian Library at Oxford (but not at LF) is to be seen in the frontispiece.

2 John Bunyan, *Some Gospel-truths Opened*, 1656, and *A Vindication of the Book Called, Some Gospel-Truths Opened*, 1657, in *MW*, 1:134, 61. FGM, pp. 8, 211.

3 Donald F. Durnbaugh, "Baptists and Quakers—Left Wing Puritans?" *QH* 62 (1973), 67–82; Craig Horle, "Quakers and Baptists 1647–1660," *BQ* 26 (1976): 344–62.

4 I am greatly indebted here and elsewhere to Theodore Dwight Bozeman's analysis of biblical primitivism and its implications for understanding the New England Puritan experience, *To Live Ancient Lives: The Primitivist Dimension in Puritanism* (Chapel Hill: University of North Carolina Press, 1988).

5 Mircea Eliade, *Myths, Dreams,and Mysteries: The Encounter Between Contemporary Faith and Archaic Realities,* trans. Philip Mairet (Harvill Press, 1960), pp. 29–30. See also chapter 8.

6 For this phrase from Baxter and Tertullian, see the following section. Bonnelyn Young Kunze, *Margaret Fell and the Rise of Quakerism* (Stanford: Stanford University Press, 1994), pp. 197–210. H. Larry Ingle, *First Among Friends: George Fox and the Creation of Quakerism* (New York: Oxford University Press, 1994), pp. 51, 111–14. See also Melvin B. Endy, Jr., "Puritanism, Spiritualism, and Quakerism: An Historiographical Essay," in *The World of William Penn,* ed. Richard S. Dunn and Mary Maples Dunn (Philadelphia: University of Pennsylvania Press, 1986), pp. 280–301. Employment of the paradign of primitivism to explain basic Quaker beliefs and practices, however, does not dismiss the importance of the social/regional origins of some customs (e.g., the use of *thee* and *thou*)—see BQPE, pp. 71–93, 160–80.

7 Andrew Forrest Scott Pearson, *Thomas Cartwright and Elizabethan Puritanism, 1535–1603,* (Cambridge: Cambridge University Press, 1925), p. 29. John Dod and Robert Cleaver, *A Plaine and Familiar Exposition of the Ten Commandments* 1605, p. 11. William Ames, *Conscience With the Power and Cases Thereof,* 1639, book 4, p. 72. Thomas Shepard, *Theses Sabbaticae,* 1649, part 2, pp. 4–5, 17 quoted. John Owen, *Of the Divine Originall* (Oxford) 1659, p. 25. Richard Baxter, preface to *The Protestants Answer to That Question, Where Was Your Church Before Luther? Wherein Popery is Proved a Novelty,* by Thomas Doolittle, 1675, sigs. A4r–A4v; I am grateful to Neil Keeble for calling my attention to this preface. Thomas Gouge, *Christian Directions,* 1675, p. 25. Thomas Goodwin, *An Exposition on the First Eleven Verses of the Second Chapter of the Epistle to the Ephesians,* part 2, 1681, in *The Works of Thomas Goodwin* (1681–1704, 5 vols.), 1:265 (second pagination). Baxter, *A Christian Directory,* 1673, p. 928. Ames, *Conscience With the Power and Cases Thereof,* 1639, p. 74.

8 Gouge, *Christian Directions,* 1675, pp. 26, 142. Richard Baxter, *The Saints Everlasting Rest,* 1650, pp. 759–60 (the section on heavenly meditation bears the date 1649). In his spiritual autobiography, the Baptist John Bunyan described his discovery of religious truth "from the relation of the four Evangelists": "But, oh! now, how was my Soul led from truth to truth by God! even from the birth and cradle of the Son of God, to his ascension and second coming from Heaven to judge the World," and concluded, "Me thought I was as if I had seen him born, as if I had seen him grow up, as if I had seen him walk thorow this world, from the Cradle to his Cross" (John Bunyan, *Grace Abounding,* ed. Roger Sharrock [Oxford: Clarendon Press, 1962], sections 119–20, pp. 37–38). See also John Bunyan, *The Doctrine of the Law and Grace Unfolded,* 1659, in *MW,* 2: 158. For the use of spiritual senses, see also Richard Sibbes, *A Breathing After God,* 1639, p. 172, and Richard L. Greaves, introduction to *MW,* 9: xxxv–xli.

9 Ernest Axon, ed., *Oliver Heywood's Life of John Angier,* Chetham Society, Remains, historical and literary . . . , n.s. number 97 (Manchester: 1937), p. 50. Bozeman, *To Live Ancient Lives,* pp. 35, 19; for further analysis see pp. 3–119 and Richard T. Hughes, ed., *The American Quest for the Primitive Church* (Urbana: University of Illinois Press, 1988). See also John R. Knott, Jr., *The Sword of the*

Spirit: Puritan Responses to the Bible (Chicago: University of Chicago Press, 1980); Neil H. Keeble, *The Literary Culture of Nonconformity in Late Seventeenth-Century England* (Athens, Georgia: University of Georgia Press, 1987).

10 See Peter Toon, "The Latter-day Glory" and Robert G. Clouse, "The Rebirth of Millenarianism," in *Puritans, the Millennium and the Future of Israel: Puritan Eschatology 1600–1660*, ed. Peter Toon (Cambridge: James Clarke, 1970) pp. 23–41, 42–65.

11 John Smyth, *The Character of the Beast*, 1609, p. 1.

12 Thomas Helwys, *A Short Declaration of the Mistery of Iniquity*, 1612, pp. 69, 209. See also W. T. Whitley, ed., *The Works of John Smyth*, 2 vols. (Cambridge: Cambridge University Press, 1915), introduction, 1: xvii–cxii; Walter H. Burgess, *John Smith the Se-Baptist, Thomas Helwys and the First Baptist Church in England* (James Clarke, 1911); William R. Estep, *The Anabaptist Story*, rev. ed. (Grand Rapids: Willian B. Eerdmans, 1975), pp. 203–35; J. W. Martin, *Religious Radicals in Tudor England* (Hambledon Press, 1989), pp. 3, 19–20, 27–28, 133. For a summary of the scholarly debate over the relationship between Continental Anabaptists and English General Baptists, see Lonnie D. Kliever, "General Baptist Origins: The Question of Anabaptist Influences," *The Mennonite Quarterly Review* 36 (1962): 291–321. From his own analysis Kliever concludes that their differences "are thought significant enough to consider the Anabaptists and the originating group of the General Baptists as dissimilar Christian traditions," and that "the distinctive features of early General Baptists are accounted for by their English Puritan Separatist background. They appeared on the scene as a leftward movement of Puritanism and a logical extension of Separatism" (p. 321). See also Stephen Brachlow, "Puritan Theology and General Baptist Origins," *BQ* 31 (1985): 179–94; Murray Tolmie, *The Triumph of the Saints: The Separate Churches of London 1616–1649* (Cambridge: Cambridge University Press, 1977), pp. 69–84; and Nuttall's thesis in *HSPFE*, discussed later. For Baptists and the issue of religious toleration, see Timothy George, "Between Pacifism and Coercion: The English Baptist Doctrine of Religious Toleration," *Mennonite Quarterly Review* 58 (1984): 30–49.

13 Champlin Burrage, *Early English Dissenters*, 2 vols. (Cambridge: Cambridge University Press, 1912), 2: 292–305, 302 quoted. MBC, pp. 171–89; Article 40, p. 185. General Baptist confession: 1651, article 48, MBC, p. 103. WHB, p. 87. On Particular Baptist origins see also Glen H. Stassen, "Anabaptist Influence in the Origin of the Particular Baptists," *Mennonite Quarterly Review* 36 (1962): 322–48; B. R. White, "Baptist Beginnings and the Kiffin Manuscript," *Baptist History and Heritage* 2 (1967): 27–37; Tolmie, *Triumph of the Saints*, pp. 50–68; UHB, pp. 56–62.

14 Thomas Tillam, *The Seventh-day Sabbath*, 1657, pp. 11, 98, 108 quoted, 50–51. See T. L. Underwood, introduction to *MW*, 4: xlv–lii; W. T. Whitley, "Seventh Day Baptists in England," *BQ* 12 (1947): 252–58; Ernest A. Payne, "More About the Sabbatarian Baptists," *BQ* 14 (1951–52): 161–66; Bryan W. Ball, *The Seventh-day Men: Sabbatarians and Sabbatarianism in England and Wales, 1600–1800* (Oxford: Oxford University Press, 1994).

15 W. T. Whitley, "Baptist Churches till 1660," Baptist Historical Society *Transactions* 2 (1911): 232–34. W. K. Jordan, *The Development of Religious Toleration in England*, 3 vols. (Allen and Unwin, 1938), 3: 457. UHB, p. 85; Ruth Butterfield, "'The Royal Commission of King Jesus': General Baptist Expansion and Growth 1640–1660," *BQ* 35 (1993): 56–80. See also J. F. V. Nicholson,

"The Office of 'Messenger' amongst British Baptists in the Seventeenth and Eighteenth Centuries," *BQ* 17 (1957–58): 206–25; WHB, pp. 90–93. For Baptist historiography see WEBSC, pp. 12–20. For Baptist bibliography see W. T. Whitley, *A Baptist Bibliography*, 2 vols. (Kingsgate Press, 1916–22) and Edward C. Starr, *A Baptist Bibliography*, 25 vols. (Philadelphia: Judson Press, 1947–76). For additional resources see Susan B. Mills, "Sources for the Study of Baptist History," *BQ* 34 (1992): 282–96.

16 BQPE, pp. 37–38. RQER, p. 121. Rosemary Anne Moore concludes that "throughout the 1650's Fox was always the leading Quaker as far as Quakers themselves were concerned" ("The Faith of the First Quakers. The Development of their Beliefs and Practices up to the Restoration" [Ph.D. thesis, University of Birmingham, 1993], p. 225, LF). See chapter 6 for the competition for leadership between Nayler and Fox. Ingle, *First Among Friends*.

17 FJN, pp. 4, 11, 12. FJN down to 1650 relies on the 1694 edition of Thomas Ellwood, who took considerable liberties with his sources. Because there is no corroborative manuscript for most of it, this portion of FJN is less reliable than the remainder. See FJN, John L. Nickalls, preface, p. xi, and Geoffrey F. Nuttall, "Reflections on William Penn's Preface to George Fox's *Journal*," *JFHS* 57 (1995): 113–17.

18 FJN, p. 35. For the Lamb's War, see Rev. 14–19, Eph. 6:10–18. BBQ, pp. 43–110. Kunze, *Margaret Fell*, pp. 13–14, 21, 53–55. A. Neave Brayshaw, *The Quakers*, 3rd ed. (New York: Macmillan, 1953), p. 75. Hooton to Fox, 11 June 1653, LF: Barclay MSS 14. Thomas Aldam to Margaret Fell, probably 1653 or 1654, LF: Barclay MSS 159. BQPE, pp. 181–82; RQER, p. 11. For the Quakers named in these two paragraphs, see *BDBR* and *DNB*. For a life of Hooton, see Emily Manners, *Elizabeth Hooton* (Headley Brothers, 1914). Joseph Besse, *A Collection of the Sufferings of the People Called Quakers*, 2 vols. (Luke Hinde, 1753).

19 Richard T. Vann, *The Social Development of English Quakerism 1655–1755* (Cambridge: Harvard University Press, 1969), pp. 72–75, 73 quoted. Vann's analysis has been challenged by Judith Jones Hurwich, "The Social Origins of the Early Quakers," *Past and Present* 48 (1970): 156–62. See also Richard T. Vann and David Eversley, *Friends in Life and Death: The British and Irish Quakers in the Demographic Transition, 1650–1900* (Cambridge: Cambridge University Press, 1992). Ernest E. Taylor, *The Valiant Sixty* (Bannisdale Press, 1947), p. 43. RQER, pp. 20–26. J. F. McGregor, "The Baptists: Fount of All Heresy," in *Radical Religion in the English Revolution*, ed. J. F. McGregor and Barry Reay (Oxford: Oxford University Press, 1984), p. 36. WHB, p. 97 quoted. Because of the relative abundance of Quaker biographical materials, in this study more attention is given to the identification of Baptist disputants than Quakers.

20 Thomas Grantham, *Hear the Church*, 1687, sig. A2r, p. 21.

21 William Penn, preface to George Fox, *The Journal of George Fox* ed. Thomas Ellwood, 1694, sigs. Br, Bv, B1r, F1r.

22 I have chosen to use the admittedly anachronistic term *radical*, for the defense of which see Richard L. Greaves, *Enemies Under His Feet: Radicals and Nonconformists in Britain, 1664–1677* (Stanford: Stanford University Press, 1990), pp. 7–8.

23 Samuel Richardson, *Some Brief Consideration On Doctor Featly his Book*, 1645, p. 3. Featly died in 1645. See note 42 for this chapter, *Humble Petition and Representation*, 1649, and McGregor, "The Baptists: Fount of All Heresy," pp. 23–63.

24 R. H., *The Character of a Quaker*, 1671, p. 1. FGM, p. 286; George Fox, "To all such as sett uppe Crosses," 1655, LF: Swarthmore MSS 2/87; "Queries to Papesh [*sic*]," n.d., LF: Swarthmore MSS 7/5; "For the Pope," 22 September 1662, LF: Swarthmore MSS 7/80, in which Fox wrote "For to doe to another as you would have another to doe to you, then they [the heathen] should kill you & burne you as you have done others, for your killinge, burninge, banishinge, Rackinge & torturinge others"; *Something in Answer to Lodowick Muggleton's Book*, 1667. Michael G. Finlayson, *Historians, Puritanism, and the English Revolution: The Religious Factor in English Politics before and after the Interregnum* (Toronto: University of Toronto Press, 1983), p. 128. BBQ, pp. 306–42. BQPE, pp. 174, 131–37. RQER, pp. 113–17. Winthrop S. Hudson, "A Supressed Chapter in Quaker History," *Journal of Religion* 24 (1944): 108–18. Thomas O'Malley, " 'Defying the Powers and Tempering the Spirit': A Review of Quaker Control over Their Publications, 1672–1689," *Journal of Ecclesiastical History*, 33 (1982): 72–88. In 1677, the London Second Day Morning Meeting examined Margaret Fell's *The Daughter of Zion Awakened* (printed later in the year) and, "several heads in it being objected against," decided that they could not print it "as it is, without it be Altered or Corrected" ("London [Second Day] Morning Meeting Minutes," 23 July 1677, p. 17, LF. FJP, Norman Penney, introduction, 1: xv–xxvii. Henry J. Cadbury, ed., *George Fox's "Book of Miracles"* (New York: Octagon Books, 1973). Geoffrey F. Nuttall, "A Letter by James Nayler Appropriated to George Fox," *JFHS* 55 (1988): 178–79. H. Larry Ingle, "George Fox as Enthusiast: An Unpublished Epistle," *JFHS* 55 (1989): 266–70; "George Fox, Historian," *QH* 82 (1993): 28–35. See also Christopher Hill, *The Experience of Defeat* (New York: Viking Press, 1984), pp. 129–69; "Quakers and the English Revolution," *JFHS* 56 (1992): 178. RQER, p. 121.

25 RQER, pp. 81–100. See also Philip F. Gura, *A Glimpse of Sion's Glory: Puritan Radicalism in New England, 1620–1660* (Middletown, Conn.: Wesleyan University Press, 1984), pp. 144–52; Jonathan M. Chu, *Neighbors, Friends, or Madmen: The Puritan Adjustment to Quakerism in Seventeenth-Century Massachusetts Bay* (Westport, Conn.: Greenwood Press, 1985), pp. 11–33.

26 MBC, pp. 171, 111, 124–61, 218–89. *The Humble Representation and Vindication*, 1654, in *The Minutes of the General Assembly of the General Baptist Churches in England*, ed. W. T. Whitley, 2 vols. (Kingsgate Press, 1909–10), 1: 1–5. WEBSC, pp. 83–84. *The Humble Petition and Representation*, 1649, p. 5. A previously lost copy of *A Declaration of Several Baptized Believers*, 1659, is in the Congregational Library, London: MSS Portfolio 2 a 39. It was criticized in Richard Hubberthorn and Edward Burrough, *An Answer to a Declaration*, 1659. *The Humble Apology*, 1660–61, in *Confessions of Faith and Other Public Documents*, ed. Edward Bean Underhill, Hanserd Knollys Society publication 10 (Haddon Brothers, 1854), pp. 343–52. WEBSC, pp. 96–97. See also B. R. White, "William Kiffin—Baptist Pioneer and Citizen of London," *Baptist History and Heritage* 2 (1967): 91–103.

27 FJN, p. 357. Margaret Fell, *A Declaration*, 1660, p. 7. Fox et al., *A Declaration from the Harmles & Innocent People of God*, 1661, pp. 1–2, 4–5. Richard L. Greaves, "Shattered Expectations? George Fox, the Quakers, and the Restoration State, 1660–1685," *Albion* 24 (1992): 237–59; *Deliver Us from Evil: The Radical Underground in Britain, 1660–1663* (New York: Oxford University Press, 1986); *Enemies Under His Feet; Secrets of the Kingdom: British Radicals from the Popish Plot to the Revolution of 1688–1689* (Stanford: Stanford University Press,

1992). See also Meredith Baldwin Weddle, "Conscience or Compromise: The Meaning of the Peace Testimony in Early New England," *QH* 81 (1992): 73–86.

28 Jerome Friedman, *Blasphemy, Immorality, and Anarchy: The Ranters and the English Revolution* (Athens, Ohio: Ohio University Press, 1987), p. 13.

29 J. F. McGregor, "Seekers and Ranters," in McGregor and Reay, *Radical Religion in the English Revolution*, pp. 121–39, pp. 129 (the emphasis is mine), 123 quoted. John Tomkins, *Piety Promoted*, 2nd ed., 3 pts. (1703–06), pt. 3 (1706), p. 119. Thomas Taylor, *Truth's Innocency*, 1697, sigs. B2r, C2r. Thomas Edwards, *Gangraena*, 1646, pp. 73, 77–78; *The Second Part of Gangraena*, 1646, p. 21; *The Third Part of Gangraena*, 1646, pp. 75, 89–90. William Erbery, *The Testimony*, 1658. William Walwyn, *A Whisper in the Eare of Mr. Thomas Edwards*, 1645. John Saltmarsh, *Sparkles of Glory*, 1647. Laurence Clarkson, *The Lost Sheep Found*, 1660, p. 19. John Jackson, *A Sober Word*, 1651, pp. 34–35. Richard Baxter, *A Key for Catholicks*, 1659, pp. 331–34, p. 332 quoted. *BDBR*.

30 J. C. Davis, *Fear, Myth and History* (Cambridge: Cambridge University Press, 1986); "Fear, Myth and Furore: Reappraising the Ranters," *Past and Present* 129 (1990): 98–103. Friedman, *Blasphemy, Immorality, and Anarchy*, pp. 236–49. Abiezer Coppe, *A Second Fiery Flying Roll*, 1649, sig. B3r (faulty pagination). John Taylor, *Ranters of Both Sexes*, 1651, p. 2. Richard Baxter, *Reliquiae Baxterianae*, 1696, pt. 1, p. 76. *BDBR*. See also A. L. Morton, *The World of the Ranters* (Lawrence and Wishart, 1970); James F. McGregor, "Ranterism and the Development of Early Quakerism," *Journal of Religious History* 9 (1977): 349–63; Nigel Smith, *Perfection Proclaimed: Language and Literature in English Radical Religion, 1640–1660* (Oxford: Clarendon Press, 1989). Friends themselves distinguished between "Civil Ranters" (antinomian Independents) and those who engaged in more objectionable behavior—see Thomas Barcroft to Margaret Fell, 26 May 1657, LF: Swarthmore MSS 1/173; Oliver Atherton to Margaret Fell, 17 December 1660, LF: Swarthmore MSS 1/134.

31 Christopher Hill, Barry Reay, and William Lamont, *The World of the Muggletonians* (Temple Smith, 1983), pp. 1–5, tell the story of the death in 1979 of possibly the last Muggletonian and the purchase of the Muggletonian archive by the British Library. John Reeve, *A Transcendent Spiritual Treatise*, 1652, pp. 5, 23. Lodowick Muggleton, *An Answer to Isaac Penington*, 1669, p. 16; Lodowick Muggleton *A Discourse Between John Reeve and Richard Leader*, 1682, p. 7. John Reeve and Lodowick Muggleton, *A Divine Looking-Glass*, 1661, pp. 100–103. William Wood to Muggleton, 9 February 1692, British Library: Additional Manuscript 60168/41. Reeve, *Transcendent Spiritual Treatise*, 1652, p. 34 quoted. See also T. L. Underwood. "'For then I should be a Ranter or a Quaker': John Bunyan and Radical Religion," in *'Awakening Words': John Bunyan and the Language of Community*, ed. David Gay and Arlette Zinck, forthcoming.

32 William Penn, *The New Witnesses*, 1672, p. 65. Fox, *Something in Answer to Lodowick Muggleton's Book*, 1667, p. 9. FJN, pp. 196–97. Muggleton, *Answer to Isaac Penington*, 1669, p. 20; Muggleton, *The Answer to William Penn*, 1673, p. 120. Lodowick Muggleton, *A Looking-Glass for George Fox*, 1668, p. 85. Fox, *Something in Answer to Lodowick Muggleton's Book*, 1667, p. 21.

33 John Downham, *A Blow at the Root*, 1650, pp. 151–52. William Kiffin, *Heart-Bleedings for Professors Abominations*, 1650. Joseph Salmon, *Heights in Depths and Depths in Heights*, 1651, p. 4. HSPFE, Mark Kishlansky quoted on the cover of the 1992 reprint. HSPFE, pp. 91–92. See also Bozeman, *To Live Ancient Lives*, pp. 364–68; Durnbaugh, "Baptists and Quakers—Left Wing Puritans?";

Horle, "Quakers and Baptists 1647–1660"; Melvin B. Endy, Jr., "The Interpretation of Quakerism: Rufus Jones and His Critics," *QH* 70 (1981): 3–21; "Puritanism, Spiritualism, and Quakerism," pp. 280–301; and H. Larry Ingle, "From Mysticism to Radicalism: Recent Historiography of Quaker Beginnings," *QH* 76 (1987), 79–94. Bozeman (p. 367) distorts Nuttall's thesis by ignoring his argument that Quakers were also "the Puritans' fiercest foes" (*HSPFE*, p. 13).

34 MBC, p. 194. WEBSC, pp. 41–44. FJN, p. 4. William Caton to Francis Howgill or Edward Burrough, 19 March 1654, LF: Swarthmore MSS 3/151.

35 FJN, p. 25. Roger Hayden, ed., *The Records of a Church of Christ in Bristol, 1640–1687*, Bristol Record Society Publication 27 (1974), p. 110. It should be noted that the Quaker Dennis Hollister had been an Independent (Hollister, *Skirts of the Whore Discovered*, 1656, p. 16) not a Baptist (Horle, "Quakers and Baptists 1647–1660," p. 347) member of the Independent-Baptist Broadmead church in Bristol. UFR, pp. 140–41, 144–45. *FPT*, p. 228. UFR, p. 353. FJN, pp. 209–10. John Beevan, *A Loving Salutation*, 1660, p. 3. Francis Howgill, *The Inheritance of Jacob Discovered*, 1656, p. 15.

36 "London [Second Day] Morning Meeting Minutes," 18 May, 10 August, 7 September, 12 October 1691, pp. 149, 150, 154; 23 May 1692, p. 170, LF. BBQ, pp. 45–46. BSPQ, pp. 228–44. FJP, 1: 375–76. FJP, 2: 5, 314 quoted. Kenneth L. Carroll, *John Perrot: Early Quaker Schismatic*, *JFHS* Supplement 33 (1971).

37 UFR, pp. 291, 307–8, 311–13, 317–18, 328–29, 330–33, 332–33 quoted; *BDBR*. Geoffrey F. Nuttall, "Another Baptist Vicar? Edmund Skipp of Bodenham," *BQ* 33 (1990): 331–34. LF: Southwark MSS 1/26 quoted, 1/27.

38 Edward Burrough to Margaret Fell, 1654, LF: Caton MSS 3/63. FJN, pp. 226, 234, 270, 285, 325; 102; 252. Baptists also disputed with others—see Arthur S. Langley, "Seventeenth-Century Baptist Disputations," *Baptist Historical Society Transactions* 6 (1918–19): 216–43. For the practice of shaking the dust off one's feet, see Matt. 10:14, Luke 9:5, Acts 13:51.

39 *Declaration of several of the People called Anabaptists, In and about the City of London* 1659, broadsheet. Richard Hubberthorn, *An Answer to a Declaration Put Forth by the General Consent of the People Called Anabaptists, In and About the City of London*, 1659, p. 5 (part by Edward Burrough). Joseph Smith, *Bibliotheca Anti-Quakeriana* (Joseph Smith, 1873). See also Joseph Smith, *A Descriptive Catalogue of Friends' Books*, 2 vols. (Joseph Smith, 1867); Hugh Barbour and Arthur O. Roberts, eds., *Early Quaker Writings 1650–1700* (Grand Rapids: William Eerdmans, 1973), pp. 567–76; Rosemary Anne Moore, "An Annotated Listing of Quaker and Anti-Quaker Publications 1652–1659," 1994, LF.

40 Luke Howard, *The Seat of the Scorner Thrown Down*, 1673, p. 3. George Whitehead, *Forgery Detected* (1690?), broadsheet. FJN, p. 669. "London [Second Day] Morning Meeting Minutes," 10 December 1674, p. 4, LF.

41 Peter Milward, *Religious Controversies of the Elizabethan Age: A Survey of Printed Sources* (Lincoln, Neb.: University of Nebraska Press, 1977); *Religious Controversies of the Jacobean Age: A Survey of Printed Sources* (Lincoln, Neb.: University of Nebraska Press, 1978). See also M. G. F. Bitterman, "The Early Quaker Literature of Defense," *Church History* 42 (1973): 203–28. Bunyan, *Some Gospel-truths Opened*, 1656, and *Vindication*, 1657, in *MW*, 1:135, 45; Isa. 36–37. FGM, pp. 8, 211. William Russel, *Quakerism Is Paganism*, 1674, p. 31. Thomas Rudyard, *The Water-Baptists Reproach Repeld*, 1673, p. 55.

42 Christopher Hill, "History and Denominational History," *BQ* 22 (1967):

65–71. Richard L. Greaves, "The Nature of the Puritan Tradition," in *Reformation, Conformity and Dissent: Essays in Honour of Geoffrey Nuttall*, ed. R. Buick Knox (Epworth Press, 1977), p. 258 quoted; "The Puritan-Nonconformist Tradition in England, 1560–1700: Historiographical Reflections," *Albion* 17 (1985): 449–86. RQER, p. 121. McGregor and Reay, *Radical Religion in the English Revolution*, p. vii. HSPFE, p. 13. For these studies of Baptists and Quakers, see notes 3, 6, 12–19, 23, 24, 27 for this chapter. In using Baptist confessions it must be kept in mind that they represent select groupings of Particular or General Baptist congregations. The General Baptist confessions employed in this study are: "The Faith and Practice of Thirty Congregations" (churches in the Midlands), 1651; "A Brief Confession or Declaration of Faith Set forth by many of us, who are (falsely) called Ana-Baptists," 1660 (churches primarily in London and vicinity); "An Orthodox Creed," 1679 (churches in the Midlands). The Particular Baptist confessions employed are: "The Confession of Faith, Of those Churches which are commonly (though falsly) called Anabaptists," 1644 (seven London churches); "A Confession of the Faith of Several Churches of Christ in the County of Somerset, and of some Churches in the Counties near adjacent," 1656; "Confession of Faith Put forth by the Elders and Brethren of many Congregations of Christians (baptized upon Profession of their Faith) in London and the Country," 1677. These confessions are printed in William L. Lumpkin, *Baptist Confessions of Faith* (Valley Forge, Pa.: Judson Press, 1969) as well as in MBC. Similar care must be exercised in employing the Westminster Confession and the Savoy Declaration.

Chapter 2

1 They were held in September 1672 at the Quakers' meeting at Devonshire House, on 28 August and 9 October 1674 at the Baptists' meeting place in the Barbican, and on 16 October 1674 at the Quakers' meeting house on Wheeler Street in Spitalfields.

2 George Whitehead, *The Christian-Quaker*, 1673, pp. 85–87. William Kiffin, *The Quakers Appeal Answer'd*, 1674, sig. A4r. William Mead, *A Brief Account*, 1674, p. 27. Thomas Plant, *A Contest for Christianity*, 1674, p. 25 quoted. Although invited, neither Penn nor Whitehead attended the 28 August meeting, the business of which was described by Kiffin as "*not to Dispute, but only to Hear and Examine Matters of Fact*, viz. *Whether* Tho. Hicks *was Guilty of that which is Objected against him*" (Kiffin, *The Quakers Appeal Answer'd*, 1674, sigs. A2r–A7v, p. 2 quoted). See also Thomas Rudyard, *The Barbican-cheat Detected*, 1674, pp. 3–11. Hicks (d. 1688?) was a Baptist minister in Devizes, Wiltshire, before becoming active in London. See G. Lyon Turner, *Original Records of Early Nonconformity under Persecution and Indulgence*, 3 vols. (T. Fisher Unwin, 1911–14), 1: 117; George Whitehead, *Forgery Detected* (1690?), broadsheet. For Hicks's other disputes with Quakers see Robert West, *Damnable Heresie Discovered*, 1673, p. 1, and *The Pride of Jordan Spoiled*, 1674, p. 3; Whitehead, *Christian-Quaker*, 1673, pp. 10, 60–61, 69.

3 MBC, pp. 227–31, 151–53. Westminster Confession, chapter 1; Savoy Declaration, chapter 1.

4 William Penn, *Reason Against Railing*, 1673, p. 150. Edward Burrough, *Something in Answer to a Booke, Called a Voice*, 1654, p. 19. William Loddington, *Quakerism No Paganism*, 1674, p. 31. Whitehead, *Christian-Quaker*, 1673, p. 49. William Ames, *A Declaration*, 1656, p. 10. It should be noted that Whitehead

sometimes considered the Bible a "historical rule" (*An Appendix*, 1673, p. 35), and James Nayler, who could describe the Scripture in spiritual terms, wrote of it as "our Rule" without adding modifiers (*Weakness Above Wickedness*, 1656, p. 13).

5 Penn, *Reason Against Railing*, 1673, p. 121. Thomas Lawson, *An Untaught Teacher*, 1655, p. 14, 1 Cor. 12:10. James Nayler, *The Boaster Bared*, 1655, p. 7. Samuel Fisher, *Rusticus ad Academicos*, 1660, pt. 4, p. 184.

6 GCP, pt. 4, p. 50. William Burnet, *The Capital Principles*, 1668, p. 19 (misprinted 91). William Russel, *Quakerism is Paganism*, 1674, p. 29. To a similar accusation made by Benjamin Keach (*The Progress of Sin*, 1684, p. 246), the former Independent James Park (1636–96) replied, "Shall I utterly renounce what is good, because a Jesuit holds the same?" (*False Fictions*, 1684, p. 8).

7 FGM, pp. 39, 141 quoted. FJN, p. 34. Lawson, *Untaught Teacher*, 1655, p. 14, 1 John 2:20. William Penn, *The Counterfeit Christian*, 1674, p. 97. Burrough, *Something In Answer to a Booke, Called a Voice*, 1654, p. 19.

8 Enoch Howet, *Quaking Principles Dashed*, 1655, p. 3. Thomas Collier, *A Looking-glass for the Quakers*, 1657, p. 13. John Griffith, *A Voice from the Word of the Lord*, 1654, p. 14, Ps. 119: 97. John Griffith (1622?–1700), who founded the Baptist congregation in Dunning's Alley in London about 1646, spent some fourteen years in prison after the Restoration for refusing to take the oath of allegiance (*DNB*). Griffith, *Voice from the Word of the Lord*, 1654, p. 13.

9 Burnet, *Capital Principles*, 1668, p. 21, John 19:28–29, Matt. 4:4–10. Griffith, *Voice from the Word of the Lord*, 1654, p. 13, John 5:39. To a similar claim by Tombes, Fisher pointed out that ἐρευνᾶτε might be rendered either indicatively or imperatively and that "Its most evident that he speaks there by way of complaint of the Scribes, for looking for life in the Scriptures, without coming to him who is the Light, ver. 40. [John 5:40] and not by way of command to search them, ye search, not search ye [the Scriptures]." (*Rusticus ad Academicos*, 1660, pt. 4, p. 179). Howet, *Quaking Principles Dashed*, 1655, p. 3, Matt. 4:4–10.

10 Henry Haggar, *Certain Considerations*, 1655, p. 52, John 12:49–50 and 15:15; 1 John 1:3. Griffith, *Voice from the Word of the Lord*, 1654, p. 14, John 10:4–5. Keach, *Progress of Sin*, 1684, p. 246, John 12:48.

11 Burrough, *Something in Answer to a Booke, Called a Voice*, 1654, p. 20, John 5:22. Nayler, *The Light of Christ*, 1656, p. 14, John 8:47. Burrough, *Something in Answer to a Booke, Called a Voice*, 1654, p. 20.

12 Penn, *Reason Against Railing*, 1673, p. 13. Fox to Friends and Baptists, 1653, LF: Swarthmore MSS 2/58. Lawson, *Untaught Teacher*, 1655, p. 6 (misprinted 9). Fisher, *Rusticus ad Academicos*, 1660, pt. 4, p. 109. Penn, *Reason Against Railing*, 1673, pp. 119–20.

13 Whitehead, *Christian-Quaker*, 1673, p. 40. George Whitehead, *The Light and Life of Christ Within*, 1668, p. 36.

14 GCP, pt. 4, p. 50. Collier, *Looking-glass*, 1657, p. 15. GCP, pt. 4, p. 49.

15 Thomas Hicks, *A Dialogue*, 1673, p. 17. Howet, *Quaking Principles Dashed*, 1655, p. 3.

16 Collier, *Looking-Glasse for the Quakers*, 1657, p. 7. Baxter thought the same: *Reliquiae Baxterianae*, 1696, pt. 1, p. 77. Jacob Bauthumley, *The Light and Dark Sides of God*, 1650, pp. 71–84, p. 77 quoted. See also Joseph Salmon, *Heights in Depths and Depths in Heights*, 1651, pp. 44–46; Laurence Clarkson, *The Lost Sheep Found*, 1660, p. 44. Richard Baxter, *A Key for Catholicks*, 1659, pp. 333–34; William Walwyn, *A Whisper in the Eare of Mr. Thomas Edwards*, 1645, sig. B2r.

17 John Reeve, *A Transcendent Spiritual Treatise*, 1652, p. 5. Lodowick Muggleton, *The Prophet Muggleton's Epistle*, 1672, p. 11. Lodowick Muggleton, *The Neck of the Quakers Broken*, 1663, pp. 57, 70. John Reeve and Lodowick Muggleton, *Verae Fidei Gloria est Corona Vitae. A Volume of Spiritual Epistles*, ed. Alexander Delamaine and Tobias Terry, 1820, p. 5. Lodowick Muggleton, *The Acts of the Witnesses*, 1699, p. 151 quoted. William Penn, *The New Witnesses Proved Old Hereticks*, 1672, sig. A3r. Lodowick Muggleton, *The Answer to William Penn*, 1673, title-page. Lodowick Muggleton, *An Answer to Isaac Penington*, 1669, p. 20. John Reeve and Lodowick Muggleton, *The Baptist's Commission Counterfeited*, p. 1, printed in Reeve and Muggleton, *Joyful News from Heaven*, 1706 (separate pagination).

18 Whitehead, *The Quakers Plainness*, 1674, p. 70. Fisher, *Rusticus ad Academicos*, 1660, pt. 4, pp. 177 quoted, 190. The issue of the mediate revelation of God through other persons is explored in relation to the ministry in chapter 6. The inwardness of immediate inspiration is discussed in chapter 7. Francis Howgill, *The Inheritance of Jacob Discovered*, 1656, p. 8. Howgill was referring to a period in his life that preceded his joining the Baptists.

19 Edward Burrough, *Something In Answer to a Book, Called Choice Experiences*, 1654, pp. 5–7. See also George Fox, "Answer to them that say the Quakers deny the scriptures," 1654, LF: Swarthmore MSS 7/76; George Fox, "Concerning Crosses," n.d., LF: Swarthmore MSS 7/87; Francis Howgill, "Queries to you Gathered Assemblies," n.d., LF: Swarthmore MSS 7/239. Penn, *Reason Against Railing*, 1673, p. 17. Burrough, *Something In Answer to a Book, Called Choice Experiences*, 1654, p. 7.

20 William Kaye, *A Plain Answer*, 1654, pp. 2, 4 quoted. Kaye, a Cambridge graduate, became curate and afterward rector of Stokesley, Yorkshire, and later served as minister of a Baptist congregation in Stokesley after being baptized in 1653 by Thomas Tillam, minister of the Baptist church in Hexham. In 1660 he was removed from his living. See Stephen Copson, "Advocate of the Reformed Protestant Religion: The Writings (1645–59) of William Kaye, Yorkshire Puritan," *BQ* 35 (1994): 279–93; A. G. Matthews, *Calamy Revised* (Oxford: Oxford University Press, 1988); *UFR*, pp. 292–93, 338–39. For Tillam, see UHB, p. 92 and *BDBR*. GCP, pt. 4, p. 48.

21 GCP, pt. 4, p. 49. Thomas Hicks, *A Continuation of the Dialogue*, 1673, sig. A4r.

22 Burrough, *Something in Answer to a Booke, Called a Voice*, 1654, p. 28. Penn, *Reason Against Railing*, 1673, p. 46. See also George Keith, *George Keith's Vindication*, 1674, p. 22. Howet, *Quaking Principles Dashed*, 1655, p. 2. See also General Baptist confession: 1679, article 27, MBC, p. 152; Particular Baptist confession: 1677, chapter 1, section 6, MBC, p. 229. Penn, *Counterfeit Christian*, 1674, p. 79. Whitehead, *Christian-Quaker*, 1673, p. 141. William Shewen, *The Universality of the Light*, 1674, p. 10. George Whitehead, *Christ Ascended*, 1669, p. 22. *FGM*, pp. 95, 206.

23 Edward Burrough, *The Son of Perdition*, 1661, p. 58. James Nayler, *The Boaster Bared*, 1655, pp. 2–3. Richard Farnworth, *The Holy Scriptures*, 1655, pp. 49, 53, James 1:21. As a result of this dispute Farnworth wrote *Truth Cleared*, 1654, to which Henry Haggar replied with *Certain Considerations*, 1655; this was answered in Farnworth's *Holy Scriptures*, 1655. Burrough, *Son of Perdition*, 1661, pp. 58–59, John 1. FGM, p. 110. Lawson, *Untaught Teacher*, 1655, p. 7. The Caffyn-Lawson dispute resulted in the writing of Lawson's *Untaught Teacher*,

1655, which evoked Caffyn's *The Deceived, and Deceiving Quakers*, 1656. Caffyn's work prompted responses from Nayler, *Light of Christ*, 1656, and in FGM. For Lawson, a Cambridge graduate and botanist, see E. Jean Whittaker, *Thomas Lawson 1630–1691: North Country Botanist, Quaker, and Schoolmaster* (York: Sessions Book Trust, 1986). Caffyn, expelled from Oxford for his Baptist views, became minister of a Baptist congregation in Horsham but had the correctness of his views on Christology and the Trinity questioned by other Baptists late in the century. See *BDBR* and London, Dean Street Church Book, Angus Collection MSS 36. G.A. f. 14, p. 1, Regent's Park College, Oxford.

24 Jeremiah Ives, *The Quakers Quaking*, 1656, pp. 33–34. Hicks, *Dialogue*, p. 18. Ives, *Quakers Quaking*, 1656, p. 6, Mark 7:13. GCP, pt. 4, p. 46. Joseph Wright, *A Testimony*, 1661, pp. 206–7. Wright (1623–1703?) signed the General Baptist confession of 1660 and with Grantham presented it to Charles II. Shortly thereafter he was reportedly imprisoned for twenty years. Toward the end of the century he was instrumental in bringing into question the orthodoxy of Matthew Caffyn (Joseph Ivimey, *A History of the English Baptists*, 4 vols. [1811–30], 2: 237–41, 265).

25 FGM, p. 111. Nayler, *Light of Christ*, 1656, p. 10. Whitehead, *Quakers Plainness*, 1674, pp. 71–72.

26 Lawson, *Untaught Teacher*, 1655, p. 3. See also FGM, p. 207; Nayler, *Weakness Above Wickedness*, 1656, pp. 4, 13; Nayler, *Light of Christ*, 1656, p. 13.

27 Burnet, *Capital Principles*, 1668, p. 20. Enoch Howet, *The Beast That Was*, 1659, p. 17. Thomas Hicks, *The Quakers Appeal Answer'd*, 1674, p. 26. Little is known about Burnet. William Sewel described him and Ives as "eminent Baptist teachers" (*The History of the Rise, Increase and Progress of the Christian People Called Quakers*, 1722, p. 478). Whitehead (*Light and Life of Christ Within*, 1668, p. 62) told of disputes with him and Ives at Chertsey and at Horne, near Horley, in Surrey on 16 and 17 June 1668, and accused him (p. 3) and Caffyn of being chiefly concerned in the Baptists' "publick reproaching and scandalizing the Truth professed by us called Quakers, both in words, preaching and print." In 1669, Horne was reported as the location of monthly conventicles held by Baptists, of whom Matthew Caffyn was the "chief seducer" (Turner, *Original Records*, 1: 145). Burnet received a license as a teacher of a Baptist congregation in Chertsey in 1672 (Turner, *Original Records*, 1: 323, 471, 2: 1017). The first three Quaker books referred to by title at the Barbican debate were by George Whitehead, George Fox the Younger, and James Parnell, respectively (Wing: W 1972, F 1995, P 533); the fourth has not been identified; the last was by Richard Farnworth (Wing: F 490). The fourth work was omitted from this list in Whitehead's response (*Quakers Plainness*, 1674, p. 71), perhaps indicating that it was mistakenly identified by Hicks as a Quaker publication.

28 Hicks, *Dialogue*, 1673, p. 41. Haggar, *Certain Considerations*, p. 1655, p. 50. Haggar is supposed to have baptized Colonel Henry Danvers, military governor at Stafford and later a noted plotter against the government. Haggar debated infant baptism at Ellesmere with Thomas Porter of Whitchurch, and may have been involved in the previously mentioned dispute with the Quakers at Harlaston. See Ivimey, *History of the English Baptists*, 2: 560, 608; A. G. Matthews, *The Congregational Churches of Staffordshire*, 1924, pp. 34–35; Matthews, *Calamy Revised*, entry for "Thomas Porter"; Henry Denne, *A Contention for Truth*, 1658, sig. A3r; *BDBR*.

29 William Shewen, *The Universality of the Light*, 1674, p. 12. Shewen

(1631?–1695), of Southwark, lived also for some time in Enfield, Middlesex. He was present at a dispute between Ives and Whitehead in the market place of Croydon, Surrey, on 24 April 1674, which prompted him to write this tract. Dennis Hollister, *The Harlots Vail Removed*, 1658, p. 37.

30 Ames, *Declaration*, 1656, p. 6. Shewen, *Universality of the Light*, 1674, pp. 11–12. James Nayler, *Deceit Brought to Day-light*, 1656, p. 10. Nayler's work replied to Thomas Collier, *A Dialogue Between a Minister of the Gospel, and an Enquiring Christian* (1656?), not extant.

31 Burnet, *Capital Principles*, 1668, p. 20. GCP, pt. 4, p. 48. As is shown in chapter 4, such external facts of history were of less importance soteriologically to Quakers than to Baptists. Keach, *Progress of Sin*, 1684, p. 248. Russel, *Quakerism is Paganism*, 1674, p. 16. Russel (d. 1702) Cambridge M.D. and General Baptist minister at High Hall, West Smithfield, was an active controversialist, engaging in disputes on infant baptism, the seventh day sabbath, and congregational singing (*BDBR*). Hicks, *Dialogue*, 1673, p. 25. Penn, *Christian-Quaker*, 1674, pp. 151–52. Shewen made a similar claim in *Universality of the Light*, 1674, p. 13. Penn, *Counterfeit Christian*, 1674, p. 36. Humphrey Wolrich, *One Warning More*, 1661, p. 8. Burrough, *Son of Perdition*, 1661, pp. 60, 65.

32 Jeremiah Ives, *Innocency Above Impudency*, 1656, p. 53. Collier, *Looking-glass for the Quakers*, 1657, p. 15. GCP, pt. 4, p. 50. Howet, *Quaking Principles Dashed*, 1655, pp. 4–5. Burnet, *Capital Principles*, 1658, sigs. B1r–B1v (faulty pagination).

33 Whitehead, *Christian-Quaker*, 1673, p. 40. Hicks, *Dialogue*, 1673, p. 17. Wright, *Testimony*, 1661, p. 225 (misprinted 125). Thomas Salthouse, *The Line of True Judgment*, 1658, p. 12. Salthouse (1630–91), employed by Judge Fell as a land steward at Swarthmoor Hall, was converted when Fox visited there in 1652, and later, as an evangelist in the West Country, became known as "the Apostle to the West" (*DNB*; BBQ, p. 203). Whitehead, *Christian-Quaker*, 1673, p. 49. Penn, *Reason Against Railing*, 1673, pp. 45–46. FJN, p. 295. FGM, p. 14, 2 Tim. 3:16–17. Griffith, *Voice from the Word of the Lord*, 1654, p. 3, 2 Tim. 3:15. See also James L. Ash, Jr., "'Oh no, it is not the Scriptures!' The Bible and the Spirit in George Fox," *QH* 63 (1974): 94–107.

34 Penn, *Reason Against Railing*, 1673, p. 36. Fisher, *Rusticus ad Academicos*, 1660, pt. 4, p. 188. Penn, *Reason Against Railing*, 1673, p. 28. Burrough, *Something in Answer to a Booke, Called a Voice*, 1654, pp. 30–31. Whitehead, *Christian-Quaker*, 1673, p. 55.

35 GCP, pt. 4, p. 50. Burrough, *Something in Answer to a Booke, Called a Voice*, 1654, p. 28. Nayler, *Boaster Bared*, 1655, p. 3.

36 Plant, *Contest for Christianity*, 1674, pp. 70–73. William Mead, *A Brief Narrative*, 1674, pp. 9, 70.

37 FGM, p. 95.

38 Alexander Parker to Margaret Fell, 5 June 1655 (?), LF: Caton MSS 3/93.

Chapter 3

1 William Jeffery, *Antichrist Made Known*, 1656, p. 69 (the emphasis is mine). Thomason's date is "Aprill 3." See also the entry for this work in British Museum, *Catalogue of the Pamphlets . . . Collected by George Thomason*, 2 vols. (Trustees of the British Museum, 1908), 2:144, and the explanation of Thomason's dating,

1:xxii. For discussion of "celestial inhabitation" see Richard Bailey, *New Light on George Fox and Early Quakerism* (Lewiston, N.Y.: Edwin Mellen Press, 1993). Although *HSPFE* set Quakerism firmly in an English Puritan and Nonconformist context (chapter 1), the possibility of some mystical/spiritualist influence, both Continental and English (e.g., Jacob Boehme, John Everard) should not be dismissed; see Donald F. Durnbaugh, "Baptists and Quakers—Left Wing Puritans?" *QH* 62 (1973): 67–82; Melvin B. Endy, Jr., "The Interpretation of Quakerism: Rufus Jones and His Critics," *QH* 70 (1981): 3–21; H. Larry Ingle, "From Mysticism to Radicalism: Recent Historiography of Quaker Beginnings," *QH* 76 (1987): 79–94.

2 William G. Bittle, *James Nayler 1618–1660, The Quaker Indicted by Parliament* (York: Sessions Book Trust, 1986), pp. 103–4.

3 Luke Howard, *The Seat of the Scorner Thrown Down*, 1673, p. 5. William Britten, *Silent Meeting, A Wonder to the World*, 1660, p. 2. See also chapter 5.

4 John Beevan, *A Loving Salutation*, 1660, p. 2. See also, Joseph Smith, *A Descriptive Catalogue of Friends' Books*, 2 vols. (Joseph Smith, 1867), 1:231. Frances Howgill, *The Inheritance of Jacob Discovered*, 1656, pp. 6, 9. FJN, p. 12. Beevan, of Leominster, Herefordshire, claimed to have left the "Puretans" to become a Baptist before joining with Quakers (pp. 2–3).

5 Howgill, *Inheritance of Jacob Discovered*, 1656, p. 9. Humphey Wolrich, *A Declaration*, 1659, p. 12.

6 Alexander Parker, *A Discovery of Satans Wiles*, 1657, p. 22. Parker (1628–89) joined with Fox in 1654 and often accompanied him on his journeys (*DNB*). Parker also wrote a short tract entitled *To All Ye Who Be Called Baptists*, 1657. John Salthouse, *The Line of True Judgment*, 1658, p. 14.

7 Dennis Hollister, *The Harlots Vail Removed*. 1658, p. 36. George Whitehead, *The Pernicious Way*, 1662, p. 30. FGM, p. 207. Jacob Bauthumley, *The Light and Dark Sides of God*, 1650, p. 4.

8 Thomas Collier, *A Looking-Glasse for the Quakers*, 1657, p. 7. Salmon, *A Rout, A Rout*, 1649, p.4; *Heights in Depths and Depths in Heights*, 1651, p. 37. Bauthumley, *Light and Dark Sides of God*, 1650, pp. 69–70, 4 quoted. John Taylor, *Ranters of Both Sexes*, 1651, p. 2. Collier, *Looking-Glasse for the Quakers*, 1657, p. 7. Richard Baxter, *A Key for Catholicks*, 1659, p. 333. John Saltmarsh, *Sparkles of Glory*, 1647, pp. 90, 255, 295. John Jackson, *A Sober Word*, 1651, pp. 44–46. William Erbery, *The Testimony*, 1658, pp. 8, 127. John Reeve, *A Transcendent Spiritual Treatise*, 1652, p. 23 quoted. Lodowick Muggleton, *An Answer to Isaac Penington*, 1669, p. 16; *A Discourse Between John Reeve and Richard Leader*, 1682, p. 7. Thomas Tompkinson, "Autobiographical Works," British Library: Additional Manuscript 42505, fols. 16r, 17v. William Penn, *The New Witnesses*, 1672, pp. 24, 38–39, 41 quoted. See also Lodowick Muggleton, *A Looking-Glass for George Fox*, 1668, p. 24; *The Neck of the Quakers Broken*, 1663, p. 55. It should also be noted that both Ranters and Muggletonians objected to the doctrine of the Trinity (Bauthumley, *Light and Dark Sides of God*, 1650, pp. 10–12; John Reeve and Lodowick Muggleton, *A Divine Looking-Glass*, 1661, pp. 36, 80–84).

9 William Penn, *The Counterfeit Christian*, 1674, p. 76 (misprinted 67), John 14:20. Thomas Lawson, *An Untaught Teacher*, 1655, p. 11, Gal. 2:20. FGM, p. 9, Col. 1:27. At the end of this work, pp. 373–75, Fox included a section listing several biblical passages, allegedly corrupted by the translators, in which fourteen of the twenty-seven "corrections" involved the translation of ἐν as "in" rather than "among," "with," and the like. Richard Farnworth, *The Holy Scriptures*,

1655, p. 55, Gal. 4:6. Edward Burrough, *The True Faith of the Gospel of Peace Contended For*, 1656, p. 25, 2 Cor. 13:5.

10 George Whitehead, *Christ Ascended*, 1669, pp 24–25, Deut. 30:14, Rom. 10. Burrough, *True Faith*, 1656, p. 22, Rom. 10:6–11. FGM, p. 8, James 1:21.

11 FGM, p. 142. Edward Burrough, *The Son of Perdition*, 1661, p. 11, 2 Cor. 6:16. Whitehead, *The Light and Life of Christ Within*, 1668, p. 12, 2 Cor. 4:6. Lawson, *Untaught Teacher*, 1655, p. 19. The issue of the distinctiveness of the Godhead's members is dealt with in the discussion of the Trinity.

12 George Whitehead, *The Christian-Quaker*, 1673, pp. 160–61. Edward Burrough, *Something in Answer to a Book, Called Choice Experiences*, 1654, p. 6 (misprinted 9). Farnworth, *Holy Scriptures*, 1655, p. 57.

13 Westminster Confession, chapter 14, section 1; chapter 13, section 1; chapter 16, section 3. Savoy Declaration, chapter 14, section 1; chapter 13, section 1; chapter 16, section 1. See also, for example, Richard Baxter, *The Catechizing of Families*, 1683, p. 179.

14 Particular Baptist confessions: 1644, article 19, MBC, pp. 179–180; 1656, article 18, p. 207; 1677, chapter 13, section 1, chapter 14, section 1, chapter 16, section 3, p. 247, 250. General Baptist confession: 1679, article 26, 29, p. 143, 145. William Russel, *Quakerism Is Paganism*, 1678, p. 8, Eph. 3:16–17. John Wigan, *Antichrist's Strongest Hold Overturned*, 1665, p. 41.

15 Matthew Caffyn, *Faith In Gods Promises*, 1661, p. 45. Jeffery, *Antichrist Made Known*, 1656, p. 69. Jeffery (b. 1616?) was a messenger of the General Baptist churches in Kent and a signatory of the 1660 General Baptist Confession (Joseph Ivimey, *A History of the English Baptists*, 4 vols. [1811–30], 2:222–24; Whitley, W. T., ed., *The Minutes of the General Assembly of the General Baptist Churches in England*, 2 vols. [Kingsgate Press, 1909–1910], 1:xxxviii).

16 Frances Howgill and Edward Burrough to Margaret Fell [December 1654?], LF: Caton MSS 3/75. Jeffery, *Antichrist Made Known*, 1656, p. 69. James Nayler, *Weakness Above Wickedness*, 1656, p. 12. Nayler's tract was apparently published after 22 June and before 19 July (see p. 25; British Museum, *Catalogue of the Pamphlets*, 2:155; Thomason's date is 18 July). See also BBQ, pp. 252–53, 255, 269. For a brief examination of this episode in the light of Nayler's alleged Familist tendencies, see Geoffrey F. Nuttall, *James Nayler: A Fresh Approach*, JFHS Supplement 26 (1954). The Quaker Dennis Hollister claimed to have been an Independent (Dennis Hollister, *The Skirts of the Whore Discovered*, 1656, p. 16) not a Baptist (Craig Horle, "Quakers and Baptists 1647–1660," BQ 26 [1976], 344–62, at p. 347) member of the Broadmead church. Thomas Hicks, *The Quaker Condemned*, 1674, p. 28.

17 William Burnet, *The Capital Principles*, 1668, p. 13. Thomas Ewins, *The Church of Christ*, 1657, p. 19. John Bunyan, *A Vindication of the Book Called, some Gospel Truths Opened*, in 1657, MW, 1:142, 124.

18 Bunyan, *Vindication*, 1657, in MW 1:153–54. Collier, *Looking-Glasse for the Quakers*, 1657, p. 9. Burnet, *Capital Principles*, 1668, p. 27.

19 Thomas Hicks, *A Dialogue*, 1673, p. 46.

20 Penn, *Counterfeit Christian*, 1674, p. 78.

21 Edward Burrough, *Truth (the Strongest of All) Witnessed Forth*, 1657, p. 8 quoted. Burrough, *Something in Answer to a Book, Called Choice Experiences*, 1654, p. 6. Penn, *Reason Against Railing*, 1673, p. 145 (misprinted 129).

22 Penn, *Counterfeit Christian*, 1674, p. 80. Whitehead, *Christian-Quaker*,

1673, p. 115. Burrough, *Something in Answer to a Book, Called Choice Experiences*, 1654, p. 6. FGM, p. 206. For "in measure" see Joseph Pickvance, *A Reader's Companion to George Fox's Journal* (Quaker Home Service, 1989), pp. 95–96.

23 Joseph Wright, *A Testimony*, 1661, p. 32.

24 Westminster Confession, chapter 8, section 2; Savoy Declaration, chapter 8, section 2. General Baptist Confessions: 1651, MBC, pp. 95–109; 1660, pp. 111–22; 1679, articles 4–6, pp. 126–28. Particular Baptist confessions: 1644, article 9, pp. 176–77; 1656, articles 12–14, p. 205 (article 13 refers to Christ as "truly God . . . and truly man"); 1677, chapter 7, sections 2, 3, pp. 239–40. However, some Baptists were satisfied neither with such affirmations nor with the Chalcedonian formula. The most notable was Matthew Caffyn, who later in the century was accused of holding to a Hoffmanite Christology. The two publications by him used in this book, however, do not betray such a tendency.

25 George Whitehead, *The Dipper Plung'd*, 1672, p. 13. In reply to a similar objection, Russel claimed that the term "person" as applied to Christ was, in fact, scriptural, for Pilate in Matt. 27:24 and Paul in 2 Cor. 2:10 had used it in this way (*Quakerism Is Paganism*, 1674, p. 18). FGM, p. 208. Whitehead, *Christian-Quaker*, 1673, p. 97. Humphrey Wolrich, *One Warning More*, 1661, p. 6. William Penn, *Reason Against Railing*, 1673, p. 20. Whitehead, *Christian-Quaker*, 1673, p. 97.

26 Penn, *Reason Against Railing*, 1673, p. 55. Wolrich, *One Warning More*, 1661, p. 10. Penn, *Reason Against Railing*, 1673, pp. 21–22. George Fox's reference to "Jesus Christ without, that dyed at Jerusalem" is exceptional (FGM, p. 206). Penn accused Hicks of Socinianism for believing that the entire Christ died (*Reason Against Railing*, 1673, p. 59). For Baptists and Socinian thought in this period, see Herbert John McLachlan, *Socinianism in Seventeenth-Century England* (Oxford: Oxford University Press, 1951), pp. 120, 218–24; UHB, pp. 126–128. George Whitehead, *An Appendix*, 1673, p. 22. Whitehead, *Christian-Quaker*, 1673, p. 141. Although Whitehead could speak of a hypostatic union, he meant by it the unity of the substance of the Father, Word, and Holy Spirit (p. 141). Burrough, *Son of Perdition*, 1661, p. 8. Wolrich, *One Warning More*, 1661, p. 21.

27 Burnet, *Capital Principles*, 1668, p. 6. GCP, pt. 4, pp. 60–61. For John Whitehead, see *DNB*.

28 Hicks, *Quaker Condemned*, 1674, p. 27, John 19:38. GCP, pt. 4, p. 58, Matt. 2:1, 4. Matthew Caffyn, *The Deceived, and Deceiving Quakers*, 1656, p. 38. GCP, pt. 4, pp. 53–54, John 1:28–40. Caffyn, *Faith in Gods Promises*, 1661, p. 40, Luke 4:20, 28, 29. Wright, *Testimony*, 1661, p. 117, Gen. 2:7, Gal. 4:4. Russel, *Quakerism Is Paganism*, 1674, p. 19.

29 John Bunyan, *Some Gospel-truths Opened*, 1656, in MW, 1:67–68. Russel, *Quakerism Is Paganism*, 1674, pp. 86–89. Howet, *Quaking Principles Dashed*, 1655, p. 9. Collier, *Looking-Glasse for the Quakers*, 1657, p. 10. GCP, pt. 4, p. 58.

30 Russel, *Quakerism Is Paganism*, 1674, p. 26. Hicks, *Quaker Condemned*, 1674, p. 28. No letter from Coale to Fox containing this passage has been found among the collections of early Quaker letters housed at LF, nor does one appear in Henry Cadbury, *Swarthmore Documents in America, JFHS* Supplement 20 (1940).

31 Josiah Coale to George Fox, 12 January 1665, LF: Barclay MSS 1/64. For a discussion of messianic language in early Quakerism, see *HSPFE*, p. 181–84. For Coale, see Geoffrey F. Nuttall, "Early Quaker Letters from the Swarthmore MSS to 1660" (typescript, 1952), p. 56, LF.

32 George Bishop to Margaret Fell, 27 October 1656, LF: Swarthmore MSS 1/188 quoted. See also Bittle, *James Nayler 1618–1660*, pp. 104–6.

33 Whitehead, *Appendix*, 1673, p. 44. Whitehead, *Pernicious Way*, 1662, p. 27. Wolrich, *Declaration*, 1659, p. 13. Whitehead, *Christian-Quaker*, 1673, p. 95. Whitehead, *The Babylonish Baptist*, 1672, p. 5.

34 Burrough, *Son of Perdition*, 1661, p. 9. Whitehead, *Christian-Quaker*, 1673, p. 96, John 3:31, 6:50–51, 53. Nayler, *Boaster Bared*, 1655, p. 6, reference probably to John 3:13 or Eph. 4:10. Burrough, *Son of Perdition*,1661, p. 10, Eph. 5:30 (wrongly given as 5:13). Salthouse, *Line of True Judgment*, 1658, p. 9, 2 Cor. 4:7. Hugh Barbour concludes that if early Quakers were not Apollinarian or Euty-chean, they perhaps verged on being Nestorian (BQPE, p. 146 n. 62). See also Maurice Creasey, "Early Quaker Christology with Special Reference to the Teach-ing of Isaac Penington" (Ph.D. thesis, University of Leeds, 1956), LF.

35 Whitehead, *The Light and Life of Christ Within*, 1668, pp. 50–51. Penn, *Christian-Quaker*, 1673, p. 103. Whitehead, *Light and Life of Christ Within*, 1668, p. 53. Penn, *Reason Against Railing*, 1673, p. 54.

36 Hicks, *A Continuation of the Dialogue*, 1673, p. 48. Jeffery, *Antichrist Made Known*, 1656, p. 58. Burnet, *Capital Principles*, 1668, p. 37, Luke 2:21 and Matt. 3:16–17. *Ibid.*, p. 37, Luke 2:10–11 (erroneously printed Luke 20), Acts 5:30–31. Caffyn, *Faith in Gods Promises*, 1661, p. 40, Luke 24:37–39. GCP, pt. 4, p. 58. Wigan, *Antichrist's Strongest Hold Overturned*, 1665, p. 45. Burnet, *Capital Principles*, 1668, p. 34.

37 Wright, *Testimony*, 1661, p. 100. GCP, pt. 4, p. 54, John 6. Russel, *Quakerism Is Paganism*, 1678, p. 20. Burnet, *Capital Principles*, 1668, p. 35.

38 William Mead, *A Brief Account*, 1674, p. 29. Hicks, *Dialogue*, 1673, p. 44. Crisp admitted making this statement, in Whitehead, *Christian-Quaker*, 1673, pp. 70–71. Stephen Crisp (1628–92) joined with Baptists in 1648, was converted to Quakerism in 1655 by Parnell in Colchester prison, and was active in Quaker ef-forts in the Netherlands and the German states (*BDBR*).

39 Russel, *Quakerism Is Paganism*, 1674, pp. 78, 86. Wigan, *Antichrist's Strongest Hold Overturned*, 1665, pp. 42–45, 45 quoted.

40 See, for example, Bunyan, *Some Gospel-truths Opened*, 1656, in MW, 1:47–49. Russel, *Quakerism Is Paganism*, 1674, p. 75. Bunyan, *Some Gospel-truths Opened*, 1656, in MW, 1:30–31, Rev. 13:8.

41 Whitehead, *Christian-Quaker*, 1673, p. 38 quoted, John 8:58. White-head, *Christ Ascended*, 1669, p. 13, Col. 1, Dan. 3:25 (Nebuchadnezzar). This in-terpretation of the episode in Daniel was widely held; see, for example, Thomas Goodwin, *Of the Knowledge of God the Father, and His Son Jesus Christ* (n.d.), vol. 2 of *The Works of Thomas Goodwin*, 5 vols. (1681–1704), p. 67. Wolrich, *One Warning More*, 1661, p. 35, John 8:56. Burrough, *True Faith*, 1656, pp. 13–14, John 17:5, 1 Cor. 10:1–4.

42 Westminster Confession, chapter 2, section 3; Savoy Declaration, chapter 2, section 3. See Goodwin, *Of the Knowledge of God the Father, and His Son Jesus Christ*, p. 1. Thomas Gouge, *The Principles of Christian Religion*, 1675, p. 2; Bax-ter, *Catechizing of Families*, 1683, p. 84. John Owen, *A Brief Declaration and Vindication of the Doctrine of the Trinity*, 1669, pp. 113–15.

43 General Baptist confessions: 1651, article 20, MBC, p. 99; 1660, article 7, p. 114; 1679, article 3, p. 126. Particular Baptist confessions: 1644, article 2, pp. 174–75; 1656, pp. 202–15; 1677, chapter 2, section 3, p. 232. When the doc-

trine was mentioned, usually only simple scriptural phrases were used, most frequently 1 John 5:7: "For there are three that bear record in heaven, the Father, the Word, and the Holy Ghost: and these three are one." Benjamin Evans, *The Early English Baptists*, 2 vols. (J. Heaton and Son, 1862–64), 2:37–40. Edward Drapes, *Gospel-glory Proclaimed*, 1649, p. 21. For Drapes, see W. T. Whitley, *A Baptist Bibliography*, index, s.v. "Drapes, Edward." Thomas Collier, *The Body of Divinity*, 1674, p. 43. GCP, pt. 1, p. 40. In opposition to Presbyterians and Independents, the following accusation of Fox against Owen is typical: "Where doth the Apostle tell us of three persons, but tels us of Father, Son and holy Ghost; but thou, out of the Masse-book, and old Common-prayer-book, who are the mutterers about three persons" (FGM, p. 26). GCP, pt. 1, p. 43. Caffyn, *Faith in Gods Promises*, 1661, p. 40, John 14:16–17.

    44 Collier, *Looking-Glasse for the Quakers*, 1657, p. 8. Wright, *Testimony*, 1661, p. 146. Henry Grigg, *The Baptist Not Babylonish*, 1672, p. 7. The first Quakers to reach America landed in Barbados late in 1655 on their way to New England. In November of the following year, Henry Fell wrote from Barbados to Margaret Fell that some Baptists had been convinced (LF: Swarthmore MSS 1/66). On 21 October 1670, nearly a year before Fox was to arrive there, Grigg wrote a letter to his "own Natural Sister" in Barbados "in which I was moved to forwarn and caution you concerning the evil and Soul-undoing Principles of the People called Quakers, to whose pernicious Doctrine I had some doubts and jealousies you were ready too much to hearken and incline unto" (Henry Grigg, *Light From the Sun*, 1672, title-page, p. 3). Her reply, written the following year during Fox's visit to the island, led Grigg to conclude that "you are now exceedingly drove away by the stress of their Delusions, and have sucked in the Venom of their poysonous Doctrine, which is no small grief and trouble to my Spirit" (*ibid.*, pp. 3–4). To point out to her the errors of these Quaker delusions, Grigg published *Light From the Sun*, 1672, to which Whitehead replied with *Babylonish Baptist*, 1672, and *Dipper Plung'd*, 1672. Grigg answered Whitehead's first reply with *Baptist Not Babylonish*, 1672, to which Whitehead responded in his *Christian-Quaker*, 1673. But there is apparently no Quaker record of Grigg's sister. Henry Grigg, about whom little is known, is included by Thomas Crosby in a list of some twenty men "who probably bore a testimony to Christ, by suffering for his sake" (*The History of the English Baptists*, 4 vols. [1738–40], 4:251–52). He was a signatory of the broadsheet *A Declaration of Several Baptized Believers* (1659), supporting full and equal liberty as well as magistracy, but declaring against the national ministry (Congregational Library, London: MSS Portfolio 2 a 39). For Fox's visit to Barbados, see H. Larry Ingle, *First Among Friends: George Fox and the Creation of Quakerism* (New York: Oxford University Press, 1994), pp. 231–35.

    45 Edward Burrough, *The Walls of Jerico Razed*, 1654, p. 3. Whitehead, *Christian-Quaker*, 1673, p. 128, John 14:18. Wolrich, *One Warning More*, 1661, p. 22. Whitehead, *Christian-Quaker*, 1673, p. 128.

    46 FGM, p. 142. Burrough, *Truth*, 1657, p. 32, Isa. 9:6. Lawson, *Untaught Teacher*, 1655, p. 16, John 10:30. Wolrich, *One Warning More*, 1661, p. 23, John 14:8–12. (erroneously printed 8:14). Whitehead, *Christ Ascended*, 1669, p. 15, Isa. 45. Whitehead, *Christian-Quaker*, 1673, p. 107. Whitehead, *Christian-Quaker*, 1673, p. 128, 1 John 5:7.

    47 Burnet, *Capital Principles*, 1668, p. 25. Caffyn, *Deceived, and Deceiving Quakers*, 1656, p. 41. Grigg, *Light From the Sun*, 1672, p. 46, Luke 24:51. Bun-

yan, *Some Gospel-truths Opened*, 1656, in MW, 1:74–75, Acts 1:9–11. Bunyan, *Vindication*, 1657, in MW, 1:124, Rom. 8:34. Howet, *Quaking Principles Dashed*, 1655, p. 9, Acts 3:21.

48 Bunyan, *Some Gospel-truths Opened*, in MW, 1:46–47, Luke 24:39–40, 50–51. GCP, pt. 4, pp. 60, 63, 57.

49 Burrough, *Walls of Jerico Razed*, 1654, p. 6.

50 Wolrich, *One Warning More*, 1661, p. 11. John Pitman and Jasper Batt, *Truth Vindicated*, 1658, p. 55, Phil. 3:20. Pitman (d. 1659?) and Batt (d. 1702), both of Street in Somerset, were among the first converted in the county and became coworkers for the Quaker cause, but Pitman probably died not long after his conversion (*FPT*, pp. 222–23, 226–28). In their tract against Collier, they claimed to have "sometimes fed on Husks" among the Baptists (*Truth Vindicated*, 1658, title-page). FGM, p. 12, Eph. 2:6 and 5:30. Whitehead, *Appendix*, 1673, p. 21. Nayler, *Boaster Bared*, 1655, p. 6, reference probably to John 3:13 or Eph. 4:10. Thomas Plant, *A Contest for Christianity*, 1674, pp. 23, 25.

51 Burrough, *Son of Perdition*, 1661, p. 9, John 3:13. Lawson, *Untaught Teacher*, 1655, p. 18, John 17:5. Whitehead, *Christ Ascended*, 1669, p. 17. Even such a seemingly direct statement as "Christ arose with the same body that was Crucified" was not above suspicion, for Quakers could speak of Christ's crucifixion in spiritual terms, and of the resurrection and ascension of Christ's body, the Church. However, Whitehead's discussion in another work of the nature of that postresurrection and preascension body in its various appearances makes it seem at least possible that he believed in the resurrection of the earthly body, although in a transformed condition (*Light and Life of Christ Within*, 1668, p. 63). Burrough, *Son of Perdition*, 1661, p. 9. Whitehead, *Christ Ascended*, 1669, p. 19. Whitehead, *Christian-Quaker*, 1673, p. 149.

52 Whitehead, *Christian-Quaker*, 1673, p. 102. Writing against Fox, Muggleton declared that "God is a single person in the form of a man, a spiritual person, and no bigger in compass than a man, and he was so from eternity, even of the same stature as the first Adam was, therefore said to be made in the image and likeness of God. Also Christ is said to be the express image of his Fathers person" (*Looking-Glass for George Fox*, 1667, p. 41). He called Fox's claim that the saints were Christ's flesh and bone "his allegorical Juggle" (p. 22). Ewins, *Church of Christ*, 1657, p. 20. Whitehead, *Christ Ascended*, 1669, p. 20.

Chapter 4

1 For Child, Burton, Spencly, and Fenn, see T. L. Underwood, MW, introduction, 1:xxiv–xxvii.

2 Burrough, *Truth*, 1657, pp. 53–55. Burrough apparently had not had a direct encounter with Bunyan (p. 3). G. Lyon Turner, ed., *Original Records of Early Nonconformity Under Persecution and Indulgence*, 3 vols. (T. Fisher Unwin, 1911–14), 1:63–68. FJN, pp. 219, 226–27.

3 John Bunyan, *Some Gospel-truths Opened*, 1656, in *MW*, 1:114. John Bunyan, *Grace Abounding*, 5th ed. (1680), section 124, p. 39. The section may also have been added to the fourth edition, which is not extant. See T. L. Underwood, *MW*, introduction 1:xxi–xxxv; MW, 4:xxv–xxxvi. See also Richard L. Greaves, "John Bunyan: Tercentenary Reflections," in *John Bunyan: A Tercentenary*, ed. T. L. Underwood, *American Baptist Quarterly* 7 (1988): 496–508; T. L. Underwood, " 'It pleased me much to contend:' John Bunyan as Controversialist,"

Church History 57 (1988): 456–69. Bunyan's congregation in Bedford included Independents and Baptists, and today as "Bunyan meeting" still maintains ties with successors of both groups: the Baptist Union and the Congregational Federation.

4 Referring to the similarities among the numerous Quaker autobiographies, Luella M. Wright comments, "As an individual, recounting the events of his life, he [the typical Quaker autobiographer] stressed those that duplicated the experiences of others within the group; as spokesman for the Society, he subordinated personal episodes in his own life to those shared by the group" (*The Literary Life of the Early Friends, 1650–1725*, [New York: Columbia University Press, 1932], p. 11). For early Quaker autobiography, see Owen C. Watkins, *The Puritan Experience* (Routledge and Kegan Paul, 1972), pp. 160–81.

5 Luke Howard, *The Seat of the Scorner Thrown Down*, 1673, p. 5. William Britten, *Silent Meeting, A Wonder to the World*, 1660, p. 2. William Britten was a national minister and then a Baptist preacher before becoming a Friend (BBQ, p. 509). Britten, *Silent Meeting*, 1660, p. 2, Luke 15:16. William Bayly, *A Short Relation*, 1659, p. 3. Ames, *Declaration*, 1656, pp. 2, 4. John Beevan, *A Loving Salutation*, 1660, p. 6.

6 Francis Howgill, *The Inheritance of Jacob Discovered*, 1656, sigs. B3r–B3v (faulty pagination). Bayly, *Short Relation*, 1659, p. 7.

7 Bayly, *Short Relation*, 1659, p. 7; Ames, *Declaration*, 1656, p. 3. Howgill, *Inheritance of Jacob Discovered*, 1655, sig. B4r (faulty pagination). Ames, *Declaration*, 1656, p. 7.

8 Bunyan, *Some Gospel-truths Opened*, 1656, in *MW*, 1:17, 20, 45 quoted, Col. 1:22. William Burnet, *The Capital Principles*, 1668, p. 42. GCP, pt. 4, p. 52.

9 Westminster Confession, chapter 8, section 5, chapter 11, section 3; Savoy Declaration, chapter 8, sections 4, 5, chapter 11, section 3. Richard Baxter, however, took exception to this penal concept of satisfaction (*The Catechizing of Families*, 1683, p. 106).

10 General Baptist confessions: 1651, MBC, pp. 95–109; 1660, pp. 111–22; 1679, article 17, p. 136. Particular Baptist confessions: 1644, article 28, p. 182; 1656, article 15, p. 205; 1677, chapter 8, section 5, p. 241.

11 Burnet, *Capital Principles*, 1668, p. 35. Bunyan, *Some Gospel-truths Opened*, 1656, in *MW*, 1: p. 36. Thomas Hicks, *A Continuation of the Dialogue*, 1673, p. 24. William Russel, *Quakerism Is Paganism*, 1674, p. 34.

12 George Fox's brief statement that Christ "made Satisfaction" (FGM, p. 63) seems to be exceptional, although George Whitehead could speak of satisfaction in the sense of Christ's sacrifice being "a most satisfactory offering" (*The Christian-Quaker*, 1673, pp. 89–90). William Penn's *The Sandy Foundation Shaken*, 1668, in which he strongly attacked this doctrine, was acclaimed by some English Socinians; see Herbert John McLachlan, *Socinianism in Seventeenth-Century England* (Oxford: Oxford University Press, 1951), p. 306.

13 George Whitehead, *The Light and Life of Christ Within*, 1668, p. 51. William Penn, *Reason Against Railing*, 1673, p. 91.

14 Whitehead, *Light and Life of Christ Within*, 1668, p. 50. Penn, *Reason Against Railing*, 1673, pp. 145–46 (p. 145 is misprinted 129).

15 Whitehead, *Christian-Quaker*, 1673, p. 103; Edward Burrough, *The Son of Perdition*, 1661, p. 4; Penn, *Reason Against Railing*, 1673, p. 21; FGM, p. 63; Whitehead, *Christian-Quaker*, 1673, p. 117.

16 See, for example, Edward Burrough's reply to Bunyan, in *The True Faith of the Gospel of Peace Contended For*, 1656, pp. 26–27, and chapter 3 earlier.

17 Whitehead, *Christian-Quaker*, 1673, pp. 105, 103; William Penn, *The Christian-Quaker*, 1674, p. 105.

18 Penn, *Reason Against Railing*, 1673, p. 20. See also Isaac Penington, *The Flesh & Blood of Christ*, 1675, pp. 9–17.

19 Joseph Wright, *A Testimony*, 1661, pp. 1–2. On rare occasions Quakers were also accused of believing Christ to be only an exemplar (Hicks, *Continuation of the Dialogue*, 1673, p. 54). They replied that although Christ was a model, he was also more than just a pattern to be copied (Whitehead, *Christian-Quaker*, 1673, p. 103).

20 Bunyan, *Some Gospel-truths Opened*, 1656, in *MW*, 1:58, Heb. 13:12, Rom. 5:15, 1 Pet. 2:24.

21 George Whitehead, *Christ Ascended*, 1669, p. 22, Heb. 6:6, Rev. 11:8. William Penn, *The Counterfeit Christian*, 1674, p. 75.

22 Whitehead, *Christian-Quaker*, 1673, p. 103. Martin Mason, *Sions Enemy Discovered*, 1659, pp. 3–4. For Mason see *DNB*. Whitehead, *Light and Life of Christ Within*, 1668, p. 17. Penn, *Christian-Quaker*, 1674, pp. 102, 105. The reference is apparently to Rom. 5:5: "And hope maketh not ashamed; because the love of God is shed abroad in our hearts by the Holy Ghost which is given unto us."

23 Henry Grigg, *Light From the Sun*, 1672, pp. 51–52. John Wigan, *Antichrist's Strongest Hold Overturned*, 1665, sig. A1r (edition A, LF).

24 Henry Grigg, *The Baptist Not Babylonish*, 1672, pp. 7–8. Thomas Hicks, *A Dialogue*, 1673, p. 88.

25 Hicks, *Continuation of the Dialogue*, 1673, p. 4. Bunyan, *Vindication*, 1657, in *MW*, 1:123–24. Russel, *Quakerism Is Paganism*, 1674, p. 22. Grigg, *Light From the Sun*, 1672, p. 14. See also GCP, pt. 4, p. 54.

26 Thomas Salthouse, *The Line of True Judgment*, 1658, p. 11, Gal. 1:15–16, 1 John 3:8. Penn, *Reason Against Railing*, 1673, p. 64.

27 Whitehead, *Christian-Quaker*, 1673, p. 75. Penn, *Christian-Quaker*, 1674, p. 97. Penn, *Reason Against Railing*, 1673, p. 63 quoted. Penn draws on the parable of the mustard seed, Matt. 13:31–32.

28 Penn, *Christian-Quaker*, 1674, p. 98, Gen. 3:15. Whitehead, *Christian-Quaker*, 1673, p. 75, Isa. 53:2. Although Nuttall has rightly pointed out that it was primarily the imagery of Gen. 3:15 rather than that of "organic growth" that lay behind Fox's references to the Seed (*HSPFE*, p. 158), the latter metaphor was not lacking in his thought (see FJP, 1:312). Penn, *Reason Against Railing*, 1673, p. 130. Wright, *Testimony*, 1661, pp. 97, 105 quoted. Hicks, *Dialogue*, 1673, p. 47.

29 Westminster Confession, chapter 3, sections 3–7, chapter 11, section 4; Savoy Declaration, chapter 3, sections 3–7, chapter 11, section 4. Particular Baptist confessions: 1677, chapter 3, sections 3–6, chapter 11, section 4, MBC, pp. 233–34; 1644, article 3, p. 175, and article 17, p. 178; 1656, article 9, p. 204. The 1656 confession makes no specific mention of the extent of Christ's work (p. 202–15).

30 General Baptist confessions: 1651, articles 17, 44, 45, MBC, pp. 99, 102–3; 1660, articles 3, 4, 8, 9, pp. 112–15; 1679, articles 9, 10, 18, pp. 129–31, 137–38.

31 See Fox's attack on Ives in FGM, p. 63.

32 Bunyan, *Some Gospel-truths Opened*, 1656, *MW*, 1:30. FGM, p. 211. Samuel Fisher, *Rusticus ad Academicos*, 1660, pt. 4, p. 182 quoted. Whitehead, *Christian-Quaker*, 1673, p. 29.

33　Westminster Confession, chapter 6, sections 2–4, article 11, section 1, article 16, section 2; Savoy Declaration, chapter 6, sections 2–4, chapter 11, section 1, chapter 16, section 2. It should be noted, however, that among those with Calvinistic sympathies, views ranged from the antinomian position, like that of John Saltmarsh (*Free Grace; Or the Flowings of Christ's Blood Freely to Sinners*, 1645, pp. 128–29, 188–89), to Richard Baxter's "conditional covenant" (*Plain Scripture Proof of Infants Church-Membership and Baptism*, 1651, p. 326). See Richard L. Greaves, *John Bunyan* (Abingdon, Berkshire: Sutton Courtenay Press, 1969), pp. 97–121.

34　Thomas Collier, *The Body of Divinity*, 1674, pp. 186, 268. Collier's Arminian tendencies sometimes brought him into controversy with other Particular Baptists. See Richard D. Land, "Controversies of English Particular Baptists (1648–1691) as Illustrated by the Career and Writings of Thomas Collier" (D.Phil. thesis, Oxford University, 1979).

35　Particular Baptist confessions: 1644, articles 4, 5, 22, MBC, pp. 175, 176, 180–81; 1656, articles 7, 20, 23, pp. 204, 207, 208; 1677, chapter 7, sections 2, 4, chapter 11, section 2, chapter 16, sections 1–5, pp. 235, 236, 244–45, 249–51. General Baptist confessions: 1651, articles 15, 25, 43, 55, 72, pp. 99, 102, 100, 104, 108; 1660, articles 2, 14, 18, pp. 112, 116, 117; 1679, articles 10, 14, 15, 20, 26, pp. 131, 133–34, 139–40, 143–44; however, article 36, p. 151, does speak of perseverance.

36　Thomas Collier, *A Looking-Glasse for the Quakers*, 1657, pp. 1–3. Hicks, *Continuation of the Dialogue*, 1673, p. 68. Wright, *Testimony*, 1661, pp. 3–4. Grigg, *Light From the Sun*, 1672, p. 11.

37　Bunyan, *Vindication*, 1657, in *MW*, 1:158–59. John Tombes, *True Old Light*, 1660, p. 67, Eph. 1:7–9 and Titus 3:4–5. Wright, *Testimony*, 1661, p. 13.

38　FGM, p. 206. Burrough, *True Faith*, 1656, p. 29, James 2:20.

39　Penn, *Counterfeit Christian*, 1674, p. 106. Burrough, *True Faith*, 1656, p. 13. Penn, *Reason Against Railing*, 1673, p. 96, James 2:21, 24.

40　Bunyan, *Vindication*, 1657, in *MW*, 1:200–201, Prov. 6:23. Wigan, *Antichrist's Strongest Hold Overturned*, 1665, pp. 16, 32, 34, 41, Rom. 3:20, Rom. 8:2. Burnet, *Capital Principles*, 1668, pp. 4, 16, Rom. 2:14–15. Matthew Caffyn, *The Deceived, and Deceiving Quakers*, 1656, pp. 12–13. Compare Baxter, *Catechizing of Families*, 1683, pp. 229–33.

41　Bunyan, *Some Gospel-truths Opened*, 1656, in *MW*, 1:45. Wright, *Testimony*, 1661, p. 41. Grigg, *Light From the Sun*, 1672, pp. 12–13. Bunyan, *Vindication*, 1657, in *MW*, 1:148–49 quoted.

42　Wigan, *Antichrist's Strongest Hold Overturned*, 1665, p. 36. Grigg, *Light From the Sun*, 1672, p. 11. Bunyan, *Vindication*, 1657, in *MW*, 1:155–57, 1 John 3:3.

43　FGM, p. 12. Fisher, *Rusticus ad Academicos*, 1660, pt. 4, p. 188. Whitehead, *Christian-Quaker*, 1673, p. 14.

44　Burrough, *True Faith*, 1656, p. 10. Whitehead, *Light and Life of Christ Within*, 1668, p. 56. Burrough, *Truth*, 1657, p. 29.

45　General Baptist confessions: 1651, MBC, p. 95–109; 1660, pp. 111–22; 1679, article 16, pp. 134–35. Particular Baptist confessions: 1644, pp. 171–89; 1656, pp. 202–15; 1677, chapter 11, section 1, pp. 244–45. Russel, *Quakerism Is Paganism*, 1674, p. 50, Rom. 4:5–8, 22–25. Bunyan, *Some Gospel-truths Opened*, 1656, in *MW*, 1:44. Wigan, *Antichrist's Strongest Hold Overturned*, 1665, p. 51.

46　See, for example, John Biddle's objection in *A Twofold Catechism*, 1654,

p. 82. For Biddle, see *DNB*. Whitehead, *Christian-Quaker*, 1673, p. 65. Penn, *Reason Against Railing*, 1673, p. 97. Ames, *Declaration*, 1656, p. 3. Burrough, *Truth*, 1657, p. 46. Penn, *Reason Against Railing*, 1673, pp. 71, 97. Dennis Hollister, *The Harlots Vail Removed*, 1658, p. 67.

47 George Whitehead, *An Appendix*, 1673, p. 36. Penn, *Christian-Quaker*, 1674, pp. 110–13; Penn, *Reason Against Railing*, 1673, p. 75; Penn, *Counterfeit Christian*, 1673, p. 108 quoted.

48 Bunyan, *Some Gospel-truths Opened*, 1656, in *MW*, 1:61, Isa. 64:6. William Kaye, *A Plain Answer*, 1654, p. 10. Bunyan, *Some Gospel-truths Opened*, 1656, in *MW*, 1:62. Hicks, *Continuation of the Dialogue*, 1673, p. 55. Grigg, *Light From the Sun*, 1672, p. 16, Rom. 6:1–10.

49 Wright, *Testimony*, 1661, p. 13. Bunyan, *Some Gospel-truths Opened*, 1656, in *MW* 1:63. Matthew Caffyn, *Faith in Gods Promises*, 1661, p. 21. Burnet, *Capital Principles*, 1668, p. 5 (misprinted 4). Collier, *Looking-Glasse for the Quakers*, 1657, p. 2. Whitehead, *Appendix*, 1673, pp. 35–37. Burrough, *Son of Perdition*, 1661, p. 5.

50 Caffyn, *Deceived, and Deceiving Quakers*, 1656, pp. 60–61. Wright, *Testimony*, 1661, p. 150. Grigg, *Light From the Sun*, 1672, p. 62. Thomas Collier, *An Answer to an Epistle*, 1657, p. 5. Enoch Howet, *Quaking Principles Dashed*, 1655, p. 17. Collier, *Looking-Glasse for the Quakers*, 1657, p. 20. Thomas Ewins, *The Church of Christ*, 1657, p. 19. Collier, *Looking-Glasse for the Quakers*, 1657, p. 10.

51 Hicks, *Dialogue*, 1673, p. 50, Job 1:8 and Ps. 119:96.

52 Jeremiah Ives, *The Quakers Quaking*, 1656, pp. 23–24, Rom. 7. Hicks, *Dialogue*, 1673, p. 51, Phil. 3:12. Bunyan, *Vindication*, 1657, in *MW*, 1:198, 1 John 1:8.

53 Collier, *Looking-Glasse for the Quakers*, 1657, p. 10. Caffyn, *Faith in Gods Promises*, 1661, p. 37.

54 Wigan, *Antichrist's Strongest Hold Overturned*, 1665, pp. 56–60, 63 quoted. Of such denunciations, Margaret Fell replied that any person who knew of Wigan and his opposition to the Quakers would "judge them [her denunciations] to be truth to thee" (quoted in Thomas Curwen, *This Is an Answer*, 1665, p. 87). In reply to a similar charge, Alexander Parker pointed out that such expressions as "Dog, Devil, Serpent, Sorcerer" were, in fact, "Scripture-Language, most of them used by Christ himself to that wicked generation of pharisaical professors, and others, by the Apostles and Ministers of Christ" (*Discovery of Satans Wiles*, 1657, p. 43). John Pendarves, *Arrowes Against Babylon*, 1656, p. 42. In reply to similar questions, George Whitehead declared that personal weaknesses did not reflect on the doctrine of perfection (*The Dipper Plung'd*, 1672, pp. 11–12) and expressed a fear that Baptists would abuse those whom he might name (*Christian-Quaker*, 1673, p. 80). Hicks, *Dialogue*, 1673, p. 55.

55 FGM, 1659, p. 254. Penn, *Reason Against Railing*, 1673, p. 101. Whitehead, *Christian-Quaker*, 1673, p. 78. FGM p. 280, Mark 3:27. Penn, *Reason Against Railing*, 1673, pp. 99–100, 1 Thess. 5:23. James Nayler, *Deceit Brought to Day-light*, 1656, p. 13. Whitehead, *Christian-Quaker*, 1673, p. 327.

56 FGM, p. 251, Job 1:8, Ps. 119:96. Salthouse, *Line of True Judgment*, 1658, p. 8, Rom. 6:6–10. Burrough, *Truth*, 1657, p. 58, 1 John 3:9, Lev. 19:1. Humphrey Wolrich, *A Declaration*, 1659, p. 20. Nayler, *Weakness Above Wickedness*, 1656, p. 13, Eph. 4:11–13, Col. 1:28.

57 Salthouse, *Line of True Judgment*, 1658, p. 19. James Nayler, *An Answer*

to Some Queries, 1656, p. 4 quoted. FGM, p. 208. Nayler, *Deceit Brought to Day-light*, 1656, p. 19.

58 Whitehead, *Christian-Quaker*, 1673, p. 168. Salthouse, *Line of True Judgment*, 1658, p. 7. The letter to which Whitehead referred was dated the 18th day, 7th month, 1657, from Tiverton, and was signed by Collier, Thomas Glass (see Joseph Ivimey, *A History of the English Baptists*, 4 vols. [New York: Oxford University Press, 1994], 2:65, 146), and Nathaniel Strange; see Geoffrey F. Nuttall, "The Baptist Western Association 1653–1658," *Journal of Ecclesiastical History* 11 (1960). It was printed together with nine other circular letters from various meetings of the Western Association (*Several Resolutions and Answers of Queries*, 1657) and was intended for the "spiritual advantage" of the churches. The only known copies (none are listed in Wing) are located at LF (lacks title-page) and at Bristol Baptist College (imperfect, pp. 7–22 only); see Nuttall, "Baptist Western Association," 213 n. 4, 214 n. 8, 218. The letter drew a reply from Thomas Salthouse, *An Epistle to the Churches of the Anabaptists So Called*, 1657, to which Collier replied with *Answer to an Epistle*, 1657. Salthouse answered with *Line of True Judgment*, 1658, to which Collier replied with *The Hypocrase and Falsehood of Thomas Salthouse* (1659?), (extant?), to which in turn Robert Wastfield responded with *An Equal Ballance*, 1659. The Tiverton letter was used in a similar manner by Joseph Pitman and Jasper Batt, *Truth Vindicated*, 1658, p. 60, and by Fox, FGM, pp. 299–301.

59 Westminster Confession, chapter 8, section 4, chapter 33, section 3; Savoy Declaration, chapter 8, section 4, chapter 32, section 3. General Baptist confessions: 1651, article 53, MBC, p. 204; 1660, article 22, pp. 118–19; 1679, article 17, p. 136. Particular Baptist confessions: 1644, article 20, p. 180; 1656, article 34, p. 213; 1677, chapter 8, section 4, chapter 32, section 3, pp. 174, 140–41.

60 Humphrey Wolrich, *One Warning More*, 1661, pp. 11, 13, Matt. 24:34. He may also have had in mind Gal. 2:20. FGM, p. 143. For the Lamb's War, see Rev. 14–19, Eph. 6:10–18; BQPE, 40–41; Douglas Gwyn, *Apocalypse of the Word* (Richmond, Ind.: Friends United Press, 1984), pp. 36–38, 193–97; Joseph Pickvance, *A Reader's Companion to George Fox's Journal* (Quaker Home Service, 1989), pp. 132–33; and H. Larry Ingle, "George Fox, Millenarian," *Albion* 24 (1992): 261–78.

61 Burrough, *Truth*, 1657, p. 15. Whitehead, *Light and Life of Christ Within*, 1668, p. 40; Whitehead, *The Pernicious Way*, 1662, p. 29; Whitehead, *The Authority of the True Ministry*, 1660, pp. 2–3 quoted.

62 Wright, *Testimony*, 1661, p. 83. Caffyn, *Faith In Gods Promises*, 1661, p. 43. Hicks, *Continuation of the Dialogue*, 1673, p. 43, Acts 1:10–11. Caffyn, *Deceived, and Deceiving Quakers*, 1656, pp. 29, 32–33, 1 Thess. 4:17. Grigg, *Light From the Sun*, 1672, pp. 21–22, 1 Cor. 1:4–7. Bunyan, *Some Gospel-truths Opened*, 1656, in *MW*, 1:84–86, 100 quoted, Matt. 24:24, 50–51, 2 Pet. 3:3.

63 Westminster Confession, chapter 32, sections 2–3; Savoy Declaration, chapter 31, sections 2–3. General Baptist confessions: 1660, article 20, MBC, p. 118; 1679, article 49, pp. 160–61. In the 1651 confession few references were made to eschatology and none to resurrection (pp. 95–109). Particular Baptist confessions: 1644, article 40, p. 185; 1656, article 29, p. 213; 1677, chapter 31, pp. 272–73.

64 Thomas Lawson, *An Untaught Teacher*, 1655, p. 22, John 5:28–29. William Shewen, *The Universality of the Light*, 1674, pp. 10–11.

65 Burrough, *Son of Perdition*, 1661, pp. 16–17. Whitehead, *Christian-Quaker*, 1673, pp. 326, 343 (misprinted 143), 2 Cor. 5:17, Eph. 4:24.

66 Burrough, *Son of Perdition*, 1661, p. 20, Job 7:9. Dennis Hollister, *The Skirts of the Whore Discovered*, 1656, p. 22 (misprinted 26), 1 Cor. 15:50. Penn, *Reason Against Railing*, 1673, p. 139, 1 Cor. 15:53–54. Whitehead, *The Christian-Quaker*, 1673, p. 323, 1 Cor. 15:42–44.

67 Penn, *Reason Against Railing*, 1673, p. 138, 1 Cor. 15:36–40. Lawson, *Untaught Teacher*, 1655, p. 22, 1 Cor. 15:44. Whitehead, *Dipper Plung'd*, 1672, p. 15, 1 Cor. 15:48. Hollister, *Skirts of the Whore Discovered*, 1656, p. 24 (misprinted 20), Phil. 3:21. Lodowick Muggleton, who thought of God as a man and who believed in the mortality of the soul (*A Looking-Glass for George Fox*, 1667, pp. 16–22), labeled the Quaker notion that people's spirits could subsist without physical bodies "the Heathen Philosophers opinion" (pp. 64–65).

68 Penn, *Reason Against Railing*, 1673, p. 138. Whitehead, *Christian-Quaker*, 1673, p. 331, 2 Cor. 5:4. Burrough, *Son of Perdition*, 1661, p. 18, Rom. 8:21–23. Penn, *Reason Against Railing*, 1673, p. 136, 1 Cor. 15:53, 2 Cor. 5:1.

69 Wright, *Testimony*, 1661, p. 60, Col. 2:12–13. GCP, pt. 4, p. 73. Bunyan, *Some Gospel-truths Opened*, 1656, in *MW*, 1:107–8, Rom. 8:5, 1 Cor. 15:50. Wright, *Testimony*, 1661, p. 72, Acts 13:36, 1 Cor. 15:52.

70 Bunyan, *Some Gospel-truths Opened*, 1656, in *MW*, 1:108. Burnet, *The Capital Principles*, 1668, p. 50. Hicks, *Dialogue*, 1673, p. 58, 1 Cor. 15:42–44. Grigg, *Light From the Sun*, 1672, p. 44.

71 Russel, *Quakerism Is Paganism*, 1674, p. 64, 2 Cor. 5:10. Caffyn, *Deceived, and Deceiving Quakers*, 1656, p. 46. Wright, *Testimony*, 1661, p. 62, 2 Tim. 2:16–18. Hicks, *Dialogue*, 1673, p. 62, 1 Cor. 15:12–17.

72 Westminster Confession, chapters 32, 33; Savoy Declaration, chapters 31, 32. General Baptist confessions: 1660, articles 4, 10, 21, MBC pp. 112–13, 115, 118; 1679, articles 49, 50, pp. 160–61. Particular Baptist confessions: 1644, article 20, p. 180; 1656, articles 40–42, p. 213; 1677, chapters 31, 32, pp. 272–74.

73 John Lawson in George Fox, *Saul's Errand to Damascus*, 1653, p. 36. For John Lawson, see Nuttall, "Early Quaker Letters from the Swarthmore Manuscripts to 1660," Typescript (1952), p. 66. Ives, *Quakers Quaking*, 1656, pp. 21, 37–38. Caffyn, *Deceived, and Deceiving Quakers*, 1656, p. 50, 2 Tim. 4:11. John Lawson in Fox, *Saul's Errand to Damascus*, 1653, p. 36. Ives, *Quakers Quaking*, 1656, p. 23. FGM, p. 64, Eph. 2:6. Nayler, *Weakness Above Wickedness*, 1656, p. 13, Ps. 16:10, Jon. 2:2, 2 Cor. 12:2–4.

74 Wright, *Testimony*, 1661, p. 78. Whitehead, *Christian-Quaker*, 1673, p. 331. FGM, pp. 290, 93, 143, 9, Rev. 19:11–20. Whitehead, *Christ Ascended*, 1669, p. 24, Rev. 21:2, 22–23. See T. L. Underwood, "Early Quaker Eschatology," in *Puritans, the Millennium and the Future of Israel: Puritan Eschatology 1600–1660* ed. Peter Toon (Cambridge: James Clarke, 1970), pp. 91–103; Douglas Gwyn, *Apocalypse of the Word*.

75 Richard Baxter, *A Key for Catholicks*, 1659, pp. 333–34. John Saltmarsh, *Sparkles of Glory*, 1647, p. 255. John Jackson, *A Sober Word*, 1651, pp. 46–48. William Erbery, *The Testimony*, 1658, p. 127. Edward Burrough, *A Trumpet of the Lord Sounded Out of Sion*, 1656, p. 29. Collier, *Looking-Glasse, for the Quakers*, 1657, p. 7. Joseph Salmon, *Heights in Depths and Depths in Heights*, 1651, pp. 43–44. Jacob Bauthumley, *The Light and Dark Sides of God*, 1650, pp. 14–24, 42–54. Bauthumley also seemed to think that God would cease to live in flesh and creatures, creatures would then give up their power and return back to God, and

"God shall be All" (*Light and Dark Sides of God*, 1650, p. 53). Abiezer Coppe, *A Second Fiery Flying Roll*, 1649, sig. B3r (faulty pagination). See also Laurence Clarkson, *A Single Eye*, 1650, pp. 10–12; *The Lost Sheep Found*, 1660, pp. 19–22. Bauthumley, *Light and Dark Sides of God*, 1650, p. 37. See also Salmon, *Heights in Depths*, 1651, pp. 46–51. Thomas Lawson to Margaret Fell, n.d., LF: Swarthmore MSS 1/242. Margaret Fell, *A Testimonie*, 1656, pp. 32–36, 36 quoted. Francis Howgill and Anthony Pearson expressed to Margaret Fell a similar fear of association with London Ranters (10 July [1654], LF: Caton MSS 3/74). Richard Baxter believed that Quakers "were but the *Ranters* turned from horrid Prophaneness and Blasphemy, to a Life of extream Austerity on the other side" (*Reliquiae Baxterianae*, 1696, pt. 1, p. 77).

76 John Reeve, *A Transcendent Spiritual Treatise*, 1652, pp. 42–7, 15. John Reeve and Lodowick Muggleton, *The Baptist's Commission Counterfeited*, pp. 27–30, in *Joyful News from Heaven*, 1706 (separate pagination); *Joyful News from Heaven*, p. 37. John Reeve and Lodowick Muggleton, *A Divine Looking-Glass*, 1661, p. 62. John Gratton, *A Journal of the Life of that Ancient servant of Christ, John Gratton*, 1720, p. 24. John Reeve and Lodowick Muggleton, *Verae Fidei*, 1820, p. 233. Muggleton had cursed her son Samuel in 1662.

77 George Fox, *Several Warnings*, 1659, p. 1.

Chapter 5

1 For Fell's imprisonment, see Isabel Ross, *Margaret Fell, Mother of Quakerism*, 2nd ed., (York: Sessions Book Trust, 1984), pp. 177–204; Bonnelyn Young Kunze, *Margaret Fell and the Rise of Quakerism*, pp. 18–20. For Wigan, see W. T. Whitley, "The Rev. Colonel John Wigan," *JFHS* 16 (1955–56): 141–42; *BDBR*.

2 John Wigan, *Antichrist's Strongest Hold Overturned*, 1655, p. 12. Thomas Curwen, *This Is an Answer*, 1665, p. 25. FJN, 171–72.

3 Westminster Confession, chapters 27–29; Savoy Declaration, chapters 28–30.

4 Quakers also objected to the use of the term *sacraments*. To John Owen, George Fox wrote, "As for thy word *Sacraments*, the Pope was the Author of them in his Common-prayer book" (FGM, p. 264). See General Baptist confessions: 1651, article 52, MBC, p. 104; 1679, article 42, p. 156; Particular Baptist confessions: 1644, articles 37, 38, 48, pp. 184, 184–85, 187; 1656, article 34, pp. 211–12; 1679, chapter 19, section 3, p. 255.

5 General Baptist confessions: 1651, articles 50, 53, MBC, pp. 103, 104; 1660, article 11, pp. 115–16; 1679, articles 27, 28, 33, pp. 144–45, 148–49. Particular Baptist confessions: 1644, article 40, p. 185; 1656, articles 24, 25, pp. 208–9; 1677, chapters 29, 30, pp. 269–72.

6 Quakers also criticized this notion. To John Owen, Fox declared, "It's God that seal's the Son, and sent him into the world, and not outward shadows" (FGM, 1659, p. 264).

7 John Tombes, *A Short Catechism About Baptism*, 1659, sig. B1r. John Bunyan, *A Confession of My Faith*, 1672, in *MW*, 4:160–64.

8 Edward Burrough, *The Son of Perdition*, 1661, pp. 23–24. Humphrey Wolrich, *One Warning More*, 1661, p. 3. Edward Burrough, *Something in Answer to a Book, Called Choice Experiences*, 1654, p. 13.

9 Wolrich, *One Warning More*, 1661, p. 8. William Penn, *Reason Against Railing*, 1673, p. 107; William Penn, *The Counterfeit Christian*, 1674, p. 101;

Penn, *Reason Against Railing*, 1673, p. 108. FGM, p. 112, 2 Cor. 4:18. Dennis Hollister, *The Harlots Vail Removed*, 1658, p. 35. Geoffrey F. Nuttall has observed that whereas orthodox Protestants emphasized the unity of Scripture and at least a partial continuity of Old and New Testaments, enthusiasts stressed the difference between the two testaments and a fuller termination of the notions and practices of the former. See the discussion of the enthusiast Walter Cradock in Geoffrey F. Nuttall, *The Welsh Saints 1640–1660* (Cardiff: University of Wales Press, 1957), pp. 34–36.

10 George Whitehead, *The Christian-Quaker*, 1673, p. 105; Robert Wastfield, *An Equal Ballance*, 1659, p. 7, 2 Thess. 2:3. Robert Wastfield (d. 1677) of Brislington, Somerset, was one of the earliest converts to Quakerism in that county. He was said to have been "serviceable in ye beginning, but declined pretty much for want of faithfulness in his Latter days" (*FPT*, pp. 226, 227, 228 quoted; "Digested Copy of the Registers of Burials of the Quarterly Meeting of Bristol and Somersetshire," LF).

11 Matthew Caffyn, *Faith in Gods Promises*, 1661, p. 30. Henry Grigg, *Light From the Sun*, 1672, p. 54. John Pendarves, *Arrowes Against Babylon*, 1656, pp. 42–43. Thomas Collier, *A Looking-Glasse for the Quakers*, 1657, p. 11. GCP, pt. 4, p. 66.

12 Wigan, *Antichrist's Strongest Hold Overturned*, 1665, p. 50. Joseph Wright, *A Testimony*, 1661, p. 50. William Jeffery, *Antichrist Made Known*, 1656, pp. 69–70, 1 Cor. 11:26, 1 John 2:24.

13 John Griffith, *A Voice from the Word of the Lord*, 1654, p. 15, Mal. 3:16–17.

14 Dennis Hollister, *The Skirts of the Whore Discovered*, 1656, p. 27 (misprinted 31). Burrough, *Something in Answer to a Book, Called Choice Experiences*, 1654, p. 13. Hollister, *Harlots Vail Removed*, 1658, p. 37.

15 James Nayler, *Deceit Brought to Day-light* 1656, p. 25.

16 Pendarves, *Arrowes Against Babylon*, 1656, p. 43. Collier, *Looking-Glasse for the Quakers*, 1657, pp. 10–11.

17 This was the only aspect of baptism mentioned in the General Baptist confession of 1651 (article 50, MBC, p. 103), and it was the primary concern in that of 1660 (article 11, pp. 115–16). The apparent lack of interest in symbolic significance was reversed, however, in the confession of 1679 (article 28, pp. 144–45).

18 1644: Articles 39–41, MBC, p. 185. 1656: article 24, pp. 208–9. Westminster Confession, chapter 28, section 1. 1677: chapter 29, MBC, pp. 269–70.

19 UHB, p. 103; Thomas Ewins, *The Church of Christ*, 1657, pp. 67–68; HBR, pp. 47–48. See also Bunyan, *Confession*, 1672, in *MW*, 4:153–87. Reciprocally, the paedobaptists of these congregations were willing to associate with Baptists as members and to allow them to follow their own particular practice. Such an association between Baptists and Independents in the same congregation was also in evidence elsewhere (see *HSPFE*, pp. 96–97). 1677: MBC, p. 287.

20 Adherence to the practice of laying on of hands was made a requirement for communion at the 1656 General Assembly (W. T. Whitley, *The Minutes of the General Assembly of the General Baptist Churches in England*, 2 vols. [Kingsgate Press, 1909–10], 1:6) and at the Kent Association meeting at Biddenden on 26 and 27th of the third month in 1657 ("A Register Booke . . . of the Congregation . . . in and about Speldhurst and Penbury in Kent," British Library: Additional Manuscript 36709, fol. 32).

21 General Baptist confession: 1679, article 28, MBC, pp. 144–45; however,

article 33 refers to the sealing quality of the Lord's Supper, p. 148. Particular Baptist confessions: 1644, article 40, p. 185; 1656, article 24, pp. 208–9; 1677, chapter 29, pp. 169–70.

22 Bunyan, *Confession*, 1672, in *MW*, 4:172.

23 Westminster Confession, chapter 28, sections 1, 6. See also Savoy Declaration, chapter 29, sections 1, 6. Particular Baptist confession: 1677, chapter 29, MBC, pp. 169–70. General Baptist confession: 1679, article 28, pp. 144–45. Particular Baptist confession: 1677, appendix, p. 278. Thomas Collier made a similar protest, adding that references to the ordinances as seals were not "Scripture language" (*The Body of Divinity*, 1674, pp. 470–71).

24 Tombes, *Short Catechism About Baptism*, 1659, sig. B3r, Rom. 6:3–4. General Baptist confession: 1679, article 28, MBC, pp. 144–45. Particular Baptist Confessions: 1644, article 40, p. 185; 1656, article 24, pp. 208–9; 1677, chapter 29, pp. 269–70. Bunyan, *Confession*, 1672, in *MW*, 4:164, Col. 2:12, Rom. 6:4.

25 WEBSC, pp. 41–44; Ernest Payne, "Baptists and the Laying On of Hands," *BQ* 15 (1955–56): 203–15; the Particular Baptist Thomas Tillam also followed this practice (UFR, p. 289). UFR, 36–37, 61, 67–68, 69–70, 188, 272–73, 290; Grantham insisted that the bread in the Lord's Supper be broken, not cut (GCP, pt. 2, p. 95. William Jeffery, *The Whole Faith of Man*, 2nd ed., 1659, p. 102; UFR, pp. 66, 223; Adam Taylor, *The History of the English General Baptists* (1818), pt. 1, pp. 421–52. Hanserd Knollys, *The Life and Death of . . . Hanserd Knollys*, 1692, p. 35; Jeffery, *Whole Faith of Man*, 1659, pp. 102–3; Taylor, *History of the English General Baptists*, pt. 1, pp. 452–55. UFR, 190, 243–44, 269. Tillam recommended the holy kiss to the Hexham church (UFR, 324). Attention to detail was also evident in the measures taken at the amicable division of the church at Biddenden, Kent, in 1678. Both groups agreed that they would make their leaders available to work together in the anointing of the sick because the Scripture (James 5:14) stipulated that it was to be administered by "elders" rather than one "elder" (Taylor, *History of the English General Baptists*, pt. 1, p. 453).

26 George Whitehead, *The Authority of the True Ministry*, 1660, p. 2. Thomas Taylor, *Certain Queries*, (1680?), in *Truth's Innocency*, 1697, p. 334. Whitehead, *Authority of the True Ministry*, 1660, pp. 9–10 quoted.

27 Luke Howard, *Love and Truth in Plainness Manifested*, 1704, pp. 7–8; Luke Howard, *The Seat of the Scorner Thrown Down*, 1673, p. 5 quoted. Howard charged that Baptists in Kent began as Particular Baptists, then changed to General Baptists and had to be baptized again (*A Looking-Glass for Baptists*, 1672, p. 5). William Bayly, *A Short Relation*, 1659, p. 7. See also Stephen Crisp, *A Memorable Account*, 1694, p. 13. Nayler, *Deceit Brought to Day-light*, 1656, p. 19. Whitehead, *Christian-Quaker*, 1673, p. 163, 2 Tim. 3:6.

28 Humphrey Wolrich, *A Declaration*, 1659, p. 31, Matt. 3:1–6. Burrough, *Son of Perdition*, 1661, p. 26. James Parnell, *The Watcher*, 1655, p. 32, Matt. 28:19. Whitehead, *Authority of the True Ministry*, 1660, p. 6. FGM, p. 64. Parnell, *Watcher*, 1655, p. 32. Nayler, *Weakness Above Wickedness*, 1656, p. 14. Nevertheless, in another work Nayler admitted this practice of Baptists to be "a little nearer in the letter" to the Scripture than that of the "Parish Teachers" (*Deceit Brought to Day-light*, 1656, p. 23). Of the latter's mode of baptism George Fox wrote, perhaps in 1654, "There is not a Word in all the Scripture to hold up the Practice of Sprinkling Infants" (*A Collection*, 1698, p. 57) and to a papist in 1668 he remarked, "To throw a little water in a child's face and say it was baptised (or christened) there was no Scripture for that" (FJN, p. 529). As might be expected, bap-

tism commanded far less attention in the controversies between Quakers and non-Baptists. In this connection, it is interesting to note that Ewins referred to several cases (the earliest, perhaps in 1651) of the use of child dedication services among Baptists (*Church of Christ*, 1657, pp. 63–65), and that Ralph Farmer, lecturer at St. Nicholas in Bristol, labelled Ewins's practice "dry Baptism" (*Sathan Enthron'd*, 1657, p. 51). See T. L. Underwood, "Child Dedication Services among British Baptists in the Seventeenth Century," *BQ* 23 (1969): 164–69.

29 Penn, *Reason Against Railing*, 1673, p. 107. See also Hollister, *Harlots Vail Removed*, 1658, pp. 10–11, Matt. 3:11. John Perrot, *The Mistery of Baptism and the Lord's Supper*, 1662, p. 14, Eph. 4:4–5. Whitehead, *Authority of the True Ministry*, 1660, p. 4. FJN, p. 231.

30 Wolrich, *Declaration*, 1659, title-page quoted, p. 31. Whitehead, *Authority of the True Ministry*, 1660, p. 8. Taylor, *Certain Queries* (1680?), p. 336, 1 Cor. 1:14. Penn, *Reason Against Railing*, 1673, p. 110, 1 Cor. 1:17.

31 Burrough, *Son of Perdition*, 1661, p. 25. John Perrot, *To All Baptists Everywhere*, 1660, broadsheet. Perrot's tiny broadsheet was written from the "Prison of Madmen" in Rome and was dated the 2nd day of the 8th month, 1660. For Perrot's sojourn in Rome, see BBQ, pp. 424–26. Burrough, *Son of Perdition*, 1661, p. 26. Humphrey Wolrich, *The Unlimited God*, 1659, pp. 1–2, 2 quoted. For Fox's reaction see BBQ, pp. 392–93.

32 Henry Grigg, *The Baptist Not Babylonish*, 1672, p. 14.

33 Grigg, *Light From the Sun*, 1672, pp. 23–24, Matt. 28:19–20. Ewins, *Church of Christ*, 1657, p. 58, Matt. 3:15. Joseph Wright, *A Testimony*, 1661, p. 39. Jeremiah Ives, *The Quakers Quaking*, 1656, p. 25.

34 Grigg, *Light From the Sun*, 1672, p. 25, Acts 8:38. Caffyn, *Deceived, and Deceiving Quakers*, 1656, p. 52, Acts 10:44–48. Ives, *Quakers Quaking*, 1656, p. 26, Acts 2. Grigg, *Light From the Sun*, 1672, p. 27, 1 Cor. 1:17. Jeremiah Ives, *Innocency Above Impudency*, 1656, p. 50, 1 Cor. 1:14, 16.

35 Caffyn, *Deceived, and Deceiving Quakers*, 1656, p. 53, 1 Cor. 1:12, 14–15. Tillam letter to "those deluded soules called Quakers," 1654, LF: Portfolio 36 no. 13. Grigg, *Baptist Not Babylonish*, 1672, p. 10, Matt. 28:20. GCP, pt. 4, p. 65.

36 His claim was in the long title of John Perrot, *To All Baptists Everywhere*, 1660. Randall Roper, *Truth Vindicated*, 1661, sigs. A4r, B3v–B4r (faulty pagination). In 1672, Roper was the minister of a Baptist congregation in East Smithfield, Middlesex (G. Lyon Turner, *Original Records of Early Nonconformity under Persecution and Indulgence*, 3 vols. [T. Fisher Unwin, 1911–14], 1:311). Enoch Howet, *Quaking Principles Dashed*, 1655, pp. 10–11.

37 FGM, p. 112. Penn, *Reason Against Railing*, 1673, p. 112. Whitehead, *Christian-Quaker*, 1673, p. 93. FGM, p. 65. Taylor, *Certain Queries* (1680?), p. 345. Wolrich, *Declaration*, 1659, p. 11. Penn, *Reason Against Railing*, 1673, pp. 107–8, Matt. 3, Acts 1.

38 Whitehead, *Authority of the True Ministry*, 1660, p. 7, Acts 11:16. Penn, *Counterfeit Christian*, 1674, p. 104, Acts 19. Wolrich, *Declaration*, 1659, pp. 33, 11 quoted, Acts 8:17–18. Richard Farnworth, *To You That Are Called by the Name of Baptists*, 1654, p. 2. Burrough, *Son of Perdition*, 1661, p. 25, Heb. 9:9. Perrot, *Mistery of Baptism and the Lord's Supper*, 1662, p. 16.

39 General Baptist confession: 1660, article 12, MBC, p. 116. Ives, *Quakers Quaking*, 1656, p. 25. Caffyn, *Deceived, and Deceiving Quakers*, 1656, p. 52. Roper, *Truth Vindicated*, 1661, sigs. C1r–C2r (faulty pagination). William Kaye, *A Plain Answer*, 1654, p. 6. Wright, *Testimony*, 1661, pp. 33, 35 quoted.

40 1644: MBC, pp. 171–89. 1656: article 25, pp. 209–10. 1677: chapter 30, sections 1, 5, MBC, pp. 270–71; Westminster Confession, chapter 29, sections 1, 5; see also Savoy Declaration, chapter 30, sections 1, 5. George Offor, ed., *The Works of John Bunyan*, 3 vols. (Glasgow: Blackie and Son, 1853), index, 3:787; John Bunyan, *Differences in Judgment About Water-Baptism*, 1673, in *MW*, 4:222–25.

41 1651: article 53, MBC, p. 104. 1660: article 13, p. 116.

42 1679: article 33, MBC, p. 148; Westminster Confession, chapter 29, section 1 (see also Savoy Declaration, chapter 30, section 1). 1679: article 32, MBC, pp. 148–89; Westminster Confession, chapter 29, section 7 (see also Savoy Declaration, chapter 30, section 7).

43 GCP, pt. 2, p. 85. See E. P. Winter, "Calvinist and Zwinglian Views of the Lord's Supper among the Baptists of the Seventeenth Century," *BQ*, 15 (1953–54): 323–29.

44 James Nayler, *The Boaster Bared*, 1655, p. 6. FGM, p. 112. Perrot, *Mistery of Baptism and the Lord's Supper*, 1662, p. 18. Hester Bird Andrews in Whitehead, *Christ Ascended*, 1669, p. 53. Andrews claimed to have become a Quaker "years before" she was excommunicated by a Baptist church in London. The bill of excommunication, dated the 17th day, 7th month, 1669, was also printed (p. 52).

45 Edward Burrough, *Something In Answer to a Booke, Called a Voice*, 1654, p. 16, Luke 22:14–20. Whitehead, *Christian-Quaker*, 1673, p. 133, Luke 22:16–18.

46 Penn, *Reason Against Railing*, 1673, pp. 109–10, 1 Cor. 11:23–34. Whitehead, *Christian-Quaker*, 1673, pp. 91–92, 1 Cor. 10, 11. Burrough, *Something in Answer to a Booke, Called a Voice*, 1654, p. 16. Penn, *Reason Against Railing*, 1673, p. 107, John 6:32–40.

47 Perrot, *To All Baptists Everywhere*, 1660, broadsheet, Col. 2:21–22.

48 Wolrich, *One Warning More*, 1661, p. 14.

49 Grigg, *Baptist Not Babylonish*, 1672, p. 19. Caffyn, *Deceived, and Deceiving Quakers*, 1656, p. 53, Luke 22:14–20, 1 Cor. 11:23–34. Ives, *Quakers Quaking*, 1656, p. 39, Matt. 26:27–28, 1 Cor. 11:23.

50 Wright, *Testimony*, 1661, p. 184, Acts 20:7. Wigan, *Antichrist's Strongest Hold Overturned*, 1665, p. 50.

51 Wright, *Testimony*, 1661, pp. 49, 7, 1 Cor. 11:26. Grigg, *Baptist Not Babylonish*, 1672, p. 11, 1 Cor. 11:26. Bunyan, *A Vindication of the Book Called, Some Gospel Truths Opened*, 1657, in *MW*, 1:138.

52 Richard Baxter, *A Key for Catholicks*, 1659, pp. 332–34. John Reeve and Lodowick Muggleton, *The Baptist's Commission Counterfeited*, p. 1, in *Joyful News from Heaven*, 1706 (separate pagination). Lodovick Muggleton, *The Acts of the Witnesses*, 1699, p. 100. John Jackson, *A Sober Word*, 1651, pp. 17–18. John Saltmarsh, *Sparkles of Glory*, 1647, pp. 78–83, 90–91, 247 quoted. William Erbery, *The Testimony*, 1658, p. 127. Abiezer Coppe, *A Fiery Flying Roll*, 1649, p. 14. Edward Burrough, *A Trumpet of the Lord Sounded Out of Sion*, 1656, p. 29.

53 Nayler, *Boaster Bared*, 1655, p. 6. William Wilson in Curwen, *This Is An Answer*, 1665, p. 8. For Wilson (d. 1682) see FJP, 2:392. Ewins, *Church of Christ*, 1657, p. 14.

54 FGM, p. 94, 2 Cor. 4:18. Fox to Friends and Baptists, 1653, LF: Swarthmore MSS 2/58. Whitehead, *Christian-Quaker*, 1673, p. 4. Penn, *Reason Against Railing*, 1673, p. 112, Luke 17:20.

55 Whitehead, *Christian-Quaker*, 1673, p. 91. Curwen, *This Is An Answer*,

1665, p. 9. For Curwen (d. 1680) see *FJP*, 2:475. Burrough, *Son of Perdition*, 1661, p. 27. Fox to Friends and Baptists, 1653, LF: Swarthmore MSS 2/58. Wolrich, *Declaration*, 1659, pp. 18–19, 1 Cor. 10:21, 11:29.

56 Grigg, *Baptist Not Babylonish*, 1672, p. 12. Howet, *Quaking Principles Dashed*, 1655, p. 11. Roper, *Truth Vindicated*, 1661, p. 23.

57 FGM, p. 94.

Chapter 6

1 For Roberts, see FJP, 1:434.

2 For the Bull and Mouth, see William Beck and T. Frederick Ball, *The London Friends' Meetings* (F. B. Kitto, 1869), p. 134. Fox replied to both of Ives's works in FGM.

3 See A. S. P. Woodhouse, *Puritanism and Liberty* (J. M. Dent, 1938), pp. 36–37; Geoffrey F. Nuttall, *Visible Saints: the Congregational Way, 1640–1660* (Oxford: Basil Blackwell, 1957); Stephen Brachlow, *The Communion of Saints, Radical Puritan and Separatist Ecclesiology 1570–1625* (Oxford: Oxford University Press, 1988). Westminster Confession, chapters 25, 26; Savoy Declaration, chapters 26, 27. General Baptist confessions: 1651, articles 50, 51, 52, MBC, pp. 102–104; 1679, articles 28–30, pp. 144–46. Particular Baptist confessions: 1644, articles 33, 35, 47, pp. 183, 184, 186; 1656, articles 24, 25, 29, pp. 208–9, 210; 1677, chapters 26, 29, pp. 264–70.

4 General Baptist confession: 1679, article 30, MBC, pp. 145–46. Particular Baptist confession: 1644, article 46, MBC, p. 186. GCP, pt. 2, p. 55.

5 GCP, pt. 2, p. 51. James Nayler, for example, wrote that it was not error "to withdraw from the Church of Rome, as they call it; nor from any who have reformed some things since the time of popery, but yet are not come to the true foundation of the Apostles, though they call themselves Nationall Churches, or Gathered Churches whatsoever" (*Love to the Lost*, 1656, p. 11).

6 Luke Howard, *The Seat of the Scorner Thrown Down*, 1673, p. 5. Francis Howgill, *The Inheritance of Jacob Discovered*, 1656, p. 9.

7 Thomas Salthouse, *The Line of True Judgment*, 1658, p. 14. Dennis Hollister, *The Harlots Vail Removed*, 1658, p. 41. A. Neave Brayshaw, *The Personality of George Fox* (Allenson, 1933), p. 66 n. 3. GCP, pt. 2, p. 176. FGM, p. 267.

8 FGM, p. 93. Salthouse, *Line of True Judgment*, 1658, pp. 15, 9. Hollister, *Harlots Vail Removed*, 1658, p. 41.

9 FGM, p. 93, Matt. 7:15. Dennis Hollister, *The Skirts of the Whore Discovered*, 1656, p. 14.

10 John Griffith, *A Voice from the Word of the Lord*, 1654, p. 14, Eph. 2:10–22. Joseph Wright, *A Testimony*, 1661, p. 186. Griffith, *Voice from the Word of the Lord*, 1654, p. 9, Jude 19.

11 Rachel Hadley King, *George Fox and the Light Within 1650–1660* (Philadelphia: Friends Book Store, 1940), p. 109.

12 BSPQ, pp. 228–44, 247–50. See also Norman Penney, biographical note in FJP, 2:375–76, and Kenneth L. Carroll, *John Perrot, Early Quaker Schismatic*, JFHS Supplement 33 (1971). Rebecca Travers, *A Testimony*, 1663, p. 16; Travers sided with Fox, however. BSPQ, pp. 251–68, 290–323. For the contending views in the Wilkinson–Story separation, compare John Wilkinson, *The Memory of that Servant of God, John Story, Revived*, 1683, with Thomas Camm, *The Line of Truth*, 1684. George Fox, "to them that was tainted with J Parots Spirit," n.d., LF:

Swarthmore MSS 7/162. Robert Barclay, *The Anarchy of the Ranters*, 1676, pp. 17, 23–25, 66–74, 81–82. Geoffrey F. Nuttall, *To the Refreshing of the Children of Light* (Wallingford, Pa.: Pendle Hill Pamphlet Number 101, 1959) p. 14. See also J. C. Davis, "Against Formality: One Aspect of the English Revolution," *Royal Historical Society Transactions* sixth series 1 (1993): 265–87; H. Larry Ingle, *First Among Friends: George Fox and the Creation of Quakerism* (New York: Oxford University Press, 1994), pp. 222–24, 255–65.

13 Benjamin Keach, *The Grand Impostor Discovered*, 1675, p. 274. General Baptist confessions: 1651, articles 70, 72, MBC, pp. 107, 108; 1679, article 34, MBC, pp. 149–50. Particular Baptist confession: 1677, article 26, sections 12, 15, pp. 267, 268. Among the General Baptists, the General Assembly also came to be endowed with similar powers (1679 confession: article 39, p. 154; see also Particular Baptist confession: 1677, chapter 26, section 15, p. 268). Thomas Hicks, *A Continuation of the Dialogue*, 1673, pp. 64–65.

14 See BSPQ, pp. 247–48. William Penn, *Reason Against Railing*, 1673, p. 122. Loddington's letter to Jeremiah Ives, in William Mead, *A Brief Account*, 1674, p. 41. See also Jospeh Fuce, *The Fall of A Great Visible Idol*, 1659, p. 24.

15 George Fox, "Answers in the Commonwelthes dayes," n.d., LF: Swarthmore MSS 7/77. Luke 10:19, Mark 16:19, Acts 4:31.

16 Among the "miracles" was the healing of the wife of the Baptist Thomas Baldock: When near death she was spoken to by Fox, and "the Lord raised her up that she was well, to the astonishment of the town and country" (FJN, 228). James Nayler reportedly raised up Dorcas Erbery after she had been dead two days. See Henry J. Cadbury, ed., *George Fox's "Book of Miracles"* (New York: Octagon Books, 1973), pp. 2–7.

17 William Kaye, *A Plain Answer*, 1654, p. 2.

18 William G. Bittle, *James Nayler 1618–1660, The Quaker Indicted by Parliament* (York: Sessions Book Trust, 1986), pp. 99–102. Maryann Feola-Castelucci, "'Warringe with ye worlde': Fox's Relationahip with Nayler," *QH* 81 (1992): 63–72. FJN, pp. 268–69.

19 Jeremiah Ives, *The Quakers Quaking*, 1656, pp. 9–17, 12 and 10 quoted. See Acts 2:1–4. James Nayler to George Fox [April–May 1656], LF: Swarthmore MSS 3/76.

20 Bittle, *James Nayler 1618–1660*, p. 102. Richard Hubberthorn to Margaret Fell, 25 November 1656, LF: Caton MSS 3/117. Winthrop S. Hudson, "A Supressed Chapter in Quaker History," *Journal of Religion* 24 (1944): 108–18. Thomas O'Malley, "'Defying the Powers and Tempering the Spirit': A Review of Quaker Control over Their Publications, 1672–1689," *Journal of Ecclesiastical History* 33 (1982): 72–88. Cadbury, *George Fox's "Book of Miracles."* Geoffrey F. Nuttall, "A Letter by James Nayler Appropriated to George Fox," *JFHS* 55 (1988): 178–79. H. Larry Ingle, "George Fox as Enthusiast: An Unpublished Epistle," *JFHS* 55 (1989): 266–70; "George Fox, Historian," *QH* 82 (1993): 28–35.

21 Humphrey Wolrich, *A Declaration*, 1659, p. 34. Richard Farnworth, *The Holy Scriptures*, 1655, p. 51, 2 Cor. 3:6. Thomas Lawson, *An Untaught Teacher*, 1655, p. 2, Jer. 23:30.

22 Hollister, *Harlots Vail Removed*, 1658, p. 70. Edward Burrough, *Something In Answer to a Book, Called Choice Experiences*, 1654, p. 8. John Taylor, *Certain Queries* (1680?), in *Truth's Innocency*, 1697, p. 336.

23 Wright, *Testimony*, 1661, p. 161. Ives, *Quakers Quaking*, 1656, p. 20. John Tombes, *True Old Light*, 1660, p. 36.

24 Samuel Fisher, *Rusticus ad Academicos*, 1660, pt. 4, p. 167. Penn, *Reason Against Railing*, 1673, p. 128. William Shewen, *The Universality of the Light*, 1674, p. 16. Edward Burrough, *The Son of Perdition*, 1661, p. 37. Fisher, *Rusticus ad Academicos*, 1660, pt. 4, p. 190. James Nayler, *An Answer to Some Queries*, 1656, p. 4.

25 Richard Hobbs, *A True and Impartial Relation*, 1672, p. 21. Hobbs was a General Baptist minister in Dover (G. Lyon Turner, *Original Records of Early Nonconformity under Persecution and Indulgence*, 3 vols. [T. Fisher Unwin, 1911–14], 1:16, 225, 442; Adam Taylor, *The History of the English General Baptists*, 2 vols. [T. Bore, 1818], 1:273–77). For this episode see BBQ, p. 426; BSPQ, pp. 216, 237, 238.

26 Thomas Rudyard replied in *The Anabaptist Preacher Unmask'd*, 1672, p. 5 quoted, and Luke Howard replied with *A Looking-Glass for Baptists*, 1672, p. 7 quoted. To the latter, Richard Hobbs answered with *The Quakers Looking-Glass Look'd Upon*, 1673, to which Howard replied with *Seat of the Scorner*, 1673, and Rudyard replied with *The Water-Baptists Reproach Repeld*, 1673.

27 Wright, *Testimony*, 1661, p. 156.

28 For these episodes see William Sewel, *The History of the Rise, Increase, and Progress of the Christian People Called Quakers*, 1722, p. 488; BSPQ, pp. 25, 246, 320. William Burnet, *The Capital Principles*, 1668, p. 23. Wright, *Testimony*, 1661, p. 156. Solomon Eccles, *The Quakers Challenge*, 1668, pp. 1–2.

29 George Whitehead, *The Light and Life of Christ Within*, 1668, p. 38, Isa. 20. Burrough, *Son of Perdition*, 1661, p. 32, 1 Sam. 19:24. Hollister, *Skirts of the Whore Discovered*, 1656, p. 31 (misprinted 25). For more on this practice, see Kenneth L. Carroll, "Quaker Attitudes toward Signs and Wonders," *JFHS* 54 (1977): 70–84; "Early Quakers and Going Naked as a Sign," *QH* 67 (1978) 69–87.

30 T. L. Underwood, "'It pleased me much to contend': John Bunyan as Controversialist," *Church History* 57 (1988): 456–69, 466 quoted. T. L. Underwood, introduction to *MW*, 1:xxxix–xl, 11 (quoted), 39.

31 Benjamin Keach, *Tropologia*, 1682, sigs. B2r–B2v. General Baptist confession: 1660, article 5, MBC p. 113 quoted. Savoy Declaration, pt. 2, section 12; *HSPFE*, pp. 78–81. General Baptist confession: 1651, article 71, MBC, pp. 107–8; 1660, article 5, pp. 209–10; 1677, chapter 26, section 11, p. 267. Henry Denne, *The Quaker No Papist*, 1659, sig. A2r, pp. 8–9.

32 Thomas Aldam, Elizabeth Hooton, et al., *False Prophets and False Teachers Discribed*, 1652, p. 3. FGM, p. 318, Gal. 1:12. Fisher, *Rusticus ad Academicos*, 1660, pp. 173–74. See also Richard L. Greaves, *The Puritan Revolution and Educational Thought* (New Brunswick: Rutgers University Press, 1969).

33 John Stubbs to Margaret Fell, 1657, LF: Abraham MSS 3; William Caton to Margaret Fell, 1658, LF: Caton MSS 3/172. BBQ, pp. 301–2. See FGM, pp. 373–75.

34 Richard Hubberthorn, *Antichristianism Reproved*, 1660, p. 5.

35 Shewen, *Universality of the Light*, 1674, p. 22. Richard Hubberthorn and Samuel Fisher, *Supplementum Sublatum*, 1661, p. 6.

36 Diane Willen, "Godly Women in Early Modern England: Puritanism and Gender," *Journal of Ecclesiastical History* 43 (1992): 561–80, p. 580 quoted. *HSPFE*, pp. 87–89; Geoffrey S. Nuttall, "The Early Congregational Conception of the Ministry and the Place of Women in It," *Congregational Quarterly* 26 (1948): 153–61; Dorothy P. Ludlow, "Shaking Patriarchy's Foundations: Sectarian Women in England, 1641–1700," in *Triumph Over Silence: Women in Protes-*

tant History, ed. Richard L. Greaves (Westport, Conn.: Greenwood Press, 1985), pp. 93–123. See also Hilda L. Smith, *Reason's Disciples: Seventeenth–Century Feminists* (Urbana: University of Illinois Press, 1982) pp. 3–17, 75–114; Richard L. Greaves, "The Role of Women in Early English Nonconformity," *Church History* 52 (1983): 299–311; Anne Laurence, "A Priesthood of She-believers: Women and Congregations in Mid-Seventeenth-Century England," in *Women in the Church*, ed. W. J. Sheils and Diana Wood, vol. 27 of *Studies in Church History*, Ecclesiastical History Society (Oxford: Basil Blackwell, 1990), pp. 345–63; Patricia Crawford, *Women and Religion in England 1500–1720* (Routledge, 1993), pp. 119–211; Diane Willen, "'Communion of the Saints': Spiritual Reciprocity and the Godly Community in Early Modern England," *Albion* 27 (1995): 19–41; T. L. Underwood, introduction, *MW*, 4:xxxvii–xliv. Robert Baillie, *A Dissuasive From the Errours of the Time*, 1645, p. 111; Robert Baillie, *Anabaptism*, 1647, p. 53 quoted. Baillie went on to describe a Baptist woman, Mrs. Attaway, as "the Mistresse of all the She-preachers in Coleman street." Thomas Edwards described one of her meetings (*The First and Second Part of Gangraena*, 3rd ed., 1646, pp. 31–32). See also the entry for Mrs. Attaway in *BDBR*.

37 Particular Baptist confession: 1656, article 25, MBC, p. 209. General Baptist confessions: 1651, pp. 95–105; 1660, pp. 111–22; 1679, pp. 124–61. T. L. Underwood, introduction, *MW* 4:xxxvii–xliv, 305–7, 325–26, 306 quoted. *GCP*, pt. 3, pp. 45, 47, 1 Cor. 14:34, 1 Tim. 2:11–12.

38 BSPQ, pp. 270–71. Thomas Ewins, *The Church of Christ*, 1657, pp. 47–48, 22. Ives, *Quakers Quaking*, 1656, p. 17. Matthew Caffyn, *The Deceived, and Deceiving Quakers*, 1656, p. 22. Thomas Hicks, *A Dialogue*, 1673, p. 71, 1 Cor. 14:34, 1 Tim. 2:11–12.

39 GCP, pt. 3, pp 45–46.

40 John Wigan, *Antichrist's Strongest Hold Overturned*, 1665, p. 50.

41 Thomas Curwen, *This Is an Answer*, 1665, pp. 70–71. Mead, *Brief Account*, 1674, pp. 9–10. Caffyn, *Deceived, and Deceiving Quakers*, 1656, p. 22. See also Hicks, *Dialogue*, 1673, p. 7; Rebecca Travers, *This Is for All*, 1664, p. 4. In addition, see Phyllis Mack, "Teaching About Gender and Spirituality in Early English Quakerism," *Women's Studies* 19 (1991): 223–37; *Visionary Women: Ecstatic Prophecy in Seventeenth-Century England* (Berkeley: University of California Press, 1992), which includes analysis of the changing role of Quaker women to 1770; Christine Trevett, *Women and Quakerism in the 17th Century* (York: Sessions Book Trust, 1991); Bonnelyn Young Kunze, *Margaret Fell and the Rise of Quakerism* (Stanford: Stanford University Press, 1994), pp. 19–20.

42 Christopher Hill, *Milton and the English Revolution* (New York: Viking Press, 1978), pp. 117–18. George Fox, *The Woman Learning in Silence*, 1656, pp. 1–2. See also George Fox, *Concerning the Living God of Truth*, 1680, p. 11; George Fox, *A Testimony for God's Truth*, 1688, pp. 11–12.

43 Whitchurch, Hants. transcripts, p. 6, Baptist Union Archives MSS 3, Regent's Park College Library, Oxford. General Baptist confessions: 1651, articles 59, 60, 61, MBC, pp. 105–6; 1660, article 16, p. 117; 1678, article 31, pp. 146–47. Particular Baptist confessions: 1644, article 38, MBC, pp. 184–85; 1656, article 32, p. 211; 1677, chapter 26, section 10, pp. 266–67. See also WHB, p. 132.

44 BBQ, p. 136. See also BSPQ, p. 360. William Britten, *Silent Meeting, A Wonder to the World*, 1660, p. 1. James Nayler, *The Boaster Bared*, 1655, p. 6. James Nayler, *Deceit Brought to Day-light*, 1656, p. 24. Edward Burrough, *The True Faith of the Gospel of Peace Contended For*, 1656, p. 29. Bunyan, *A Vindica-*

tion of the Book Called, Some Gospel-Truths Opened, 1657, in *MW,* 1:205. For "hireling" ministers see John 12:11–13.

45 William Penn, *The Christian-Quaker,* 1674, p. 127.

46 Burnet, *Capital Principles,* 1668, p. 23. Wright, *Testimony,* 1661, p. 154. Whitehead, *Light and Life of Christ Within,* 1668, p. 37, Acts 1:4. See also Burrough, *Son of Perdition,* 1661, p. 41, and Richard Bauman, *Let Your Words Be Few: Symbolism of Speaking and Silence Among Seventeenth-Century Quakers* (Cambridge: Cambridge University Press, 1983).

47 See BBQ, pp. 123–25, 166–67; BSPQ, pp. 526–27. Wigan, *Antichrist's Strongest Hold Overturned,* 1665, p. 49. Wright, *Testimony,* 1661, p. 164. Enoch Howet, *Quaking Principles Dashed,* 1655, p. 10. Hicks, *Dialogue,* 1673, p. 80. Griffith, *Voice from the Word of the Lord,* 1654, p. 6. Howet, *Quaking Principles Dashed,* 1655, p. 10. Wright, *Testimony,* 1661, pp. 156–57.

48 Burrough, *Son of Perdition,* 1661, pp. 30, 39, Heb. 12:21, Ps. 38, Rom. 8. FGM, p. 318, Phil. 2:12. See also George Fox, "Concerning quaking & trembling," 1653, LF: Swarthmore MSS 2/64.

49 Bauman, *Let Your Words Be Few,* pp. 120–36, 20–31, 30 quoted. See also J. Vernon Jensen, "Communicative Functions of Silence," *Etc.: A Review of General Semantics* 30 (1973): 249–57. Burrough, *Son of Perdition,* 1661, p. 42. Wolrich, *Declaration,* 1659, p. 9. Nayler, *Boaster Bared,* 1655, p. 6. Wolrich, *Declaration,* 1659, p. 9. Hicks, *Continuation of the Dialogue,* 1673, p. 66.

50 Horton Davies, *The Worship of the English Puritans* (Dacre Press, 1948), pp. 172–73. GCP, pt. 2, pp. 112–16, and W. T. Whitley, ed., *The Minutes of the General Assembly of the General Baptist Churches in England,* 2 vols. (Kingsgate Press, 1909–10), 1:27–28. See also Particular Baptist confession: 1677, chapter 22, section 5, MBC, p. 260. London, Maze Pond Minute Book, p. 3, Baptist Union Archives MSS 2, Regent's Park College Library, Oxford. UHB, p. 112.

51 FJN, pp. 164, 377. George Fox and Richard Hubberthorn, *Truth's Defence,* 1653, pp. 21–23. FJP, 1:442. Kenneth L. Carroll, "Singing in the Spirit in Early Quakerism," *QH* 73 (1984): 1–13. See also, favorably, Thomas Holme to Margaret Fell [c. 5 April 1654], LF: Swarthmore MSS 1/190; Margaret Newby to Margaret Fell, 25 November 1655, LF: Swarthmore MSS 1/359; but, negatively, John Grave to Margaret Fell [1654?], LF: Swarthmore MSS 4/232; Richard Hubberthorn to Margaret Fell, 16 September [1656], LF: Swarthmore MSS 3/153.

52 Nayler, *Boaster Bared,* 1655, p. 6. Kaye, *Plain Answer,* 1654, pp. 12–14. FJN, p. 35. Burrough, *Something in Answer to a Book, Called Choice Experiences,* 1654, p. 15.

53 General Baptist confessions: 1651, postscript, MBC, p. 109; 1660, article 25, p. 120; 1679, article 45, p. 158. Particular Baptist confessions: 1644, article 44, p. 187; 1656, article 44, p. 214; 1677, chapter 24, pp. 262–63. BQPE, p. 197. BSPQ, pp. 18–20. UHB, p. 81. BQPE, pp. 156, 199. Richard L. Greaves, "Shattered Expectations? George Fox, the Quakers, and the Restoration State, 1660–1685," *Albion* 24 (1992): 247–48.

54 WHB, p. 101. UHB, p. 81. WEBSC, pp. 102–3. See also General Baptist confessions: 1651, article 60, MBC, p. 105; 1660, article 16, p. 117. Particular Baptist confession: 1644, article 38, pp. 184–85.

55 Kaye, *Plain Answer,* 1654, pp. 11–12. See Stephen Copson, "Advocate of the Reformed Protestant Religion: The Writings (1645–59) of William Kaye, Yorkshire Puritan," *BQ* 35 (1994): 279–93. According to Copson, Kaye encouraged a national religious settlement in which all churches could be united around

believers' baptism, a rite that "was not inevitably linked to one form of church government" but "could be appropriated by all (excepting episcopal and Papal)" (p. 283). FJN, p. 297.

56 FGM, p. 318.

57 John Tombes, *A Supplement*, 1660, p. 18.

58 1679, article 48, MBC, pp. 159–60. 1677, article 23, MBC, pp. 261–62, 187 n. UHB, pp. 90–92. One such opponent of oaths, Samuel Hodgkin, is listed wrongly by Whitley (WHB, p. 104) along with Tombes, Denne, and Ives, as supporting their lawfulness. See Samuel Hodgkin's tract, *A Caution to the Sons of Sion*, 1660, and Whitley, introduction, *Minutes of the General Assembly of the General Baptist Churches*, 1:xxxviii.

59 In 1660 the following works favoring the use of oaths were published by three leading Baptists: Henry Denne, *An Epistle Recommended to All the Prisons*, Jeremiah Ives, *The Great Case of Conscience Opened*, and John Tombes, *A Serious Consideration of the Oath of the Kings Supremacy*. To the first two, Samuel Fisher replied with *One Antidote More* (1660?). To Tombes's work, Richard Hubberthorn responded with *Antichristianism Reproved*, 1660. Tombes replied with *A Supplement*, 1660, in which he also made reference to Fisher. In answer to this work by Tombes, Hubberthorn and Fisher joined forces in *Supplementum Sublatum*, 1661. Tombes replied to this, and to Fisher's *One Antidote More*, in his *Sephersheba*, 1662.

60 Hubberthorn, *Antichristianism Reproved*, 1660, p. 3. Tombes, *Sephersheba*, pt. 1, p. 91; Tombes, *Serious Consideration*, 1660, p. 16 quoted. Denne, *Epistle Recommended to All the Prisons*, 1660, p. 3, Gen. 21:23–24. Tombes, *Serious Consideration*, 1660, p. 10, Deut. 29:14. Ives, *Great Case of Conscience Opened*, 1660, p. 9 (misprinted 10), Rom. 1:9, 2 Cor. 1:23, Phil. 1:8. Denne, *Epistle Recommended to All the Prisons*, 1660, p. 4, Rev. 10:5–6. Denne, *Quaker No Papist*, 1659. Denne, *Epistle Recommended to All the Prisons*, 1660, p. 4, Ps. 132:11.

61 Hubberthorn, *Antichristianism Reproved*, 1660, p. 4. Fisher, *One Antidote More* (1660?), p. 12. Hubberthorn and Fisher, *Supplementum Sublatum*, 1661, pp. 1–2. Fisher, *One Antidote More* (1660?), pp. 27–28, 17 quoted.

62 Hubberthorn, *Antichristianism Reproved*, 1660, p. 11. Burrough, *Son of Perdition*, 1661, p. 56. Sewel claimed that Ives was imprisoned for refusing to take an oath, but having admonished two former prisoners for submitting to it, he himself changed his mind and took it (*History of the Rise, Increase, and Progress of the Quakers*, pp. 522–25). Fisher, *One Antidote More* (1660?), p. 3. Hubberthorn and Fisher, *Supplementum Sublatum*, 1661, p. 5. Tombes, *Supplement*, 1660, p. 16.

63 See A. Neave Brayshaw's discussion in *The Quakers*, 3rd ed. (New Tork: Macmillan, 1953), pp. 128–30. For enumeration and explanation of these oaths, see FPT, pp. 346, 354–57. See also BBQ, pp. 446–47, and BSPQ, pp. 23–24; Bauman, *Let Your Words Be Few*, pp. 95–119. Craig W. Horle, *The Quakers and the English Legal System 1660–1688* (Philadelphia: University of Pennsylvania Press, 1988), pp. 161–253.

64 For troubles caused by such refusal see BBQ, chapter 19. Howet, *Quaking Principles Dashed*, 1655, p. 14, Exod. 20. Ives, *Quakers Quaking*, 1656, p. 39, Acts 26:25. Nayler, *Boaster Bared*, 1655, p. 7. Alexander Parker, *A Discovery of Satans Wiles*, 1657, p. 40. Nayler, *Deceit Brought to Day-light*, 1656, pp. 14–15. Burrough, *Son of Perdition*, 1661, p. 50, the first of two pages of the same number. In responding to a reference by Keach about the Quakers' refusal of hat honor

(*Progress of Sin*, 1684, pp. 244–45), Park demanded scriptural precedent for the practice of removing the hat (*False Fictions*, 1684, p. 6). Barbour has pointed out that Quakers echoed the "bitterness of the tenants toward noblemen, clergy, and tithes" characteristic of the north of England in earlier decades, and were "thoroughly radical in their instinctive reactions to all the claims of the highborn and mighty" (BQPE, pp. 76, 84).

65 Ives, *Quakers Quaking*, 1656, p. 40. Henry Haggar, *Certain Considerations*, 1655, p. 56. Kaye, *Plain Answer*, 1654, p. 14.

66 Wright, *Testimony*, 1661, p. 180.

67 Richard Baxter, *A Key for Catholicks*, 1659, pp. 332–34. John Saltmarsh, *Sparkles of Glory*, 1647, sig. A11v, pp. 105, 149–53, 290–92. William Walwyn, *A Whisper in the Eare of Mr. Thomas Edwards*, 1645, sig. B2r, p. 6. John Jackson, *A Sober Word*, 1651, p. 45. William Erbery, *The Testimony*, 1658, pp. 53–54, 198–201, 312. Laurence Clarkson, *The Lost Sheep Found*, 1660, pp. 19, 38. Jacob Bauthumley, *The Light and Dark Sides of God*, 1650, p. 79. Abiezer Coppe, *A Fiery Flying Roll*, 1649, p. 5. John Reeve, *A Transcendent Spiritual Treatise*, 1652, p. 38. John Reeve and Lodowick Muggleton, *The Baptist's Commission Counterfeited*, pp. 1–2, 5, 10, in *Joyful News from Heaven*, 1706 (separate pagination). John Reeve, *Sacred Remains*, 1706, p. 66; Reeve, *Transcendent Spiritual Treatise*, 1652, pp. 7, 11. John Reeve and Lodowick Muggleton, *Verae Fidei*, 1820, p. 24.

68 Reeve, *Transcendent Spiritual Treatise*, 1652, p. 5. William Penn, *The New Witnesses*, 1672, pp. 61–62. Lodowick Muggleton, *A Looking-Glass for George Fox*, 1668, p.8; Lodowick Muggleton, *The Neck of the Quakers Broken*, 1663, p. 52; Lodowick Muggleton, *The Answer to William Penn*, 1673, p. 123. George Fox, *Something in Answer to Lodowick Muggleton's Book*, 1667, p. 27. Quakers also heard voices, of course, and had similar criticisms made of them—see Thomas Morford to Margaret Fell, 4 January [1657], LF: Swarthmore MSS 4/75; chapter 7 hereafter. In Maryland, Richard Beard was reportedly convinced of the truth of Quakerism when "in a miraculous way" he was struck down by "a clap of thunder" (Robert Clarkson to Elizabeth Harris, 14 January 1658, LF: Swarthmore MSS 3/7).

69 Salthouse, *Line of True Judgment*, 1658, pp. 1–2.

70 Wigan, *Antichrist's Strongest Hold Overturned*, 1665, pp. 53–54.

Chapter 7

1 John Tombes, *True Old Light Exalted Above Pretended New Light*, 1660, title page quoted. BDBR. FJN, 297.

2 Such controversies in person or in print engaged Burrough, Nayler, Penn, Whitehead, Bunyan, Collier, Grigg, and Ives, among others.

3 See Westminster Confession, chapter 6, chapter 10, section 4; Savoy Declaration, chapter 6, chapter 10, section 4; Perry Miller, *The New England Mind: The Seventeenth Century* (Cambridge: Harvard University Press, 1954), pp. 29, 187, 210, 216.

4 UFR, pp. 73–74, 83–84. For opposition to Quakers by a church that Denne served, see UFR, index, "Quakers." Henry Denne, *The Drag-net of the Kingdom of Heaven*, 1646, p. 91. Braithwaite (following Robert Barclay, *The Inner Life of the Religious Societies of the Commonwealth*, 1876, p. 163, and Rufus M. Jones, *Studies in Mystical Religion*, [Macmillan, 1909], pp. 422–23) concluded that "Denne, the most powerful preacher among the General Baptists, ad-

vocated the doctrine of the Inner Light in *The Drag-net, etc.*, a book published in 1646, before Fox had begun his public preaching" (BBQ, p. 12). In fact, Denne used here what he termed the "allegory" of John 1:9 to support his contention as a General Baptist that God gives the opportunity for salvation to *all* people. Nor do other references to light or inwardness support Braithwaite's conclusion. See T. L. Underwood, "The Baptist Henry Denne and the Quaker Doctrine of the Inner Light," *QH* 56 (1967): 34–40.

5 John Wigan, *Antichrist's Strongest Hold Overturned*, 1665, p. 33.

6 John Tombes, *True Old Light*, 1660, p. 16, Gen. 1:16. Thomas Hicks, *A Dialogue*, 1673, p. 4. William Penn, *The Christian-Quaker*, 1674, pp. 116–17.

7 George Whitehead, *The Christian-Quaker*, 1673, p. 29.

8 FJN, 295–96, John 1:1–7.

9 Penn, *Christian-Quaker*, 1674, p. 116.

10 Wigan, *Antichrist's Strongest Hold Overturned*, 1665, p. 25. Hicks, *A Continuation*, 1673, sig. A4r. Wigan, *Antichrist's Strongest Hold Overturned*, 1665, p. 25. William Burnet, *The Capital Principles*, 1668, p. 11. Wigan, *Antichrist's Strongest Hold Overturned*, 1665, p. 25. Enoch Howet, *Quaking Principles Dashed*, 1655, pp. 6–7. For "the candle" see Prov. 20:27.

11 Richard Hubberthorn, *The Light of Christ*, 1660, p. 3. Penn, *Christian-Quaker*, 1674, p. 12. George Whitehead, *An Appendix*, 1673, p. 28. For this characteristic, see especially Benjamin Ives's *The Quakers Quaking*, 1656. Commenting on the practice, Ellwood stated, "He seemed, I confess, well read in the fallacies of logic, and was, indeed, rather ready than true and sound in framing Syllogisms" (*The History of the Life of Thomas Ellwood*, 1714, p. 312). Jeremiah Ives, *A Sober Request*, 1674, broadsheet. Ives requested that such a meeting be held separately from any that Quakers might plan with Hicks, but Shewen replied, "J. I. as so, is not worth disputing with: but [Quakers] . . . will be ready to do it, both by Life and Doctrine, against all their Opposers" (*A Brief Return*, 1674, broadsheet). Apparently the meeting never took place. Shewen, *Brief Return*, 1674, broadsheet quoted.

12 James Nayler, *The Boaster Bared*, 1655, p. 5. Enoch Howet, *Quaking Principles Dashed*, 1655, p. 5. Edward Burrough, *The Walls of Jerico Razed*, 1654, pp. 5–6.

13 Tombes, *True Old Light*, 1660. p. 17. John Bunyan, *Some Gospel-truths Opened*, 1656, in *MW*, 1:55, Rom. 1:20. John Bunyan, *A Vindication of the Book Called, Some Gospel-Truths Opened*, 1657, in *MW*, 1:147 quoted. Bunyan, *Vindication*, 1657, *MW*, 1:147–48 quoted.

14 George Whitehead, *The Light and Life of Christ Within*, 1668, p. 30. FGM, p. 208. William Smith, *The Lying Spirit*, 1658, p. 6. Whitehead, *Appendix*, 1673, p. 28.

15 Penn, *The Christian-Quaker*, 1674, p. 115.

16 Edward Burrough, *Truth (the Strongest of All) Witnessed Forth*, 1657, p. 19. Richard Farnworth, *The Holy Scriptures*, 1655, p. 43. Humphrey Wolrich, *A Declaration*, 1659, p. 34.

17 FJN, 296.

18 James Nayler, *An Answer to Some Queries*, 1656, John 8:12, Luke 17:21, 2 Cor. 4:6–7, Col. 1:27.

19 George Whitehead, *The Quakers Plainness*, 1674, p. 74.

20 John Owen stated, "Non dicitur Christum illuminare omnem hominem venientem in mundum, sed quod ipse veniens in mundum omnem hominem illu-

minat" (*Pro Sacris Scripturis*, 1658, pp. 113–14). Acccording to Richard Baxter, "All that come into the world of nature, he enlighteneth with the light of Nature. . . . And all that come into the world of grace he enlighteneth with the light of supernatural Revelation" (*The Quakers Catechism*, 1655, p. 7). Unlike other Baptists, Ives spoke of a single enlightening, but he achieved the same result as his fellow controversialists by interpreting Christ's enlightening of all persons as providing the means by which all might come to him, the light, if they chose, and by insisting that all people did not have this light within them. Although Ives's Arminianism is evident in his interpretation, it would not have prevented him from accepting the approach used by Calvinistic Baptists.

21 Tombes, *True Old Light*, 1660, pp. 16–17. Wigan, *Antichrist's Strongest Hold Overturned*, 1665, pp. 43–44. Bunyan, *Some Gospel-truths Opened*, 1656, in *MW*, 1:55–56. Henry Grigg, *Light From the Sun*, 1672, pp. 8–9.

22 Thomas Collier, *A Looking-Glasse for the Quakers*, 1657, p. 14. Henry Grigg, *The Baptist Not Babylonish*, 1672, p. 18. Wigan, *Antichrist's Strongest Hold Overturned*, 1665, p. 42.

23 Bunyan, *Some Gospel-truths Opened*, 1656, in *MW*, 1:56–57. Bunyan, *Vindication*, 1657, in *MW*, 1:144 quoted. Edward Burrough, *The True Faith of the Gospel of Peace Contended For*, 1656, p. 17.

24 William Penn, *Reason Against Railing*, 1673, pp. 34–35. Farnworth, *Holy Scriptures*, 1655, p. 54. Whitehead, *The Christian-Quaker*, 1673, p. 67. Penn, *Christian-Quaker*, 1674, p. 32. James Nayler, *The Light of Christ*, 1656, p. 16.

25 Whitehead, *Christian-Quaker*, 1673, p. 109. Samuel Fisher, *Rusticus ad Academicos*, 1660, pt. 4, p. 184. Farnworth, *Holy Scriptures*, 1655, p. 54, John 14:16, 12:1–11. William Penn, *The Counterfeit Christian*, 1674, p. 59, 1 John 1:11. Hicks, *Dialogue*, 1673, p. 3. Grigg, *Baptist Not Babylonish*, 1672, p. 18.

26 FGM, p. 95. Whitehead, *Appendix*, 1673, p. 30. Thomas Hicks, for example, exclaimed, "One while 'tis the Divine essence, 'tis Christ, 'tis increated; another while, 'tis not Christ himself, but only his gift, or appearance, a seed, a measure of Light, a witness for God . . . Their sayings hereabouts are so cross and thwarting, that 'tis almost impossible for a man to know when they speak as they think, or think as they speak" (*A Continuation of the Dialogue*, 1673, sig. A3v). Penn, *Reason Against Railing*, 1673, p. 15. Hugh Barbour rightly concluded that Friends "spoke of Light, the Spirit, and Christ within so interchangeably that no uniform distinction can be made clear" (BQPE, p. 110). For discussion of such interchangeability in Fox's journals, see Aimo Seppänen, "The Inner Light in the Journals of George Fox: A Semantic Study" (thesis for the Licentiate in Philosophy, Helsinki University, 1965), especially pp. 39, 54–55, 128, 191, LF.

27 Thomas Collier, *An Answer to an Epistle*, 1657, p. 11. Thomas Hicks, *The Quaker Condemned*, 1674, p. 6.

28 John Pendarves, *Arrowes Against Babylon*, 1656, p. 43. Pendarves (ca. 1623–56), Particular Baptist and Fifth Monarchist, was born in Cornwall, graduated B.A. from Exeter College, Oxford, and was a lecturer at Wantage, Berkshire, before joining with Baptists (BDBR).

29 Hicks, *Quaker Condemned*, 1674, p. 14. Matthew Caffyn, *The Deceived, and Deceiving Quakers*, 1656, pp. 10–11, 14. Henry Haggar, *Certain Considerations*, 1655, pp. 49–50, Matt. 6:23.

30 Whitehead, *Christian-Quaker*, 1673, p. 112, Rom. 10:8. Nayler, *Answer to Some Queries*, 1656, p. 6. To Nayler's use of Luke 17:21, Jeremiah Ives replied that ἐντὸζ ought to be translated "among" rather than "within" (*Innocency Above*

Impudency, 1956, p. 45). Tombes commented, "Whereunto I answer, 1. That the particle translated (*within you*) may be as well, and to my apprehension more truly rendered (*among you*) which is the translation in the Margin. 2. That the sense is, the kingdome is not to be expected as a future thing; but as it is Mat. 12.28. *The kingdome of God is come unto you.* Luke 10:9 The kingdome of God is come nigh unto you: which is not meant of light within, but the preaching of the Gospel, of the presence of the Messiah (who was among them, Joh. 1.26.) without them; the light within each man cannot be meant by the kingdome of God" (*True Old Light,* p. 54). Thomas Salthouse, *The Line of True Judgment,* 1658, p. 13. FGM, p. 3.

31 Penn, *Christian-Quaker,* 1674, pp. 26–27, Deut. 30:11–13. James Parnell, *The Watcher,* 1655, p. 2. Farnworth, *Holy Scriptures,* 1655, pp. 52–53, Ps. 119:11, 130. Penn, *Christian-Quaker,* 1674, pp. 28–30.

32 Haggar, *Certain Considerations,* 1655, p. 50. Hicks, *Dialogue,* 1673, pp. 10–11.

33 FGM, p. 38, Isa. 49.6. Paul and Barnabas, however, seem to have used this passage in a different way, interpreting themselves as the light sent (Acts 13:47). Fisher, *Rusticus ad Academicos,* 1660, pt. 4, p. 178. Penn, *Christian-Quaker,* 1674, pp. 42–52. H. G. Wood notes that the bulk of Penn's quotations from the ancient philosophers were taken from Thomas Stanley's *History of Philosophy,* 1658 ("William Penn's *Christian Quaker,*" in *Children of Light,* ed. H. H. Brinton [New York: Macmillan, 1938], p. 8). Penn, *Reason Against Railing,* 1673, pp. 12–13. Penn, *Christian-Quaker,* 1674, pp. 80–84, 120. "Swear not at all" is found in Matt. 5:34 (see also chapter 6).

34 Bunyan, *Some Gospel-truths Opened,* 1656, in *MW,* 1:56–57. Ives, *Innocency Above Impudency,* 1656, p. 45, Rom. 2:14. Tombes, *True Old Light,* 1660, p. 68.

35 Nayler, *Deceit Brought to Day-light,* 1656, p. 11.

36 FGM, p. 64. Burrough, *True Faith,* 1656, p. 18. Fisher, *Rusticus ad Academicos,* 1660, pt. 4, p. 171.

37 Nayler, *Weakness Above Wickedness,* 1656, p. 21.

38 Ives, *Innocency Above Impudency,* 1656, p. 37. *FGM,* p. 64. William Shewen, *The Universality of the Light,* 1674, p. 15, Eph. 5:8.

39 Nuttall regards Fox's numerous attempts to appeal to the inner light in wicked persons as strong evidence of his fundamental belief that even the wicked had the Spirit (*HSPFE,* p. 161). Thomas Curwen, *This Is an Answer,* 1665, p. 24. Burrough, *True Faith,* 1656, p. 20. Fisher, *Rusticus ad Academicos,* 1660, pt. 4, p. 170, John 12:35.

40 Ives, *Innocency Above Impudency,* 1656, p. 37. Bunyan, *Some Gospel-truths Opened,* 1656, in *MW,* 1:22–23, Rom. 8:9. Caffyn, *Deceived, and Deceiving Quakers,* 1656, p. 20, John 14:17. Ives, *Quakers Quaking,* 1656, pp. 36–37. Burnet, *Capital Principles,* 1668, p. 9.

41 Edward Burrough, *The Son of Perdition,* 1661, p. 45. FGM, p. 38. Whitehead, *Christian-Quaker,* 1673, p. 15. Penn, *Reason Against Railing,* 1673, p. 15.

42 FJN, p. 34. Francis Howgill, *The Inheritance of Jacob Discovered,* 1656, pp. 11–12. Ames, *Declaration,* 1656, p. 8, Eph. 2:14. Grigg, *Light From the Sun,* 1672, pp. 7–10. Wigan, *Antichrist's Strongest Hold Overturned,* 1665, p. 10. Burnet, *Capital Principles,* 1668, p. 11.

43 Bunyan, *Vindication,* 1657, in *MW,* 1:165. Hicks, *Dialogue,* 1673, p. 82. GCP, pt. 4, p. 71.

44 Benjamin Keach, *The Progress of Sin,* 1684, pp. 247–48. James Park re-

sponded by asking, "How can the Light of the glorious Gospel, that shines in Peoples Hearts, be ignorant or know nothing of the glorious Gospel of Jesus Christ [?]" (*False Fictions*, 1684, p. 15).

45 Whitehead, *Christian-Quaker*, 1673, pp. 88–89. Nayler, *Weakness Above Wickedness*, 1657, p. 11. Whitehead, *Appendix*, 1673, p. 31.

46 Whitehead, *Christian-Quaker*, 1673, p. 21, John 3:16–17. Shewen, *Universality of the Light*, 1674, p. 13. Burrough, *Truth*, 1657, p. 35. Fisher, *Rusticus ad Academicos*, 1660, pt. 4, p. 175. Whitehead, *Dipper Plung'd*, 1672, p. 8, reference probably to Rom. 1:19–20.

47 Penn, *Christian-Quaker*, 1674, p. 37.

48 Tombes, *True Old Light*, 1660, p. 40. Bunyan, *Vindication*, 1657, in *MW*, 1:166, Rom. 9:16–22.

49 Haggar, *Certain Considerations*, 1655, p. 53. Collier, *Looking-Glasse for the Quakers*, 1657, p. 9. Haggar, *Certain Considerations*, 1655, p. 51, Isa. 8:20. Tombes, *True Old Light*, 1660, pp. 71–72.

50 Penn, *Reason Against Railing*, 1673, p. 35. Fisher, *Rusticus ad Academicos*, 1660, pt. 4, p. 183. Parnell, *Watcher*, 1655, p. 45. Parnell (1636–56), of Retford near Nottingham, visited Fox in Carlisle prison and was converted. As a travelling preacher he encountered Baptists at Fenstanton, Huntingdonshire, to whom he addressed forty-three queries printed in *Watcher*. He died in prison at Colchester Castle (*BDBR*).

51 William Ames, letter to the Baptists at Sunderland, Durham, 21 April 1656, LF: Portfolio 1A 6.

52 GCP, pt. 4, p. 1. Hicks, *Dialogue*, 1673, p. 85. Tombes, *True Old Light*, 1660, p. 54, 51. For this estrangement see chapters 3 and 6, and BBQ, pp. 247–50. Pendarves, *Arrowes Against Babylon*, 1656, p. 45. Tombes, *True Old Light*, 1660, p. 53. Kaye, *Plain Answer*, 1654, p. 5.

53 See Richard Baxter, *The Certainty of a World of Spirits, Fully Evinced by Unquestionable Histories of Apparitions and Witchcrafts, Operations, Voices, &c.*, 1691. See also Amelia Mott Gummere, *Witchcraft and Quakerism* (Philadelphia: Biddle Press, 1908); Alan Macfarlane, *Witchcraft in Tudor and Stuart England* (Routledge and Kegan Paul, 1970); Brian P. Levack, *The Witch-hunt in Early Modern Europe*, (Longman, 1987); Sue Friday, "Witchcraft and Quaker Convincements: Lynn, Massachusetts, 1692," *QH* 84 (1995): 89–115.

54 James Blackley's tract, *A Lying Wonder Discovered*, 1659, was also signed by George Whitehead and three others. (For Blackley, see BBQ, p. 296). The anonymous tract, *Strange & Terrible Newes from Cambridge*, 1659, is catalogued in the British Library under Mary Philips; p. 4 is quoted. See T. L. Underwood, introduction, *MW*, 1:xxviii–xxix.

55 Ralph James was licensed in 1672 as a Baptist preacher at North Willingham, Lincolnshire (not Leicestershire as in Turner). G. Lyon Turner, *Original Records of Early Nonconformity under Persecution and Indulgence*, 3 vols. (J. Fisher Unwin, 1911–14), 1:579, 584, 585. James apparently told the story of these events, which had occurred some nine years before (*The Quakers Subterfuge*, 1672, p. 13) at a dispute between Independents and Quakers in 1671 or 1672. The circulation of the story in London brought requests for its printed substantiation, leading to the publication of James's tract. To it Thomas Rudyard replied with *The Anabaptists Lying Wonder*, 1672, and *The Anabaptist Preacher Unmask'd*, 1672. To these James responded with *Quakers Subterfuge*, 1672, which evoked a rejoinder from Robert Ruckhill in *The Quakers Refuge*, 1673, and another from William

Smith in *The Baptists Sophistry Discovered*, 1673. Rudyard, of London, possessed a knowledge of law, which he employed in the Quaker cause. In 1682, he went to North America (FJP, 2:420.) and in 1685 to Barbados, where he died in 1692. A moral lapse apparently led to the severance of his connection with Friends. See Alfred W. Braithwaite, *Thomas Rudyard: Early Friends' "Oracle of Law"*, *JFHS* Supplement 27 (1956). Little is known of Robert Ruckhill except that he lived in Lincolnshire. The deaths of a daughter in 1644, a son in 1675, and his wife in 1693 are recorded in Digested Copy of the Registers of Burials of the Quarterly Meeting of Lincolnshire, LF. Smith (d. 1673), of Besthorpe, Nottinghamshire, was an Independent minister before joining with the Quakers in 1658 (*DNB*).

56 Bauthumley, *The Light and Dark Sides of God*, 1650, sigs. A4r–A4v, pp. 71–84. William Erbery, *The Testimony*, 1658, pp. 8, 138, 127. John Jackson, *Strength in Weakness*, 1655, pp. 12–14, p. 14 quoted. Edward Burrough, *A Trumpet of the Lord Sounded Out of Sion*, 1656, pp. 28–29. Richard Farnworth, *The Ranters Principles*, 1654, p. 3. James Nayler, *What the Possession of the Living Faith Is*, 1659, p. 61. Margaret Fell, *A Testimonie of the Touch-Stone*, 1666, p. 27. Anthony Pearson to George Fox, 18 July 1654, LF: Swarthmore MSS 3/34. Numerous disputes with Ranters were reported by Friends, including ones with Jacob Bauthumley and Joseph Salmon—William Dewsbury to [George Fox], [1654], LF: Swarthmore MSS 3/22; Henry Fell to Margaret Fell, 3 November 1656, LF: Swarthmore MSS 1/66. See also FJN. Lodowick Muggleton, *The Prophet Muggleton's Epistle*, 1672, p.11 Lodowick Muggleton, *A Looking-Glass for George Fox*, 1667, pp. 38–39. Isaac Penington, *Observations on Some Passages of Lodowick Muggleton*, 1668, p. 14.

57 Smith, *Baptists Sophistry Discovered*, 1673, p. 17. Fisher, *Rusticus ad Academicos*, 1660, pt. 4, pp. 183–84.

58 Fisher, *Rusticus ad Academicos*, 1660, pt. 4, p. 183. Richard Baxter, who often referred to the similarities of Quakers and papists, commented on their use of the term "infallible Spirit": "we hear the croakings of your Papist guides in that word (*infallible*)" (*The Quakers Catechism*, 1655, p. 9). William Russel, *Quakerism Is Paganism*, 1674, p. 57. Hicks, *Dialogue*, 1673, p. 27. For a typical refutation of such stories see Whitehead, *Christian-Quaker*, 1673, p. 56. Penn, *Reason Against Railing*, 1673, p. 11.

59 Whitehead, *Christian-Quaker*, 1673, pp. 34–35.

60 *FPT*, pp. 119–21.

Chapter 8

1 Mircea Eliade, *Myths, Dreams, and Mysteries: The Encounter Between Contemporary Faith and Archaic Realities*, trans. Philip Mairet (Harvill Press, 1960), pp. 29–30. Eliade also concludes that "The initiation of a transhuman model, the repetition of an exemplary scenario and the breakaway from profane time through a moment which opens out into the Great Time, are the essential marks of 'mythical behaviour'—that is, the behaviour of the man of the archaic societies, who finds the very source of his existence in the myth" (p. 30).

2 Nigel Smith, ed., *A Collection of Ranter Writings from the 17th Century*, (Junction Books, 1983), p. 10. For a different conclusion regarding Muggletonians and Quakers, see Rosemary Anne Moore, "The Faith of the First Quakers: The Development of their Beliefs and Practices up to the Restoration" (Ph.D. thesis, University of Birmingham, 1993), p. 25, LF.

3 Richard Baxter, *The Saints Everlasting Rest*, 1650, p. 759.

4 John Bunyan, *Grace Abounding*, ed. Roger Sharrock (Oxford: Clarendon Press, 1962), section 124, p. 39. John Bunyan, *Some Gospel-truths Opened*, 1656, in *MW*, 1:58. Henry Grigg, *Light From the Sun*, 1672, pp. 21–22. John Beevan, *A Loving Salutation*, 1660, p. 2.

5 FJN, p. 4. William Penn, *Reason Against Railing*, 1673, p. 17. Thomas Ellwood, *Forgery No Christianity*, 1674, pp. 71–72. See also James Nayler, *An Answer to Some Queries*, 1656, p. 3; Humphrey Wolrich, *A Declaration to the Baptists*, 1659, pp. 7–8; John Perrot, "To the Assembly of Baptists," n.d., LF: Swarthmore MSS 5/30.

6 Thomas Ellwood, *Forgery No Christianity*, 1674, pp. 71–72. Samuel Howe, *Sufficiency of the Spirits Teaching Without Humane Learning*, 1639, reprinted 1655, p. 40. Edward Barber, *A True Discovery of the Ministry of the Gospel*, 1645, pp. 1–2. However, Barber also required the minister to be converted "by the Word outwardly, and so a baptized or dipt Disciple" (p. 1). Thomas Collier, *A General Epistle to the Universal Church*, 1649, p. 46, in *The Second Volume of the Works of Thomas Collier*, 1649. J. L. Nickalls, "George Fox's Library," *JFHS* 28 (1931): 8.

7 FJN, 392.

8 See Michael Hill, *A Sociology of Religion* (New York: Basic Books, 1973), pp. 140–204; Bryan Wilson, *Religion in Sociological Perspective* (Oxford: Oxford University Press, 1982), pp. 89–147; Bryan Wilson, *Religious Sects: A Sociological Study* (New York: McGraw-Hill, 1970).

9 See WEBSC, pp. 23–92; J. F. McGregor, "The Baptists: Fount of All Heresy," in *Radical Religion in the English Revolution*, ed. J. F. McGregor and B. Reay (Oxford: Oxford University Press, 1984), pp. 23–63; and RQER, pp. 103–22. As previously discussed, Perrot objected to the Quaker "requirement" of removing the hat during prayer, and Wilkinson and Story to the organization and standardized practice Fox was trying to impose—all on the grounds that the working of the Spirit (the inner light) in individuals was thus being suppressed.

10 Richard L. Greaves, "Shattered Expectations? George Fox, the Quakers, and the Restoration State, 1660–1685," *Albion* 24 (1992): 237–59. Craig Horle, *The Quakers and the English Legal System, 1660–1688* (Philadelphia: University of Pennsylvania Press, 1988). In contrast to the vigorous evangelistic approach of the earlier period, see the account of the gradual conversion to Quakerism by 1693 of the young husbandman Josiah Langdale, whose Quaker employers had for years not even raised the subject of religion with him (RQER, pp. 103–4).

11 Vavasor Powell, *The Bird in the Cage*, 1661, p. 71 (I am grateful to Richard L. Greaves for this reference). R. H., *The Character of a Quaker*, 1671, p. 1. Margaret Fell, "To Friends and Brethren and Sistern," 1700, LF: Portfolio 25: 66. Margaret Fell, "An Epistle to Friends," 1698, in *A Brief Collection*, 1710, p. 535. See also Isabel Ross, *Margaret Fell, Mother of Quakerism*, 2nd. ed. (York: Sessions Book Trust), pp. 379–80.

12 *The Quakers Ballad*, 1674, broadsheet. Grigg, *Baptist Not Babylonish*, 1672, sigs. A2r–A3r. Ann Hughes, "The Pulpit Guarded: Confrontations between Orthodox and Radicals in Revolutionary England," in *John Bunyan and His England, 1628–88*, ed. Anne Laurence, W. R. Owens, and Stuart Sim (Hambledon Press, 1990), pp. 3–50, 40 quoted.

Bibliography

Place of publication is London unless otherwise noted.

Primary Sources

Manuscripts

British Library

"A Register Booke . . . of the Congregation . . . in and about Speldhurst and Penbury in Kent." Additional Manuscript 36709.
Thomas Tompkinson. "Autobiographical Works." Additional Manuscript 42505.
William Wood. Letter to Lodowick Muggleton. Additional Manuscript 60168/41.

Congregational Library, London

A Declaration of Several Baptized Believers. 1659. Manuscript Portfolio 2 a 39.

Regent's Park College Library, Oxford

London, Dean Street Church Book. Angus Collection Manuscripts 36. G.A. f. 14.
London, Maze Pond Minute Book. Baptist Union Archives Manuscripts 2.
Whitchurch, Hants. transcripts, Baptist Union Archives Manuscripts 3.

Library of the Religious Society of Friends, London

Abraham Manuscripts.
A. R. Barclay Manuscripts.

William Caton Manuscripts.
Digested Copy of the Registers of Burials of the Quarterly Meeting of Bristol and
    Somersetshire.
Digested Copy of the Registers of Burials of the Quarterly Meeting of Lin-
    colnshire.
London [Second Day] Morning Meeting Minutes.
Portfolio 1A6.
Portfolio 25:66
Portfolio 36 no. 13.
Swarthmore Manuscripts.
Southwark Manuscripts.

Published Primary Sources

Aldam, Thomas, Elizabeth Hooton, et al. *False Prophets and False Teachers Dis-
    cribed*, 1652.
Ames, William, the Puritan. *Conscience With the Power and Cases Thereof*, 1639,
    Book 4.
Ames, William, the Quaker. *A Declaration*. 1656.
Baillie, Robert. *A Dissuasive From the Errours of the Time*, 1645.
———. *Anabaptism*, 1647.
Baptist Western Association. *Several Resolutions and Answers of Queries*, 1657.
Barber, Edward. *A True Discovery of the Ministry of the Gospel*, 1645.
Barclay, Robert. *The Anarchy of the Ranters*, 1676.
Bauthumley, Jacob. *The Light and Dark Sides of God*, 1650.
Baxter, Richard. *The Saints Everlasting Rest*, 1650.
———. *Plain Scripture Proof of Infants Church-Membership and Baptism*, 1651.
———. *The Quakers Catechism*, 1655.
———. *A Key for Catholicks*, 1659.
———. *A Christian Directory*, 1673.
———. *The Catechizing of Families*, 1683.
———. *The Certainty of a World of Spirits, Fully Evinced by Unquestionable Histories
    of Apparitions and Witchcrafts, Operations, Voices, &c.*, 1691.
———. *Reliquiae Baxteriannae*, 1696.
Bayly, William. *A Short Relation*, 1659.
Beevan, John. *A Loving Salutation*, 1660.
Biddle, John. *A Twofold Catechism*, 1654.
Blackley, James. *A Lying Wonder Discovered*, 1659.
Britten, William. *Silent Meeting, A Wonder to the World*, 1660.
Bunyan, John. *Some Gospel-truths Opened*, 1656.
———. *A Vindication of the Book Called, Some Gospel-Truths Opened*, 1657.
———. *The Doctrine of the Law and Grace Unfolded*, 1659.
———. *A Confession of My Faith*, 1672.
———. *Differences in Judgment About Water-Baptism*, 1673.
———. *Grace Abounding*, edited by Roger Sharrock. Oxford: Clarendon Press,
    1962.
———. *The Miscellaneous Works of John Bunyan*. Edited by Roger Sharrock. 13 vols.
    Oxford: Clarendon Press, 1976–94.
Burnet, William. *The Capital Principles*, 1668.
Burrough, Edward. *Something in Answer to a Book, Called Choice Experiences*, 1654.

———. *Something in Answer to a Booke, Called a Voice*, 1654.

———. *The Walls of Jerico Razed*, 1654.

———. *The True Faith of the Gospel of Peace Contended For*, 1656.

———. *A Trumpet of the Lord Sounded Out of Sion*, 1656.

———. *Truth (the Strongest of All) Witnessed Forth*, 1657.

———. *The Son of Perdition*, 1661.

Caffyn, Matthew. *The Deceived, and Deceiving Quakers*, 1656.

———. *Faith in Gods Promises*, 1661.

Camm, Thomas. *The Line of Truth*, 1684.

Clarkson, Laurence. *A Single Eye*, 1650.

———. *The Lost Sheep Found*, 1660.

Collier, Thomas. *A General Epistle to the Universal Church*, in *The Second Volume of the Works of Thomas Collier*, 1649.

———. *A Dialogue Between a Minister of the Gospel, and an Enquiring Christian*, (1656?), not extant.

———. *An Answer to an Epistle*, 1657.

———. *A Looking-Glasse for the Quakers*, 1657.

———. *The Hypocrase and Falsehood of Thomas Salthouse* (1659?), extant?

———. *The Body of Divinity*, 1674.

Coppe, Abiezer. *A Fiery Flying Roll*, 1649.

———. *A Second Fiery Flying Roll*, 1649.

Crisp, Stephen. *A Memorable Account*, 1694.

Curwen, Thomas. *This Is an Answer*, 1665.

A Declaration of Several Baptized Believers, 1649.

Declaration of several of the People called Anabaptists, In and about the City of London, 1659.

Denne, Henry. *The Drag-net of the Kingdom of Heaven*, 1646.

———. *A Contention for Truth*, 1658.

———. *The Quaker No Papist*, 1659.

———. *An Epistle Recommended to All the Prisons*, 1660.

Dod, John, and Robert Cleaver. *A Plaine and Familiar Exposition of the Ten Commandments*, 1605.

Doolittle, Thomas. *The Protestants Answer to That Question, Where Was Your Church Before Luther? Wherein Popery is Proved a Novelty*. With a preface by Richard Baxter, 1675.

Downham, John. *A Blow at the Root*, 1650.

Drapes, Edward. *Gospel-glory Proclaimed*, 1649.

Eccles, Solomon. *The Quakers Challenge*, 1668.

Edwards, Thomas. *Gangraena*, 1646.

———. *The Second Part of Gangraena*, 1646.

———. *The Third Part of Gangraena*, 1646.

———. *The First and Second Part of Gangraena*, 3rd ed., 1646.

Ellwood, Thomas. *The History of the Life of Thomas Ellwood*, 1656.

———. *Forgery No Christianity*, 1674.

Erbery, William. *The Testimony*, 1658

Ewins, Thomas. *The Church of Christ*, 1657.

Farmer, Ralph. *Sathan Enthron'd*, 1657.

Farnworth, Richard. *The Ranters Principles*, 1654.

———. *To You That Are Called by the Name of Baptists*, 1654.

———. *Truth Cleared*, 1654.

———. *The Holy Scriptures*, 1655.

Fell, Margaret. *A Testimonie*, 1656.

———. *A Declaration*, 1660.

———. *A Testimonie of the Touch-Stone*, 1666.

———. *The Daughter of Zion Awakened*, 1677.

———. *An Epistle to Friends*, 1698. In *A Brief Collection*, 1710.

Fisher, Samuel. *One Antidote More*, 1660?

———. *Rusticus ad Academicos*, 1660.

Fox, George. *Saul's Errand to Damascus*, 1653.

———. *The Woman Learning in Silence*, 1656.

———. *The Great Mistery of the Great Whore Unfolded*, 1659.

———. *Several Warnings*, 1659.

———. *Something in Answer to Lodowick Muggleton's Book*, 1667.

———. *Concerning the Living God of Truth*, 1680.

———. *A Testimony for God's Truth*, 1688.

———. *A Collection*, 1698.

———. *The Journal of George Fox*. Edited by Thomas Ellwood, 1694.

———. *The Journal of George Fox*. Edited by Norman Penney. 2 vols. Cambridge: Cambridge University Press, 1911.

———. *The Journal of George Fox*. Edited by John L. Nickalls. Religious Society of Friends, 1975.

Fox, George, and Richard Hubberthorn. *Truth's Defence*, 1653.

Fox, George, et al. *A Declaration from the Harmles & Innocent People of God*, 1661.

Fuce, Joseph. *The Fall of A Great Visible Idol*, 1659.

Goodwin, Thomas. *The Works of Thomas Goodwin*. 5 vols. 1681–1704.

Gouge, Thomas. *Christian Directions*, 1675.

———. *The Principles of Christian Religion*, 1675.

Grantham, Thomas. *Christianismus Primitivus*, 1678.

———. *Hear the Church*, 1687.

Gratton, John. *A Journal of the Life of that Ancient servant of Christ, John Gratton*, 1720.

Griffith, John. *A Voice from the Word of the Lord*, 1654.

Grigg, Henry. *The Baptist Not Babylonish*, 1672.

———. *Light From the Sun*, 1672.

H., R. *The Character of a Quaker*, 1671.

Haggar, Henry. *Certain Considerations*, 1655.

———. *The Holy Scriptures*, 1655.

Helwys, Thomas. *A Short Declaration of the Mistery of Iniquity*, 1612.

Hicks, Thomas. *A Dialogue*, 1673.

———. *A Continuation of The Dialogue*, 1673.

———. *The Quaker Condemned*, 1674.

———. *The Quakers Appeal Answer'd*, 1674.

Hobbs, Richard. *A True and Impartial Relation*, 1672.

———. *The Quakers Looking-Glass Look'd Upon*, 1673.

Hodgkin, Samuel. *A Caution to the Sons of Sion*, 1660.

Hollister, Dennis. *The Skirts of the Whore Discovered*, 1656.

———. *The Harlots Vail Removed*, 1658.

Howard, Luke. *A Looking-Glass for Baptists*, 1672.

———. *The Seat of the Scorner Thrown Down*, 1673.

———. *Love and Truth in Plainness Manifested*, 1704.
Howe, Samuel. *Sufficiency of the Spirits Teaching Without Humane Learning*, 1639, reprinted 1655.
Howet, Enoch. *Quaking Principles Dashed*, 1655.
———. *The Beast That Was*, 1659.
Howgill, Francis. *The Inheritance of Jacob Discovered*, 1656.
Hubberthorn, Richard. *An Answer to a Declaration Put Forth by the General Consent of the People Called Anabaptists, In and About the City of London*, 1659.
———. *Antichristianism Reproved*, 1660.
———. *The Light of Christ*, 1660.
Hubberthorn, Richard, and Edward Burrough. *An Answer to a Declaration*, 1659.
Hubberthorn, Richard, and Samuel Fisher. *Supplementum Sublatum*, 1661.
The Humble Apology, 1660–61.
The Humble Petition and Representation, 1649.
The Humble Representation and Vindication, 1654.
Ives, Jeremiah. *Innocency Above Impudency*, 1656.
———. *The Quakers Quaking*, 1656.
———. *The Great Case of Conscience Opened*, 1660.
———. *A Sober Request*, 1674.
Jackson, John. *A Sober Word*, 1651.
———. *Strength in Weakness*, 1655.
James, Ralph. *The Quakers Subterfuge*, 1672.
Jeffery, William. *Antichrist Made Known*, 1656.
———. *The Whole Faith of Man*. 2nd ed., 1659.
Kaye, William. *A Plain Answer*, 1654.
Keach, Benjamin. *The Grand Impostor Discovered*, 1675.
———. *Tropologia*, 1682.
———. *The Progress of Sin*, 1684.
Keith, George. *George Keith's Vindication*, 1674.
Kiffin, William. *Heart-Bleedings for Professors Abominations*, 1650.
———. *The Quakers Appeal Answer'd*, 1674.
Knollys, Hanserd. *The Life and Death of . . . Hanserd Knollys*, 1692.
Lawson, Thomas. *An Untaught Teacher*, 1655.
Loddington, William. *Quakerism No Paganism*, 1674.
Mason, Martin. *Sions Enemy Discovered*, 1659.
Mead, William. *A Brief Account*, 1674.
———. *A Brief Narrative*, 1674.
Muggleton, Lodowick. *The Neck of the Quakers Broken*, 1663.
———. *A Looking-Glass for George Fox*, 1668.
———. *An Answer to Isaac Penington*, 1669.
———. *The Prophet Muggleton's Epistle*, 1672.
———. *The Answer to William Penn*, 1673.
———. *A Discourse Between John Reeve and Richard Leader*, 1682.
———. *The Acts of the Witnesses*, 1699.
Nayler, James. *The Boaster Bared*, 1655.
———. *An Answer to Some Queries*, 1656.
———. *Deceit Brought to Day-light*, 1656.
———. *The Light of Christ*, 1656.
———. *Love to the Lost*, 1656.
———. *Weakness Above Wickedness*, 1656.

——. *What the Possession of the Living Faith is*, 1659.

Owen, John. *Pro Sacris Scripturis*, 1658.

——. *Of the Divine Originall*, Oxford, 1659.

——. *A Brief Declaration and Vindication of the Doctrine of the Trinity*, 1669.

Park, James. *False Fictions*, 1684.

Parker, Alexander. *To All Ye Who Be Called Baptists*, 1657.

——. *A Discovery of Satans Wiles*, 1657.

Parnell, James. *The Watcher*, 1655.

Pendarves, John. *Arrowes Against Babylon*, 1656.

Penington, Isaac. *Observations on Some Passages of Lodowick Muggleton*, 1668.

——. *The Flesh & Blood of Christ*, 1675.

Penn, William. *The Sandy Foundation Shaken*, 1668.

——. *The New Witnesses Proved Old Hereticks*, 1672.

——. *Reason Against Railing*, 1673.

——. *The Christian-Quaker*, 1674.

——. *The Counterfeit Christian*, 1674.

Perrot, John. *To All Baptists Everywhere*, 1660.

——. *The Mistery of Baptism and the Lord's Supper*, 1662.

Pitman, John, and Jasper Batt. *Truth Vindicated*, 1658.

Plant, Thomas. *A Contest for Christianity*, 1674.

Powell, Vavasor. *The Bird in the Cage*, 1661.

The Quakers Ballad, 1674.

Richardson, Samuel. *Some Brief Consideration On Doctor Featly his Book*, 1645.

Reeve, John. *A Transcendent Spiritual Treatise*, 1652.

——. *Sacred Remains*, 1706.

Reeve, John, and Lodowick Muggleton. *A Divine Looking-Glass*, 1661.

——. *Joyful News from Heaven*, 1706.

——. *The Baptist's Commission Counterfeited*. In *Joyful News from Heaven*, 1706 (separate pagination).

——. *Verae Fidei Gloria est Corona Vitae. A Volume of Spiritual Epistles*. Edited by Alexander Delamaine and Tobias Terry. 1820.

Roper, Randall. *Truth Vindicated*, 1661.

Ruckhill, Robert. *The Quakers Refuge*, 1673.

Rudyard, Thomas. *The Anabaptists Lying Wonder*, 1672.

——. *The Anabaptist Preacher Unmask'd*, 1672.

——. *The Water-Baptists Reproach Repeld*, 1673.

——. *The Barbican-cheat Detected*, 1674.

Russel, William. *Quakerism Is Paganism*, 1674.

Salmon, Joseph. *A Rout, A Rout*, 1649.

——. *Heights in Depths and Depths in Heights*, 1651.

Salthouse, Thomas. *An Epistle to the Churches of the Anabaptists So Called*, 1657.

——. *The Line of True Judgment*, 1658.

Saltmarsh, John. *Free Grace; Or the Flowings of Christ's Blood Freely to Sinners*, 1645.

——. *Sparkles of Glory*, 1647.

Savoy Conference. *A Declaration of the Faith and Order Practised in the Congregational Churches in England*, 1659.

Several Resolutions and Answers of Queries, 1657.

Sewel, William. *The History of the Rise, Increase, and Progress of the Christian People Called Quakers*, 1722.

Shepard, Thomas. *Theses Sabbaticae*, 1649, Pt. 2.

Shewen, William. *A Brief Return*, 1674.
———. *The Universality of the Light*, 1674.
Sibbes, Richard. *A Breathing After God*, 1639.
Smith, William. *The Lying Spirit*, 1659.
———. *The Baptists Sophistry Discovered*, 1673.
Smyth, John. *The Character of the Beast*, 1609.
Stanley, Thomas. *History of Philosophy*, 1658.
Strange & Terrible Newes from Cambridge, 1659.
Taylor, John. *Ranters of Both Sexes*, 1651.
Taylor, Thomas. *Certain Queries*, 1680?
———. *Truth's Innocency*, 1697.
Tillam, Thomas. *The Seventh-day Sabbath*, 1657.
Tombes, John. *A Short Catechism About Baptism*, 1659.
———. *A Serious Consideration of the Oath of the Kings Supremacy*, 1660.
———. *A Supplement*, 1660.
———. *True Old Light*, 1660.
———. *Sephersheba*, 1662.
Tomkins, John. *Piety Promoted*. 2nd ed., 3 pts., 1703–06
Travers, Rebecca. *A Testimony*, 1663.
———. *This Is for All*, 1664.
Walwyn, William. *A Whisper in the Eare of Mr. Thomas Edwards*, 1645.
Wastfield, Robert. *An Equal Ballance*, 1659.
West, Robert. *Damnable Heresie Discovered*, 1673.
———. *The Pride of Jordan Spoiled*, 1674.
Westminster Assembly. *The Confession of Faith, and the Larger and Shorter Catechisms, First Agreed Upon by the Assembly of Divines at Westminster*, 1650.
Whitehead, George. *The Authority of the True Ministry*, 1660.
———. *The Pernicious Way*, 1662.
———. *The Light and Life of Christ Within*, 1668.
———. *Christ Ascended*, 1669.
———. *The Babylonish Baptist*, 1672.
———. *The Dipper Plung'd*, 1672.
———. *An Appendix*, 1673.
———. *The Christian-Quaker*, 1673.
———. *The Quakers Plainness*, 1674.
———. *Forgery Detected*, 1690?
Wigan, John. *Antichrist's Strongest Hold Overturned*, 1665.
Wilkinson, John. *The Memory of that Servant of God, John Story, Revived*, 1683.
Wolrich, Humphrey. *A Declaration*, 1659.
———. *One Warning More*, 1661.
Wright, Joseph. *A Testimony*, 1661.

Secondary Sources

Unpublished Material

Creasey, Maurice. "Early Quaker Christology with Special Reference to the Teaching of Isaac Penington." Ph.D. thesis, University of Leeds, 1956. LF.
Land, Richard D. "Controversies of English Particular Baptists (1648–1691) as Illustrated by the Career and Writings of Thomas Collier." D.Phil. thesis, Oxford University, 1979. Regent's Park College Library, Oxford.

Moore, Rosemary Anne. "The Faith of the First Quakers. The Development of their Beliefs and Practices up to the Restoration." Ph.D. thesis, University of Birmingham, 1993. LF.

Nuttall, Geoffrey, F. "Early Quaker Letters from the Swarthmore Manuscripts to 1660." Typescript, 1952. LF.

Seppänen, Aimo. "The Inner Light in the Journals of George Fox: A Semantic Study." Thesis for the Licentiate in Philosophy, Helsinki University, 1965. LF.

Articles

Ash, James L., Jr. "'Oh no, it is not the Scriptures!' The Bible and the Spirit in George Fox." *Quaker History* 63 (1974): 94–107.

Bitterman, M. G. F. "The Early Quaker Literature of Defense." *Church History* 42 (1973): 203–28.

Brachlow, Stephen. "Puritan Theology and General Baptist Origins." *Baptist Quarterly* 31 (1985): 179–94.

Butterfield, Ruth. "'The Royal Commission of King Jesus': General Baptist Expansion and Growth 1640–1660." *Baptist Quarterly* 35 (1993): 56–80.

Carroll, Kenneth L. "Quaker Attitudes Toward Signs and Wonders." *Journal of the Friends' Historical Society* 54 (1977): 70–84.

———. "Early Quakers and Going Naked as a Sign." *Quaker History* 67 (1978): 69–87.

———. "Singing in the Spirit in Early Quakerism." *Quaker History* 73 (1984): 1–13.

Clouse, Robert G. "The Rebirth of Millenarianism." In *Puritans, the Millennium and the Future of Israel: Puritan Eschatology 1600–1660*, edited by Peter Toon. Cambridge: James Clark, 1970.

Copson, Stephen. "Advocate of the Reformed Protestant Religion: The Writings (1645–59) of William Kaye, Yorkshire Puritan." *Baptist Quarterly* 35 (1994): 279–93.

Davis, J. C. "Fear, Myth and Furore: Reappraising the Ranters." *Past and Present* 129 (1990): 98–103.

———. "Against Formality: One Aspect of the English Revolution." *Royal Historical Society Transactions* 3 (1993): 265–87.

Durnbaugh, Donald F. "Baptists and Quakers—Left Wing Puritans?" *Quaker History* 62 (1973): 67–82.

Endy, Melvin B., Jr. "The Interpretation of Quakerism: Rufus Jones and His Critics." *Quaker History* 70 (1981): 3–21.

———. "Puritanism, Spiritualism, and Quakerism: An Historiographical Essay." In *The World of William Penn*, edited by Richard S. Dunn and Mary Maples Dunn. Philadelphia: University of Pennsylvania Press, 1986.

Feola–Castelucci, Maryann. "'Warringe with ye worlde': Fox's Relationship with Nayler." *Quaker History* 81 (1992) 63–72.

Friday, Sue. "Witchcraft and Quaker Convicements: Lynn, Massachusetts, 1692." *Quaker History* 84 (1995): 89–115.

George, Timothy. "Between Pacifism and Coercion: The English Baptist Doctrine of Religious Toleration." *Mennonite Quarterly Review* 58 (1984): 30–49.

Greaves, Richard L. "The Nature of the Puritan Tradition." In *Reformation, Conformity and Dissent: Essays in Honour of Geoffrey Nuttall*, edited by R. Buick Knox. Epworth Press, 1977.

———. "The Role of Women in Early English Nonconformity." *Church History* 52 (1983): 299–311.

———. "The Puritan-Nonconformist Tradition in England, 1560–1700: Historiographical Reflections." *Albion* 17 (1985) 449–86.

———. "John Bunyan: Tercentenary Reflections," in *John Bunyan: A Tercentenary*, edited by T. L. Underwood. *American Baptist Quarterly* 7 (1988): 496–508.

———. "Shattered Expectations? George Fox, the Quakers, and the Restoration State, 1660–1685." *Albion* 24 (1992): 237–59.

Hill, Christopher. "History and Denominational History." *Baptist Quarterly* 22 (1967): 65–71.

———. "Quakers and the English Revolution." *Journal of the Friends' Historical Society* 56 (1992): 178.

Horle, Craig. "Quakers and Baptists 1647–1660." *Baptist Quarterly* 26 (1976): 344–62.

Hudson, Winthrop S. "A Suppressed Chapter in Quaker History." *Journal of Religion* 24 (1944): 108–18.

Hughes, Ann. "The Pulpit Guarded: Confrontations between Orthodox and Radicals in Revolutionary England." In *John Bunyan and His England, 1628–88*, edited by Anne Laurence, W. R. Owens, and Stuart Sim. Hambledon Press, 1990.

Hurwich, Judith Jones. "The Social Origins of the Early Quakers." *Past and Present* 48 (1970): 156–62.

Ingle, H. Larry. "From Mysticism to Radicalism: Recent Historiography of Quaker Beginnings." *Quaker History* 76 (1987): 79–94.

———. "George Fox as Enthusiast: An Unpublished Epistle." *Journal of the Friends' Historical Society* 55 (1989): 266–70.

———. "George Fox, Millenarian." *Albion* 24 (1992): 261–78.

———. "George Fox, Historian." *Quaker History* 82 (1993): 28–35.

Jensen, J. Vernon. "Communicative Functions of Silence." *Etc.: A Review of General Semantics* 30 (1973): 249–57.

Kliever, Lonnie D. "General Baptist Origins: The Question of Anabaptist Influences." *Mennonite Quarterly Review* 36 (1962): 291–321.

Langley, Arthur S. "Seventeenth-Century Baptist Disputations." *Baptist Historical Society Transactions* 6 (1918–19): 216–43.

Laurence, Anne. "A Priesthood of She-believers: Women and Congregations in Mid-Seventeenth-Century England." In *Women in the Church*, edited by W. J. Sheils and Diana Wood, vol. 27 of *Studies in Church History*, Ecclesiastical History Society. Oxford: Basil Blackwell, 1990.

Ludlow, Dorothy P. "Shaking Patriarchy's Foundations: Sectarian Women in England, 1641–1700." In *Triumph Over Silence: Women in Protestant History*, edited by Richard L. Greaves. Westport, Conn.: Greenwood Press, 1985.

Mack, Phyllis. "Teaching about Gender and Spirituality in Early English Quakerism." *Women's Studies* 19 (1991): 223–37.

McGregor, James F. "Ranterism and the Development of Early Quakerism." *Journal of Religious History* 9 (1977): 349–63.

———. "Seekers and Ranters." In *Radical Religion in the English Revolution*, edited by J. F. McGregor and Barry Reay. Oxford: Oxford University Press, 1984.

———. "The Baptists: Fount of All Heresy." In *Radical Religion in the English Revolution*, edited by J. F. McGregor and Barry Reay. Oxford: Oxford University Press, 1984.

Mills, Susan B. "Sources for the Study of Baptist History." *Baptist Quarterly* 34 (1992): 282–96.

Nicholson, J. F. V. "The Office of 'Messenger' amongst British Baptists in the Seventeenth and Eighteenth Centuries." *Baptist Quarterly* 17 (1957–58): 206–25.

Nickalls, J. L. "George Fox's Library." *Journal of the Friends' Historical Society* 28 (1931): 8.

Nuttall, Geoffrey F. "The Early Congregational Conception of the Ministry and the Place of Women in It." *Congregational Quarterly* 26 (1948): 153–61.

———. "The Baptist Western Association 1653–1658." *Journal of Ecclesiastical History* 11 (1960): 213–18.

———. "A Letter by James Nayler Appropriated to George Fox." *Journal of the Friends' Historical Society* 55 (1988): 178–79.

———. "Another Baptist Vicar? Edmund Skipp of Bodenham." *Baptist Quarterly* 33 (1990): 331–34.

———. "Reflections on William Penn's Preface to George Fox's *Journal.*" *Journal of the Friends' Historical Society* 57 (1995): 113–17.

O'Malley, Thomas. "'Defying the Powers and Tempering the Spirit': A Review of Quaker Control over Their Publications, 1672–1689." *Journal of Ecclesiastical History* 33 (1982): 72–88.

Payne, Ernest A. "More about the Sabbatarian Baptists." *Baptist Quarterly* 14 (1951–52): 161–66.

———. "Baptists and the Laying On of Hands." *Baptist Quarterly* 15 (1955–56): 203–15.

Stassen, Glen H. "Anabaptist Influence in the Origin of the Particular Baptists." *Mennonite Quarterly Review* 36 (1962): 322–48.

Toon, Peter. "The Latter-day Glory." In *Puritans, the Millennium and the Future of Israel: Puritan Eschatology 1600–1660*, edited by Peter Toon. Cambridge: James Clark, 1970.

Underwood, T. L. "The Baptist Henry Denne and the Quaker Doctrine of the Inner Light." *Quaker History* 56 (1967): 34–40.

———. "Child Dedication Services among British Baptists in the Seventeenth Century." *Baptist Quarterly* 23 (1969): 164–69.

———. "Early Quaker Eschatology." In *Puritans, the Millennium and the Future of Israel: Puritan Eschatology 1600–1660*, edited by Peter Toon. Cambridge: James Clarke, 1970.

———. "'It pleased me much to contend': John Bunyan as Controversialist." *Church History* 57 (1988): 456–69.

———. "'For then I should be a Ranter or a Quaker': John Bunyan and Radical Religion," in *'Awakening Words': John Bunyan and the Language of Community*, edited by David Gay and Arlette Zinck, forthcoming.

Weddle, Meredith Baldwin. "Conscience or Compromise: The Meaning of the Peace Testimony in Early New England." *Quaker History* 81 (1992): 73–86.

White, B. R. "Baptist Beginnings and the Kiffin Manuscript." *Baptist History and Heritage* 2 (1967): 27–37.

———. "William Kiffin—Baptist Pioneer and Citizen of London," *Baptist History and Heritage* 2 (1967): 91–103.

Whitley, W. T. "Baptist Churches till 1660." Baptist Historical Society *Transactions* 2 (1911): 232–234.

———. "Seventh Day Baptists in England." *Baptist Quarterly* 12 (1947): 252–58.

——. "The Rev. Colonel John Wigan." *Journal of the Friends' Historical Society* 16 (1955–56): 141–42.

Willen, Diane. "Godly Women in Early Modern England: Puritanism and Gender." *Journal of Ecclesiastical History* 43 (1992): 561–80.

——. " 'Communion of the Saints': Spiritual Reciprocity and the Godly Community in Early Modern England." *Albion* 27 (1995): 19–41.

Winter, E. P. "Calvinist and Zwinglian Views of the Lord's Supper among the Baptists of the Seventeenth Century." *Baptist Quarterly* 15 (1953–54): 323–29.

Wood, H. G. "William Penn's *Christian Quaker*." In *Children of Light*, edited by H. H. Brinton. New York: Macmillan, 1938.

Books

Axon, Ernest, ed. *Oliver Heywood's Life of John Angier*. Remains, Historical and Literary . . . , n.s. no. 97. Manchester: Chetham Society, 1937.

Bailey, Richard. *New Light on George Fox and Early Quakerism*. Lewiston, N.Y.: Edwin Mellen Press, 1993.

Ball, Bryan W. *The Seventh-day Men: Sabbatarians and Sabbatarianism in England and Wales, 1600–1800*. Oxford: Oxford University Press, 1994.

Barbour, Hugh. *The Quakers in Puritan England*. New Haven: Yale University Press, 1964. Reprint, Richmond, Ind.: Friends United Press, 1985.

Barbour, Hugh, and Arthur O. Roberts, eds. *Early Quaker Writings 1650–1700*. Grand Rapids: William Eerdmans, 1973.

Barclay, Robert. *The Inner Life of the Religious Societies of the Commonwealth*. 1876.

Bauman, Richard. *Let Your Words Be Few: Symbolism of Speaking and Silence among Seventeenth-Century Quakers*. Cambridge: Cambridge University Press, 1983.

Beck, William, and T. Frederick Ball. *The London Friends' Meetings*. F. B. Kitto, 1869.

Besse, Joseph. *A Collection of the Sufferings of the People Called Quakers*. 2 vols. Luke Hinde, 1753.

Bittle, William G. *James Nayler 1618–1660, The Quaker Indicted by Parliament*. York: Sessions Book Trust, 1986.

Bozeman, Theodore Dwight. *To Live Ancient Lives: The Primitivist Dimension in Puritanism*. Chapel Hill: University of North Carolina Press, 1988.

Brachlow, Stephen. *The Communion of Saints: Radical Puritan and Separatist Ecclesiology 1570–1625*. Oxford: Oxford University Press, 1988.

Braithwaite, Alfred W. *Thomas Rudyard: Early Friends' "Oracle of Law."* Journal of the Friends' Historical Society Supplement 27 (1956).

Braithwaite, William C. *The Beginnings of Quakerism*. 2nd ed. Revised by Henry J. Cadbury. Cambridge: Cambridge University Press, 1955.

——. *The Second Period of Quakerism*. 2nd ed. Revised by Henry J. Cadbury. Cambridge: Cambridge University Press, 1961.

Brayshaw, A. Neave. *The Personality of George Fox*. Allenson, 1933.

——. *The Quakers*. 3rd ed. New York: Macmillan, 1953.

Brinton, H. H., ed. *Children of Light*. New York: Macmillan, 1938.

British Museum. *Catalogue of the Pamphlets . . . Collected by George Thomason*. 2 vols. Trustees of the British Museum, 1908.

Burgess, Walter H. *John Smith the Se-Baptist, Thomas Helwys and the First Baptist Church in England.* James Clarke, 1911.

Burrage, Champlin. *Early English Dissenters.* 2 vols. Cambridge: Cambridge University Press, 1912.

Cadbury, Henry. *Swarthmore Documents in America. Journal of the Friends' Historical Society* Supplement 20 (1940).

Cadbury, Henry J., ed. *George Fox's "Book of Miracles."* New York: Octagon Books, 1973.

Carroll, Kenneth L. *John Perrot: Early Quaker Schismatic. Journal of the Friends' Historical Society* Supplement 33 (1971).

Chu, Jonathan M. *Neighbors, Friends, or Madmen: The Puritan Adjustment to Quakerism in Seventeenth-Century Massachusetts Bay.* Westport, Conn.: Greenwood Press, 1985.

Crawford, Patricia. *Women and Religion in England 1500–1720.* Routledge, 1993.

Crosby, Thomas. *The History of the English Baptists.* 4 vols. 1738–40.

Davies, Horton. *The Worship of the English Puritans.* Dacre Press, 1948.

Davis, J. C. *Fear, Myth, and History.* Cambridge: Cambridge University Press, 1986.

Eliade, Mircea. *Myths, Dreams, and Mysteries: The Encounter Between Contemporary Faith and Archaic Realities.* Translated by Philip Mairet. Harvill Press, 1960.

Evans, Benjamin. *The Early English Baptists.* 2 vols. J. Heaton and Son, 1862–64.

Estep, William R. *The Anabaptist Story.* Rev. ed. Grand Rapids: William B. Eerdmans, 1975.

Finlayson, Michael G. *Historians, Puritanism, and the English Revolution: the Religious Factor in English Politics before and after the Interregnum.* Toronto: University of Toronto Press, 1983.

Friedman, Jerome. *Blasphemy, Immorality, and Anarchy: The Ranters and the English Revolution.* Athens, Ohio: Ohio University Press, 1987.

Greaves, Richard L. *John Bunyan.* Abingdon, Berkshire: Sutton Courtenay Press, 1969.

———. *The Puritan Revolution and Educational Thought.* New Brunswick: Rutgers University Press, 1969.

———. *Deliver Us from Evil: The Radical Underground in Britain, 1660–1663.* New York: Oxford University Press, 1986.

———. *Enemies Under His Feet: Radicals and Nonconformists in Britain, 1664–1677.* Stanford: Stanford University Press, 1990.

———. *Secrets of the Kingdom: British Radicals from the Popish Plot to the Revolution of 1688–1689.* Stanford: Stanford University Press, 1992.

Greaves, Richard L., ed. Vol. 9 of *The Miscellaneous Works of John Bunyan,* edited by Roger Sharrock. Oxford: Clarendon Press, 1981.

Greaves, Richard L., and Robert Zaller, eds. *Biographical Dictionary of British Radicals.* 3 vols. Brighton: Harvester Press, 1982–84.

Gummere, Amelia Mott. *Witchcraft and Quakerism.* Philadelphia: Biddle Press, 1908.

Gura, Philip F. *A Glimpse of Sion's Glory: Puritan Radicalism in New England, 1620–1660.* Middletown, Conn.: Wesleyan University Press, 1984.

Gwyn, Douglas. *Apocalypse of the Word.* Richmond, Ind.: Friends United Press, 1984.

Hayden, Roger, ed. *The Records of a Church of Christ in Bristol, 1640–1687.* Bristol Record Society Publication 27, 1974.

Hill, Christopher. *Milton and the English Revolution*. New York: Viking Press, 1978.
———. *The Experience of Defeat*. New York: Viking Press, 1984.
Hill, Christopher, Barry Reay, and William Lamont. *The World of the Muggletonians*. Temple Smith, 1983.
Hill, Michael. *A Sociology of Religion*. New York: Basic Books, 1973.
Horle, Craig W. *The Quakers and the English Legal System 1660–1688*. Philadelphia: University of Pennsylvania Press, 1988.
Hughes, Richard T., ed. *The American Quest for the Primitive Church*. Urbana: University of Illinois Press, 1988.
Ingle, H. Larry. *First Among Friends: George Fox and the Creation of Quakerism*. New York: Oxford University Press, 1994.
Ivimey, Joseph. *A History of the English Baptists*. 4 vols. 1811–30.
Jones, Rufus M. *Studies in Mystical Religion*. Macmillan, 1909.
Jordan, W. K. *The Development of Religious Toleration in England*. 3 vols. Allen and Unwin, 1938.
Keeble, Neil H. *The Literary Culture of Nonconformity in Late Seventeenth-Century England*. Athens, Georgia: University of Georgia Press, 1987.
King, Rachel Hadley. *George Fox and the Light Within 1650–1660*. Philadelphia: Friends Book Store, 1940.
Knott, John R., Jr. *The Sword of the Spirit: Puritan Responses to the Bible*. Chicago: University of Chicago Press, 1980.
Kunze, Bonnelyn Young. *Margaret Fell and the Rise of Quakerism*. Stanford: Stanford University Press, 1994.
Levack, Brian P. *The Witch-hunt in Early Modern Europe*. Longman, 1987.
Lumpkin, William L. *Baptist Confessions of Faith*. Valley Forge, Pa.: Judson Press, 1969.
Macfarlane, Alan. *Witchcraft in Tudor and Stuart England*. Routledge and Kegan Paul, 1970.
Mack, Phyllis. *Visionary Women: Ecstatic Prophecy in Seventeenth-Century England*. Berkeley: University of California Press, 1992.
Manners, Emily. *Elizabeth Hooton*. Headley Brothers, 1914.
Martin, J. W. *Religious Radicals in Tudor England*. Hambledon Press, 1989.
Matthews, A. G. *The Congregational Churches of Staffordshire*. 1924.
———. *Calamy Revised*. Oxford: Oxford University Press, 1988.
McGlothlin, William J., ed. *Baptist Confessions of Faith*. Philadelphia: American Baptist Publication Society, 1911.
McLachlan, Herbert John. *Socinianism in Seventeenth-Century England*. Oxford: Oxford University Press, 1951.
Miller, Perry. *The New England Mind: The Seventeenth Century*. Cambridge: Harvard University Press, 1954.
Milward, Peter. *Religious Controversies of the Elizabethan Age: A Survey of Printed Sources*. Lincoln, Neb.: University of Nebraska Press, 1977.
———. *Religious Controversies of the Jacobean Age: A Survey of Printed Sources*. Lincoln, Neb.: University of Nebraska Press, 1978.
Morton, A. L. *The World of the Ranters*. Lawrence and Wishart, 1970.
Nuttall, Geoffrey F. *James Nayler: A Fresh Approach*. Journal of the Friends' Historical Society Supplement 26 (1954).
———. *The Welsh Saints 1640–1660*. Cardiff: University of Wales Press, 1957.
———. *Visible Saints: the Congregational Way, 1640–1660*. Oxford: Basil Blackwell, 1957.

———. *To the Refreshing of the Children of Light.* Wallingford, Pa.: Pendle Hill Pamphlet Number 101, 1959.

———. *The Holy Spirit in Puritan Faith and Experience.* Oxford: Basil Blackwell, 1946; reprint, Chicago: University of Chicago Press, 1992.

Offor, George, ed. *The Works of John Bunyan.* 3 vols. Glasgow: Blackie and Son, 1853.

Pearson, Andrew Forrest Scott. *Thomas Cartwright and Elizabethan Puritanism, 1535–1603.* Cambridge: Cambridge University Press, 1925.

Penney, Norman, ed. *The First Publishers of Truth. Journal of the Friends' Historical Society,* Supplement 1–5, 1904.

Pickvance, Joseph. *A Reader's Companion to George Fox's Journal.* Quaker Home Service, 1989.

Reay, Barry. *The Quakers and the English Revolution.* New York: St. Martin's Press, 1985.

Ross, Isabel. *Margaret Fell, Mother of Quakerism.* 2nd ed. York: Sessions Book Trust, 1984.

Smith, Hilda L. *Reason's Disciples: Seventeenth-Century Feminists.* Urbana: University of Illinois Press, 1982.

Smith, Joseph. *Bibliotheca Anti-Quakeriana.* Joseph Smith, 1873.

———. *A Descriptive Catalogue of Friends' Books.* 2 vols. Joseph Smith, 1867.

Smith, Nigel. *A Collection of Ranter Writings from the 17th Century.* Junction Books, 1983.

———. *Perfection Proclaimed: Language and Literature in English Radical Religion, 1640–1660.* Oxford: Clarendon Press, 1989.

Starr, Edward C. *A Baptist Bibliography.* 25 vols. Philadelphia: Judson Press, 1947–76.

Stephen, Leslie, and Sidney Lee, eds. *The Dictionary of National Biography.* 22 vols. Oxford University Press, 1949–50.

Taylor, Adam. *The History of the English General Baptists.* 2 vols. T. Bore, 1818.

Taylor, Ernest E. *The Valiant Sixty.* Bannisdale Press, 1947.

Tolmie, Murray. *The Triumph of the Saints: The Separate Churches of London 1616–1649.* Cambridge: Cambridge University Press, 1977.

Trevett, Christine. *Women and Quakerism in the 17th Century.* York: Sessions Book Trust, 1991.

Turner, G. Lyon. *Original Records of Early Nonconformity under Persecution and Indulgence.* 3 vols. T. Fisher Unwin, 1911–14.

Underhill, Edward Bean, ed. *The Records of the Churches of Christ Gathered at Fenstanton, Warboys, and Hexham, 1644–1720.* Vol. 9. Hanserd Knollys Society, Haddon Brothers, 1854.

———. *Confessions of Faith and Other Public Documents.* Vol. 10. Hanserd Knollys Society, Haddon Brothers, 1854.

Underwood, Alfred C. *A History of the English Baptists.* Kingsgate Press, 1947.

Underwood, T. L., ed. Vol. 1 of *The Miscellaneous Works of John Bunyan,* edited by Roger Sharrock. Oxford: Clarendon Press, 1980.

———, ed. Vol. 4 of *The Miscellaneous Works of John Bunyan,* edited by Roger Sharrock. Oxford: Clarendon Press, 1989.

Vann, Richard T. *The Social Development of English Quakerism 1655–1755.* Cambridge: Harvard University Press, 1969.

Vann, Richard T., and David Eversley. *Friends in Life and Death: The British and Irish Quakers in the Demographic Transition, 1650–1900.* Cambridge: Cambridge University Press, 1992.

Watkins, Owen C. *The Puritan Experience.* Routledge and Kegan Paul, 1972.

White, B. R. *The English Baptists of the Seventeenth Century.* Baptist Historical Society, 1983.

Whitley, W. T. *A Baptist Bibliography.* 2 vols. Kingsgate Press, 1916–22.

———. *A History of British Baptists.* Kingsgate Press, 1932.

Whitley, W. T., ed. *The Minutes of the General Assembly of the General Baptist Churches in England.* 2 vols. Kingsgate Press, 1909–10.

Whitley, W. T., ed. *The Works of John Smyth.* 2 vols. Cambridge: Cambridge University Press, 1915

Whittaker, E. Jean. *Thomas Lawson 1630–1691: North Country Botanist, Quaker, and Schoolmaster.* York: Sessions Book Trust, 1986.

Wilson, Bryan. *Religious Sects: A Sociological Study.* New York: McGraw-Hill, 1970.

———. *Religion in Sociological Perspective.* Oxford: Oxford University Press, 1982.

Wing, Donald. *Short-title Catalogue of Books Printed in England, Scotland, Ireland, Wales, and British America, and of English Books Printed in Other Countries, 1641–1700.* 2nd ed. New York: Modern Language Association of America, 1972–88.

Woodhouse, A. S. P. *Puritanism and Liberty.* J. M. Dent, 1938.

Wright, Luella M. *The Literary Life of the Early Friends, 1650–1725.* New York: Columbia University Press, 1932.

Index

Abingdon, Berkshire, 61
Aldam, Thomas, 10
Aldersgate, London, 82
Allhallows the Great, London, 15
Ames, William (the Puritan), 6–7
Ames, William (the Quaker), 16, 22,
  29, 53, 112, 115
Amsterdam, 8
Andrews, Hester Bird, 78, 153 n. 44

Baillie, Robert, 91
Baldock, Thomas, 155 n. 16
Baptism, 5, 8–9, 11, 15–17, 69,
  72–77, 81, 83, 86, 101, 136
  n. 31
Baptists, General (Arminian), 8–9,
  11–13, 17, 21, 38, 53, 56–57,
  59, 60, 72, 77, 82–83, 92–93,
  95–96, 111, 114, 120, 125 n. 1,
  132 n. 42, 151 n. 27
Baptists, Particular (Calvinistic), 8–9,
  12–13, 15, 17–18, 21, 53,
  56–57, 66, 72–73, 77, 91, 93,
  95–96, 111, 113–14, 120, 125
  n. 1, 132 n. 42, 145 n. 34, 151
  n. 27

Baptists, Seventh Day, 9, 82, 86, 136
  n. 31
Barbados, 141 n. 44, 165 n. 55
Barber, Edward, 121
Barbican, London, 29, 48, 132 n. 1
Barbour, Hugh, 162 n. 26
Barclay, Robert, 12, 85
Batt, Jasper, 48, 142 n. 50
Bauman, Richard, 94
Bauthumley, Jacob, 25, 36, 65, 148
  n. 75, 165 n. 56
Baxter, Richard, 6–8, 13–14, 84,
  101, 106, 119, 121, 149 n. 75,
  162 n. 20
Bayley, Charles, 89
Bayly, William, 16, 53
Beard, Richard, 160 n. 68
Bedford, 51, 143 n. 3
Bedfordshire, 51–52
Beech-lane, London, 82, 87
Beevan, John, 16, 53, 137 n. 4
Berkshire, 162 n. 28
Besse, Joseph, 10
Besthorpe, Nottinghamshire, 165
  n. 55
Biddenden, Kent, 150 n. 20, 151 n. 25